M000035718

Praise for
Dim Sum Bonds

"A good 3-D view on the Dim Sum bond market—drilling down all the way from the macro factors that gave rise to this universe to the micro aspects of issuing details, while at the same time, providing a round-table perspective from the government, the issuers, the investors, and the investment banks."

—Edwin Chan, Managing Director, Head of Asian Credit Research, UBS, and No. 1 ranked analyst for Asian G3 bonds by *The Asset* and *FinanceAsia*

"This book is a very useful reference for those international investors who consider investing in the offshore RMB bond market for either an appreciation or a higher carry in the RMB. It is also a convenient guide to the dim sum bond market. I highly recommend treasurers of companies who haven't tapped this important funding source read this book."

—Jingxin Deng, Director, Lead Portfolio Manager of Global Credit Investment, China Investment Corporation, Hong Kong

"The dim sum bond market is not just another up-and-coming EM bond market. With the internationalization of the RMB and China being the second largest economy in the world, the dim sum bond market is quickly attracting investors and issuers from around the world. The growth (and the destiny) of the dim sum bond market, I believe, will be similar to the development of the Yankee bond market over the past 20 years. This timely and well-researched reference book written by both market practitioner and academic researchers is a must-read."

—Thomas Kwan, Head of Fixed Income, Harvest Global Investments Limited, Hong Kong

"A very useful and insightful reference to anyone who wants to comprehend the profound implication of the development of the dim sum bond market and what it means to the global capital market in the future. I believe market participants and researchers will benefit from the authors' great insights, while investors will gain from better appreciation of the risks, opportunities, and the significance of this asset class."

—Arthur Lau, Managing Director, Head of Fixed Income Asia ex Japan and Co-Portfolio Manager, Emerging Markets, PineBridge Investments Asia Ltd., Hong Kong, and voted the most astute bond investor in Hong Kong by *The Asset* in 2007 and 2008

"This book is essential reading for all existing and intended RMB debt market participants in Hong Kong, the biggest RMB off-shore centre."

—Philip Li, Managing Director, China Chengxin (Asia Pacific)
Credit Ratings Company Limited, and former chairman
of the Hong Kong Capital Markets Association

"This book will help fill a gap in knowledge about the rapidly growing offshore Chinese Renminbi market and specifically the 'dim sum' bond market in Hong Kong. This timely book will help investors, bankers, regulators, and academics better understand China's currency as it becomes more international and as companies look to raise funds in RMB via Hong Kong and other offshore financial centers."

—George Long, CFA, Chairman, and Chief Investment Officer, LIM
Advisors Limited, Hong Kong, the founding president of the
Hong Kong Society of Financial Analysts, and the founding
chairman of the Hong Kong Chapter of the Alternative
Investment Management Association (AIMA)

"An excellent investment handbook on dim sum bonds for practitioners. The authors have great insights on the structure and evolution of the offshore RMB bond market."

—Richard Mak, CFA, Head of Advisory Services—Asia, Pictet & Cie,
and former president of the Hong Kong Society of Financial Analysts

"Kudos to the authors of this book for providing a very comprehensive source of information about the development of the dim sum bond market. As buy-side investment advisors for private banking clients in Asia, we see the trend of the growing importance of the RMB in asset allocation. The burgeoning demand for offshore RMB-denominated investments is a major driving force behind the dim sum bond market. I strongly recommend this book to anyone who wants to understand the dim sum bond market."

—Maggie Tsui, Managing Director, Deputy Head of Investment Services,
Asia, BNP Paribas Wealth Management, Hong Kong

"The rise of China has brought its capital markets into the global limelight. The internationalization and convertibility of its currency, the renminbi, are imminent. This book provides a very timely and comprehensive study of the dim sum bond market from both a historical and risk-reward perspectives. It also provides insights into how this asset class would continue to grow and the challenges it will face along the way. Fung, Ko, and Yau's book should be made a compulsory reading for any investor who has an interest in the renminbi and China's offshore bond market."

—Michael Yong-Haron, CFA, Managing Director, Credit Suisse Private Banking Division, Greater China

"In *Dim Sum Bonds*, Fung, Ko, and Yau provide a fascinating account of the dim sum bond market from relative obscurity a few years ago to a leading position in the growing offshore RMB bond market. The book presents cases of the landmark dim sum bond issues, which illustrates clearly the issuers' perspectives. This book is a must-read for anybody who wants to know this market in Hong Kong."

—Jimin Guo, Ph.D., CFA, Executive Director, China Galaxy Securities, Beijing

"Fung, Ko, and Yau have done a superb job in sizing up the development of the offshore RMB bond market to date and laying out the opportunities and risks ahead. The book is an indispensable reference tool for anyone investing or contemplating investing in this budding market."

—David Lai, CFA, Investment Director, Fixed Income, Eastspring Investments (Singapore) Limited

"This book provides an easy-to-follow road map and delivers crystal clear details on every aspect of the dim sum bond market. It is a must-read for both seasoned professionals and novices alike."

—Lee Kerk Phua, CFA, Chief Strategist, Phillip Mutual Malaysia

"*Dim Sum Bonds* offers insight into one of the more complex aspects of China's efforts to become a major player in global financial markets. It explains in detail the internationalization of the RMB and China's efforts to create an alternative global reserve currency. This book is a must-read for academics and practitioners interested in understanding the remarkable developments now taking place in China's capital markets."

—Keith Ferguson, Chief Investment Officer, University of Washington, Seattle

"This book is an outstanding achievement that brings the reader into the world of dim sum bonds—the offshore renminbi bond market. The combined practitioner and academic experience of the authors is well translated into this book that gives not only a detailed overview of the dim sum bond market, but also a thorough quantitative analysis of the bond characteristics in this fledgling market. A must-read!"

"Fung, Ko, and Yau have authored a timely reference that sheds light on a nascent yet soon to be vital financial instrument in the global marketplace. The authors address the development of the dim sum bond market and its role in supporting the Renminbi as a global reserve currency in a way that is both entertaining and informative, both in breadth and depth. Readers, whether fixed income and equity professionals or investors, will find this book a useful desk resource today and even more so as the market begins to mature."

Dim Sum Bonds

Founded in 1807, John Wiley & Sons is the oldest independent publishing company in the United States. With offices in North America, Europe, Australia and Asia, Wiley is globally committed to developing and marketing print and electronic products and services for our customers' professional and personal knowledge and understanding.

The Wiley Finance series contains books written specifically for finance and investment professionals as well as sophisticated individual investors and their financial advisors. Book topics range from portfolio management to e-commerce, risk management, financial engineering, valuation and financial instrument analysis, as well as much more.

For a list of available titles, visit www.WileyFinance.com.

Dim Sum Bonds

The Offshore Renminbi (RMB)-Denominated Bonds

HUNG-GAY FUNG
GLENN KO
JOT YAU

WILEY

Published by John Wiley & Sons, Inc., Hoboken, New Jersey.
Published simultaneously in Canada.

For general information on our other products and services or for technical support, please contact our Customer Care Department within the United States at (800) 762-2974, outside the United States at (317) 572-3993 or fax (317) 572-4002.

Wiley publishes in a variety of print and electronic formats and by print-on-demand. Some material included with standard print versions of this book may not be included in e-books or in print-on-demand. If this book refers to media such as a CD or DVD that is not included in the version you purchased, you may download this material at http://booksupport.wiley.com. For more information about Wiley products, visit www.wiley.com.

Library of Congress Cataloging-in-Publication Data:

Fung, Hung-gay.
  Dim sum bonds : the offshore renminbi (RMB)-denominated bonds / Hung-Gay Fung, PhD, Glenn Ko, CFA, and Jot Yau, PhD, CFA.
    pages cm.—(Wiley finance series)
  Includes index.
  ISBN 978-1-118-43479-6 (cloth)—ISBN 978-1-118-83964-5 (ePDF)—
ISBN 978-1-118-83963-8 (ePub) 1. Bonds—China. 2. Banks and banking, Foreign—China. 3. Renminbi. I. Ko, Glenn. II. Yau, Jot. III. Title.
  HG4651.F86 2014
  332.63'230951—dc23

                                                    2013035586

Printed in the United States of America

10 9 8 7 6 5 4 3 2 1

To my wife, Linda; my daughter, Anna;
and my brothers and sister

—Hung-Gay Fung

To my family

—Glenn Ko

To Marie

—Jot Yau

Contents

Preface

As you are reading this preface, we know that the title of this book, *Dim Sum Bonds,* has done its job piquing your curiosity. We hope you will find this book interesting and "dim sum" meals satisfying.

Whenever we mentioned to our friends and colleagues that we were working on a book on "dim sum bonds," all of them[1] were in awe with no exception. Many of our friends, colleagues, and professional acquaintances thought that we had reinvented ourselves, switching our lifelong careers in finance/investment research and management to culinary art. A friend actually said to one of us,[2] "I didn't know that you were a chef!" We are, of course, more than happy to explain, elucidate, and explicate what dim sum bonds are and will be. We wouldn't mind having this type of 3 "E's" conversations over "dim sum" luncheons for years to come.

"Dim sum," in Cantonese[3] refers to a variety of tiny, bite-sized, steamed food that is usually served for breakfast or lunch. It is supposed to be a small, hot meal that goes with Chinese tea. A traditional dim sum meal would have "Ha Gau" (shrimp dumpling) and "Siu Mai" (pork and mushroom dumpling), whereas fusion dim sum would have food crossing over from different Chinese regions as well as Western cuisines.

The term *dim sum bonds* is used to refer to the offshore renminbi (RMB)-denominated bonds issued in Hong Kong, where "dim sum" is served in most restaurants.[4] Since the dim sum bond market made its debut in 2007, China has been contemplating establishing offshore RMB bond markets at other locations such as Taiwan, Singapore, London, and Paris. In this book, we focus on the dim sum bond market, the offshore RMB market in

---

[1] More specifically, those living outside Asia.

[2] More specifically, Jot Yau.

[3] Cantonese refers to the language that originated in the vicinity of Canton (i.e., Guangzhou), the capital city of the province of Guangdong in southern China. It also refers to the people or things that come from that area.

[4] For the credit of the use of the term *dim sum bonds* to refer to the offshore RMB-denominated bonds issued in Hong Kong, see Robert Minikin and Kelvin Lau, *The Offshore Renminbi: The Rise of the Chinese Currency and Its Global Future.* John Wiley & Sons Singapore Pte. Ltd., 2013, p. xv.

Hong Kong, emphasizing the experience and perspective of major market participants, although we also discuss how other offshore RMB bond markets are in the making in light of the development and growth in the dim sum bond market. This approach is like introducing readers to the traditional dim sum such as "Ha Gau" and "Siu Mai," while ordering some fusion dim sum for different flavors and tastes.

The purpose of this book is to provide a panoramic view of the Hong Kong offshore RMB-denominated bond market that has played a pivotal role in China's grand scheme of making the RMB a global reserve currency by providing an investment option to holders of offshore RMB as part of the strategy for internationalizing the RMB. As China does not allow free flow of funds in and out of the mainland, its domestic financial market is basically closed to foreign investors. Since many companies issuing offshore RMB (dim sum) bonds have operations in mainland China, investing in these dim sum bonds offers investors an opportunity to participate in the upside of the Chinese economy.

We discuss and analyze the dim sum bond market from the vantage points of issuers, investors, investment banks, and the Chinese government. We hope our readers appreciate the dynamics among all market participants affecting the growth, opportunities, and challenges in this nascent market. The dim sum bond market in Hong Kong has grown rapidly over the past few years. Given limited investment options for the offshore RMB deposits and expectations of RMB appreciation, the dim sum bond market was more of a seller's or issuer's market until more recently. Issuers would thus be able to obtain lower-cost funding through dim sum bond issues, whereas investors were willing to buy dim sum bonds for lower yields.

Now, the dim sum bond market is maturing. We outline changes that have taken place thus far in the dim sum bond market. For example, the more active involvement of institutional investors, such as the long-only funds and hedge funds, has made the dim sum bond market become more investor friendly. Also, the yields of dim sum bonds are now more reflective of issuers' credit quality, while terms and conditions such as covenants and the requirement of credit ratings are converging toward those of the Asian U.S. dollar bonds.

Moreover, we explain the intricacies in the primary dim sum bond issue origination process and contrast the main difference between them with those of the Asian U.S. dollar bond issues, which lies in the premarketing efforts due to differing issuer and investor profiles.

Overall, we believe the prospects of the dim sum bond market are promising despite challenges ahead. We expect the RMB will become an increasingly accepted currency worldwide, albeit the path it takes in the course of RMB internationalization will have obstacles. Worldwide circulation of the

RMB will support a sustainable growth of the global offshore RMB bond markets, including those to be developed over the long term, although the immediate future of the Hong Kong's nascent dim sum bond market depends very much on the Chinese and world economy. Changes in China's policy could present significant challenges to Hong Kong's dim sum bond market. The recently announced policy of the Chinese government authorizing RMB clearing banks in Taiwan and Singapore and thereby giving birth to offshore RMB bond markets in both countries is an example. Likewise, expansion of the Renminbi Qualified Foreign Institutional Investor (RQFII) program beyond Hong Kong will pose a threat to the dim sum bond market, although the program itself encourages international investors to hold more RMB, a positive toward the RMB internationalization efforts. Nevertheless, we believe the growth of the dim sum bond market in Hong Kong will benefit from the burgeoning offshore RMB pools around the world (e.g., Taiwan, Singapore, London, Paris, and New York), although dim sum bonds will account for a lower share of the overall offshore RMB pool.

All told, the dim sum bond market deserves attention from retail and institutional investors, issuers from different countries and industries, and investment bankers, as well as government regulators and policymakers. Practitioners, such as financial advisers, wealth and asset managers, and bond and currency traders, may find the dim sum bond market offers global investors a potentially viable asset class for portfolio diversification.

ORGANIZATION OF THIS BOOK

As mentioned, we present the dim sum bond market from the perspective of four major players in the market: the Chinese government, issuers, investors, and investment banks/bookrunners. From the Chinese central government's perspective, the development of the dim sum bond market is part of a grand scheme aiming at making the RMB a global reserve currency. It is part of the national multipronged strategy in internationalizing the RMB, controlling capital flows into China so as to provide price stability and harness inflation in mainland China, as well as developing a funding channel for tapping foreign capital. The Chinese government will thus continue to support the growth of the dim sum bond market.

From the issuers' perspective, Chinese corporations consider the dim sum bond market as an alternative to the Asian U.S. dollar (USD) bond market for lower-cost and shorter-tenor funding. The dim sum bonds are typically shorter in maturity (three years vs. five years-plus for Asian USD bonds). Many of the earlier dim sum bonds are unrated and without USD bond covenants. As such, issuers turned to the dim sum bond market for lower-cost funding with less demanding requirements on credits and covenants. Nonetheless, we note that terms and conditions of dim sum bonds are converging with those of the Asian USD bonds given the increasing participation of institutional investors. The rapidly growing of the dim sum bond market was also under the backdrop that the onshore credit environment was tightening as the Chinese government tried to rein in credit growth, issuers had resorted to the offshore bond markets for funding needs. In addition, for private corporations, the dim sum bond market provides funding, which they cannot easily obtain onshore in the CNY market. Corporations can also obtain goodwill with the Chinese government by supporting the activities in this offshore market that help China to achieve its goal of internationalizing the RMB. Finally, corporations raising capital in the capital markets may gain publicity.

From the investors' perspective, dim sum bonds provide risk-averse investors investment options, as well as exposure to take advantage of the RMB appreciation, if any. Investors can obtain yield pickup over CNH deposits through investing in dim sum bonds. Investors now ask for benchmark RegS deal size, greater variety in terms of credits and tenor, ratings, and stricter covenants, closer to those of Asian USD bonds.

From the investment banks/bookrunners' perspective, the dim sum bond market represents new business opportunities from issuers in China for bond origination as well as for sales and trading. More business opportunities in dim sum bonds will probably come from potential issuers who are not yet ready for Asian USD bond issues with regard to their smaller operating scales, credit profile, and credit ratings. While the size of the dim sum bond issue, on average, is generally smaller, the fee income from bond origination and trading could be less attractive as compared with those of Asian USD bonds since fee income is tied to bond issue size. The smaller issue size also implies thin trading liquidity. Nevertheless, the size and potential growth of the dim sum bond market could be tremendous. Furthermore, investment banks can establish a relationship with potential dim sum bond issuers as they may eventually become repeat customers for future investment banking business.

To present the perspectives of the players in the dim sum bond market, we have separate chapters focusing on the characteristics of dim sum bonds and the dim sum bond market (Chapter 2), investors' investment objectives and the performance of dim sum bonds (Chapter 3), motivations of issuers (Chapter 4), and the investment banks/bookrunners' role in the dim sum bond issuing process (Chapter 5). We present cases of landmark issues by type of issuer (Chapter 6): mainland Chinese financial institutions (e.g., Chinese Development Bank), the Chinese central government (e.g., Ministry of Finance), supranational agencies (e.g., Asian Development

Bank), China-incorporated foreign banks (the Bank of East Asia [China] Limited), and Chinese corporations incorporated outside the mainland China and listed in Hong Kong (e.g., Sinotruk [Hong Kong] Limited), and foreign corporations (e.g., McDonald's Corporation). We also present two cases of special credit enhancement structures (Beijing Capital Land Ltd. and Gemdale Corporation). We discuss the salient features of each landmark issue to highlight the evolving market development. We also present the benchmark issues for 10-, 15-, and 20-year bonds. We conclude with Chapter 7, in which we also provide an outlook of the future development of the dim sum bond market.

The source of data used in the analysis is Bloomberg unless stated otherwise. The time period for the analysis we use throughout the book is July 1, 2007, to December 31, 2012, referred to as 2007–2012 for brevity. We sincerely hope that this book becomes a valuable resource for the investment community, corporations, sovereign and sub-sovereign entities, supranational agencies, regulators, policymakers, and academics. Any errors or omissions are ours.

We hope you enjoy reading this book as much as we enjoyed writing it.

Bon appétit!

Hung-Gay Fung
Glenn Ko
Jot Yau

Acknowledgments

We would like to express our heartfelt gratitude to numerous colleagues and market practitioners who have generously shared their knowledge and expertise in enlightening us on dim sum bonds. Many of them have shared with us their distinct perspectives and insights on the subject. We greatly appreciate the quality of our numerous chats and discussions with them over the phone, coffee, lunch, or dinner. We thank them for the invaluable time they spent with us in helping us in this daunting writing endeavor.

We are grateful to our friends and families who have provided us lots of love, encouragement, and support during the time we spent on writing. In particular, Jot would like to thank Ray and Judy Chan, Keith Ferguson, Chee Shuen Fong, Tommy Y. W. Lai, Hei Wai Lee, Teresa Ling, the Pothan family, Susan F. Poon, Gary M.C. Shiu, Eddie and Doreen Wai, Vincent Yuen, and Kenneth Yung. To Dustin Ho, his design recommendation was greatly appreciated.

Finally, we wish to thank our editors, Bill Falloon, Stacey Fischkelta, and Meg Freeborn, and coordinator Tiffany Charbonier, for their guidance and patience throughout the project.

Acronyms and Key Terms

A

ADB	Asian Development Bank
APMEA	Asia-Pacific, Middle East, and Africa
ASEAN	Association of Southeast Asian Nations
A-share	Chinese shares listed on mainland exchanges for domestic investors

B

BOCMMHK	Bank of Communications Limited, Hong Kong branch
BECL	Beijing Capital Land Ltd.
BEA	Bank of East Asia
BIS	Bank of International Settlement
BOC	Bank of China
BOCHK	Bank of China (Hong Kong)
B-share	Chinese shares listed on mainland exchanges in foreign currencies
BVI	British Virgin Islands

C

CAF	Corporacion Andina de Fomento
CBRC	China Banking Regulatory Commission
CCB	China Construction Bank
CD	Certificate of Deposit
CDB	China Development Bank
CEPA	Closer Economic Partnership Arrangement
CICC	China International Capital Corporation Limited
CNH	Chinese yuan (RMB) deliverable in Hong Kong
CNL	Chinese yuan (RMB) deliverable in London

CNT	Chinese yuan (RMB) deliverable in Taiwan
CNY	Chinese yuan
CSRC	China Securities Regulatory Commission

D

| DBRS | Dominion Bond Rating Service, a Toronto-based credit rating firm |
| DIP | Debt issuance program |

E

EBITDA	Earnings before interest, taxes, depreciation, and amortization
EIPU	Equity Interest Purchase Undertaking (deed)
EMTN	Euro medium-term note
ETF	Exchange-traded fund

F

FDI	Foreign direct investment
FRN	Floating rate note
FXCD	Fixed interest rate certificate of deposit

G

| GAAP | Generally accepted accounting principles |
| GMTN | Global medium-term note |

H

HKEx	Hong Kong Exchanges and Clearing Limited
HKMA	Hong Kong Monetary Authority
H-share	Mainland Chinese shares listed on the Hong Kong Stock Exchange
HY	High yield

I

| ICBC | Industrial and Commercial Bank of China |
| IFC | International Finance Corporation |

IFRS	International Financial Reporting Standards
ISO	International Organization for Standardization

L

LIBOR	London Interbank Offered Rate

M

MD&A	Management's discussion and analysis of financial conditions
MICEX	Moscow Interbank Currency Exchange
MNC	Multinational corporation
MOF	Ministry of Finance
MOFCOM	Ministry of Commerce
MTN	Medium-term note

N

NDF	Nondelivery RMB forward contract
NDRC	National Development and Reform Commission

O

OBU	Offshore banking unit

P

PB	Private banking
PBOC	People's Bank of China
PRC	People's Republic of China

Q

QFB	Qualifying Full Bank
QFII	Qualified Foreign Institutional Investor
QIB	Qualified Institutional Buyer

R

RMB	Renminbi
RegS	Regulation S
RQFII	Renminbi Qualified Foreign Institutional Investor

S

SAFE	State Administration of Foreign Exchange
SAIC	State Administration for Industry and Commerce
SAR	Special administrative region
SCB	Standard Chartered Bank
SDR	Special drawing right
SHIBOR	Shanghai Interbank Offered Rate
SGX-ST	Singapore Exchange
SOE	State-owned enterprise
SME	Small and medium enterprise
S&P	Standard & Poor's
SPV	Special purpose vehicle

X

XBER	Berlin Exchange
XFRA	Frankfurt Exchange
XHKG	Hong Kong Stock Exchange
XLUX	Luxembourg Stock Exchange
XSTU	Stuttgart Stock Exchange

CHAPTER 1

New Market—Developments, Opportunities, and Challenges

1.1 INTRODUCTION

Since its economic reforms in late 1978, China's economic growth has been robust, at around 9 percent per annum despite signs of slowing down in the wake of the 2008 global financial crisis.[1] The sustainable and solid economic growth has catapulted China into the second-largest economy after the United States, so it is natural that China seeks to play a bigger role in the world economy. One major policy goal of the Chinese government in the coming decade is to make its currency, the renminbi (RMB),[2] a global reserve currency, and thus internationalizing the RMB has become a strategic goal.

Since March 2009, Governor Zhou of the People's Bank of China (PBOC) has urged the International Monetary Fund (IMF) to include the RMB as part of the special drawing rights (SDRs). A major obstacle to embracing the RMB as a global reserve currency is its limited convertibility outside China. The inclusion of the RMB as a global reserve currency along with the U.S. dollar and the euro by other countries requires that the RMB must be fully convertible into other currencies and widely circulated outside China for trade settlement.[3] Thus, China has strategically designed economic policies vying to gain the global reserve currency status for the RMB.

---

[1] At the time of this writing, the GDP growth rate of China is estimated to be 7.5 percent in 2013 by the Organization for Economic Co-operation and Development and the Chinese government.

[2] Renminbi (RMB) is the currency of the People's Republic of China, whereas yuan (i.e., the dollar in Chinese) is the unit of the currency.

[3] See Fung and Yau (2012).

China has a tight control on its capital account for monitoring the fund flows across its borders to avoid speculation and shocks from international markets, while the current account on international trade has been opening up to promote trade. In addition, China has switched its fixed exchange rate to pegging it against the U.S. dollar to a basket of currencies of its key trading partners. Fluctuations of the RMB exchange rate against the U.S. dollar are still under the control of the Chinese government, with a trading band widening over time. Fluctuations in the foreign exchange rate have a huge impact on China's economy in terms of trade and capital flows. Thus, the stability of the RMB value remains one of key policy concerns of the Chinese government.

To help internationalize its currency, China has taken several steps in developing different offshore RMB currency trading centers, such as Hong Kong, Tokyo, London, and New York. In March 2011, China published the 12th Five-Year Plan for the National Economic & Social Development, which interestingly contains a chapter elaborating on the significant functions and positioning of Hong Kong in the implementation of China's economic development plan. It is clear that China will support Hong Kong in consolidating and enhancing its competitive position in being an international financial, trade, and shipping center, and in becoming an offshore RMB hub for trade and investment. On many occasions, Chinese leaders have reiterated their continual support with policies that strengthen the economic ties with Hong Kong, which was promulgated in the Closer Economic Partnership Arrangement (CEPA) of 2004, which is a free trade agreement between China and Hong Kong removing barriers of trade and investment and eliminating the tariff between the two economies.

As the cross-border trade between Hong Kong and China increased and the RMB trade settlement rose accordingly, corporations had started to accumulate RMB funds in Hong Kong. Meanwhile, individuals had accumulated RMB deposits as they made a one-way bet on RMB appreciation. Hong Kong banks had accumulated the most offshore RMB deposits. As individuals were looking for opportunities to enhance returns in addition to currency appreciation, offshore RMB bonds would offer an option for risk-averse investors. For corporations that receive RMB through trade settlement, offshore RMB bonds would provide a ready tool for flexible treasury management—for liquidity and yield. With the opportunity to invest in RMB-denominated assets other than RMB bank deposits, investors, banks, and foreign governments would be more willing to hold the RMB in their portfolios, enhancing the RMB's worldwide circulation.

In light of the availability of RMB outside China, the dim sum bond market thus came into being as part of China's grand economic policy in making the RMB a global reserve currency. The dim sum bond market is also compatible with the goal of developing the domestic bond market and reducing Chinese companies' reliance on debt finance from bank loans. By issuing dim sum sovereign bonds in the offshore market, investors essentially extend a low-interest-rate loan to the Chinese government, while the Chinese government can finance a myriad of investments, such as huge infrastructure projects and foreign asset acquisitions. Likewise, corporations issuing dim sum bonds can raise funds offshore as an alternative to domestic borrowing. With competition from offshore markets, the domestic financial markets in China may develop into more efficient markets with greater depth than they otherwise might have if China did not pursue these policies. The keen competition from offshore markets may also make Chinese banks and companies more competitive.[4]

As part of its grand policy for internationalizing the RMB, the Chinese government has been promoting cross-border trade settlement in RMB and has planned to gradually open up its capital accounts. China's Ministry of Commerce (MOFCOM) has allowed foreign direct investment (FDI) in RMB since September 2011. This policy could have profound implications for harnessing asset speculation and inflation in mainland China. Regardless of the origin of the FDI and in what currency, as long as China's inward FDI is exchanged into RMB and flows through Hong Kong, it will have minimal impact on China's foreign reserve and money supply. The offshore RMB trading center in Hong Kong, where most impact from FDI into China will be felt, plays a crucial role in minimizing the inflationary and speculation pressures in China due to inward FDI while helping China to maintain its monetary and exchange rate policy independence. This is probably the reason why Hong Kong has received the blessing of the Chinese central government for developing into an offshore RMB center, serving as a buffer zone for China for the purpose of controlling hot money flows into China and curbing inflation and speculation due to these money inflows.[5]

The Chinese government envisions utilizing Hong Kong as part of the grand strategy to achieve its goal toward internationalizing the RMB. Hong Kong is well positioned in assisting and supporting the rapid development of China's policy objective, especially in the development of an offshore RMB-denominated bond market. Hong Kong has been ranked consistently among the top financial centers in the world for many years. It has served as an international center for raising capital for the Chinese government and mainland Chinese firms. Free trading of the RMB in Hong Kong has been in effect for a few years, and it is expected to pave the way for trading offshore RMB bonds in other hubs in the future.

To summarize, the offshore RMB market has been developed as part of a multipronged strategy of the Chinese government to (1) internationalize

---

[4] See Fung, Tzau, and Yau (2013b).

[5] See Fung and Yau (2013).

the RMB to become a global reserve currency, (2) control smooth cross-border capital flows to China so as to harness the inflation in mainland China, and (3) develop an offshore RMB bond market as a means to tapping foreign capital. The timeline of the historical events in the offshore RMB market is presented in Vignette 1.1.

VIGNETTE 1.1 EVOLUTION OF THE OFFSHORE RMB MARKET

Date	Events
December 2003	The Hong Kong Monetary Authority (HKMA) announced CNY business on a trial basis in Hong Kong.
February 2004	Personal RMB banking business and RMB deposits allowed in Hong Kong and Macau; Bank of China (Hong Kong) designated as RMB clearing bank.
December 2005	Settlement agreement on RMB business for designated business customers.
January 2007	Qualified mainland financial institutions permitted to issue RMB bonds in Hong Kong (dim sum bonds).
July 2007	China Development Bank (CDB) issued the first offshore RMB bond (dim sum bond) in Hong Kong.
December 2008	China signed its first bilateral local currency swap arrangement with South Korea.
July 2009	Pilot RMB trade settlement scheme for five mainland Chinese cities with Hong Kong and Macau.
September 2009	China's Ministry of Finance launched three tranches of dim sum bonds to retail and institutional investors.
February 2010	National Development and Reform Commission (NDRC) issued Elucidation of Supervisory Principles and Operational Arrangements Regarding Renminbi Business in Hong Kong.
June 2010	Extension of RMB trade settlement scheme to 20 mainland provinces and all overseas countries and regions.
July 2010	Restrictions on offshore RMB business mostly lifted; RMB interbank market formed. Debut of the first landmark issue of dim sum bonds: Hopewell Highway Infrastructure, the first nonfinancial dim sum issuer and the first issuing entity incorporated in Hong Kong.

Date	Events
September 2010	Hong Kong exchanges launched clearing system for potential listing of RMB denominated bonds and stocks.
December 2010	Extension of the number of domestic exporters in the pilot scheme for cross-border trade settlement in RMB from original 365 to over 67,000; the first synthetic RMB bond issued.
January 2011	Pilot program allowing some mainland nonfinancial enterprises to settle overseas direct investments in CNH.
April 2011	The first CNH IPO by Hui Xian Real Estate Investment Trust.
August 2011	Vice Premier Li Keqiang visited Hong Kong, announcing concessions on FDI and Renminbi Qualified Foreign Institutional Investor (RQFII); RMB trade settlement scheme expanded to the whole of China.
December 2011	China Securities Regulatory Commission (CSRC) granted its first batch of licenses under RQFII scheme.
January 2012	Hong Kong's three note-issuing banks published RMB interbank offered rates; Hong Kong Securities and Futures Commission approved 17 RQFII products.
March 2012	All onshore eligibility restrictions for CNY trade settlement scheme were removed; HKMA, Bank Negara Malaysia, and Euroclear Bank launched a pilot program for cross-border debt securities settlement, including dim sum bonds.
April 2012	HSBC issued the first offshore RMB bond in London.
June 2012	HKMA introduced a new RMB term funding facility for Hong Kong.
February 2013	Taiwan commenced RMB business on the island.
May 2013	ICBC's branch kicked off its RMB clearing service in Singapore.

Sources: Fung, Tzau, and Yau (2013a, 2013b); Fung, Wu, and Yau (2013); Fung and Yau (2012, 2013); Minikin and Lau (2013).

The RMB-denominated bonds issued and settled outside mainland China are known as offshore RMB bonds. There are two main types of offshore RMB-denominated bonds issued in Hong Kong: CNH bonds or "dim sum" bonds that are issued and settled based on the offshore RMB exchange rates (i.e., CNH exchange rates), and synthetic RMB bonds that are settled in U.S. dollars based on the onshore RMB rates (i.e., CNY exchange rates).[6] CNY (Chinese yuan) is the official International Organization for Standardization (ISO) code for the RMB, China's mainland/onshore currency, whereas CNH is the unofficial term for China's offshore currency circulating outside the mainland, primarily in Hong Kong, which is also referred to as the offshore RMB. Thus, offshore RMB bonds issued in Hong Kong are called CNH bonds or "dim sum" bonds. We use the terms *CNH bonds* and *dim sum bonds* interchangeably in this book. We specifically analyze the development and characteristics of the offshore RMB bond (dim sum bond) market in this book.

1.2 OVERVIEW OF THE DIM SUM BOND MARKET

Although the dim sum bond market is at present only a small fraction of the total RMB bond market as compared to the onshore bond market, its growth rate has exceeded all expectations and reached many milestones within a short span of time. The first dim sum bonds were issued in Hong Kong in July 2007 by China Development Bank (CDB), one of the three banks in China responsible for raising funds for large infrastructure projects, such as the Three Gorges Dam and Shanghai Pudong International Airport. The first Chinese government dim sum bonds were issued by the Ministry of Finance (MOF) in three tranches for a total amount of RMB6 billion in October 2009.

In July 2010, Hopewell Highway Infrastructure was the first foreign entity issuing dim sum bonds. The first foreign multinational corporation to issue dim sum bonds was McDonald's Corporation, a U.S. corporation, with an issue of RMB200 million in September 2010, while Sinotruk (Hong Kong) Limited was the first red-chip corporation (i.e., a Chinese company incorporated outside the mainland and listed in Hong Kong) that issued RMB2.7 billion worth of dim sum bonds in October 2010. The Asian Development Bank (ADB) was the first supranational organization that raised capital (RMB1.2 billion) in dim sum bonds listed and traded on an exchange.

---

[6] We consider dim sum bonds as a replacement of synthetic RMB bonds as the development of the CNH market allows fixed income investors to expose to RMB directly. We discuss this in more detail in Chapter 2.

From the debut of the first dim sum bond in July 2007 to the end of 2012, there were 797 dim sum bonds issued by 150 issuers, including supranational agencies, banks, corporations, and governments for a total of RMB401.52 billion. In the early years of the market development, there were few issues: five each in 2007 and 2008 for a total amount of RMB10 billion and RMB12 billion, respectively. There was little progress made in 2009 and 2010 with 8 and 28 issues, respectively, for a total of RMB51.68 billion. However, the market took off in 2011 with 290 issues, for a total amount of RMB152.01 billion. For the year 2012, the total value of dim sum bonds issued was RMB175.83 billion with 461 issues (Figure 1.1). The stupendous growth in this market reflects the might of the Chinese government, which also has the will to make RMB a global reserve currency. As such, this market will have significant impact on China and world financial markets.

Comparing to the amount of the RMB deposits in Hong Kong (i.e., CNH deposits) since 2007, the total RMB amount of dim sum bonds has only taken up a small fraction of the potential demand, suggesting that the dim sum bond market has room for future growth (Figure 1.2).

The impressive growth in the dim sum bond market has attracted a lot of interest from investors who cannot directly invest in China but want to participate in this fast-growing offshore RMB market. To many investors, investing in offshore RMB bonds is a proxy play for RMB appreciation. Thus, since the inception of the dim sum bond market in 2007, the investor demand has been the primary driver of growth for the dim sum bond market. In contrast, the supply of dim sum bonds is highly dependent on capital market sentiments as discretionary capital expenditure, rather than refinancing, is the major use of funds raised in Asian debt capital markets.

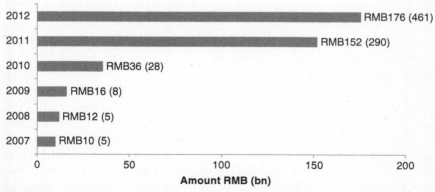

FIGURE 1.1 Dim sum bond amount and number of issues by year (2007–2012)

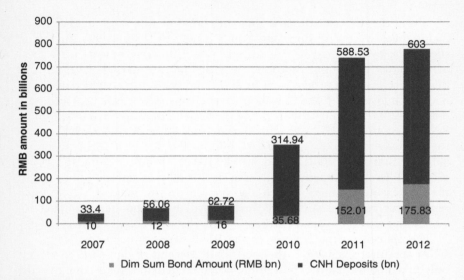

FIGURE 1.2   RMB deposits in Hong Kong (CNH deposits) and amount of dim sum bonds issued by year (2007–2012)

In the case of discretionary capital expenditure, issuers tend to be more demanding on bond pricing (i.e., lower yield), and the supply is more elastic since issuers could choose to delay capital expenditure and not issue bonds if they consider funding costs of the bond issues too high. However, in the case of refinancing, the supply is considerably less elastic, as issuers have repayment obligations to meet in a timely manner regardless of funding costs and capital market sentiments. In other words, the supply in the dim sum bond market is rather opportunistic because Asian bond issuers tend to raise funds for funding discretionary expenditure.

1.3 POLICIES SUPPORTING THE GROWTH OF OFFSHORE RENMINBI

As mentioned earlier, the establishment of the dim sum bond market is part of a multipronged strategy for internationalizing the RMB. Specifically, the dim sum bond market provides an investment conduit for the RMB earned from international trade. Without an investment outlet, circulation of RMB outside China would be limited and the willingness to hold and use RMB for trade purposes curtailed. In this section, we review recent Chinese government policies that are explicitly formulated to support the growth of the offshore

RMB (CNH). We sum up the discussion on the impact of these policies on the offshore RMB market by way of suggesting the implications for the dim sum bond market with respect to foreign investors and domestic issuers.

1.3.1 Trade Settlement in RMB and RMB Bilateral Local Currency Swap Agreements

China has long planned its currency to play an increasingly important role in the global financial system. The rise in the RMB's value relative to the U.S. dollar in early 2008 put many Chinese exporters in a less competitive position when competing with exporters from countries with a stable or depreciating currency against the U.S. dollar (see Figure 1.3). Thus, it is important for Chinese exporters to diversify the currency denomination of trade settlement away from the U.S. dollar and steer it toward the RMB.

The ability to settle trade in RMB would greatly reduce the exchange risk in the future, and hence bilateral local currency swap arrangements with foreign central banks are actively promoted in light of this broader policy target. Bilateral local currency swap agreements permit foreign central banks to sell the RMB to their local importers who want to buy Chinese goods. This is particularly useful for importers struggling to obtain trade financing in RMB in the wake of the 2007–2008 global financial crisis. As such, the bilateral local currency swap agreement policy is consistent with China's desire to participate in the Group of 20's efforts to support trade financing. As more trade settlements are denominated in RMB and with the bilateral local currency swap arrangements, China's trading partners are

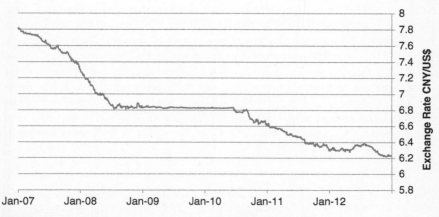

FIGURE 1.3 The exchange rates of RMB (CNY/US$) (2007–2012)

more willing to hold RMB for settlement purposes. Thus, trade settlement in RMB also helps promote RMB as a global reserve currency and diversify China's foreign currency reserve away from U.S. dollars. The purpose for both countries signing the bilateral local currency swap agreement is to avoid their currency risk against the U.S. dollar since they no longer have to exchange their currency via the U.S. dollar.

Bilateral local currency swap arrangements do not signal full RMB convertibility, but they are an important step toward it. The recent acceleration in the reform schedule by the Chinese authorities appears to suggest that the prospect of partial convertibility, especially between China and its major regional trading partners, may be closer than many believe. When there are enough RMBs floating around outside China, it indicates that the Chinese currency is used widely around the world, promoting investment in the Chinese bond market.

The Chinese authorities broadened the scope of the RMB trading program in December 2010 by increasing the number of qualified exporters from a few hundred to over 67,000, who can use the RMB in trading their goods. It is expected that "by 2015, half of China's trade with the emerging markets will settle in RMB, which will result in $2 trillion–equivalent worth of transactions per annum."[7] The use of the RMB to settle cross-border trade has grown strongly. RMB-denominated trade transactions now make up about 12 percent of China's total trade, while China has pledged to further ease the restrictions on cross-border capital flows that will encourage more RMB trade settlements.[8]

A growing number of companies in Europe are choosing to settle trade transactions in RMB to improve their position in price negotiations when doing business with partners with China according to a survey by Deutsche Bank in 2012.[9] A total of 102 companies were surveyed from the United Kingdom, Germany, and the Netherlands, and 20 percent of the respondents had already invoiced their trading partners in RMB. The remaining 80 percent indicated that a switch to invoicing in RMB was in the pipeline. Survey results show that companies using RMB could help reduce prices by an average of 4.8 percent in negotiations with Chinese business partners, while about 60 percent of the responding companies had a China business turnover of less than RMB10 million (US$1.57 million). The use of RMB in trade settlement is expected to increase in Latin American countries as well since the trade

---

[7] See Carnevale (2011), p. 10.

[8] See "China Banker Sees Lower Bar for Yuan Globalization," http://online.wsj.com/article 4578116470309984856.html?KEYWORDS=China+Renminbi+trade

[9] See www.financeasia.com/News/313660,more-european-smes-to-invoice-in-rmb.aspx

volume between Latin America and China is increasing (e.g., the trade in natural resources between Brazil and China). In 2009, China had displaced the United States as Brazil's largest trading partner, and in 2011 alone the Brazilian-Chinese trade volume rose by 34.5 percent to $84.2 billion.[10] China has a target of 20 percent to 30 percent RMB trade settlement among all trade in the long run.[11] Thus, there is still a long way to go.

1.3.2 Offshore RMB Currency Trading

Global trading in RMB allows businesses to buy and sell the currency to finance trade investment and borrowing. It is noted that Hong Kong accounts for 75 percent of China's RMB trade settlement (RMB506 billion), affirming its major role in RMB trading.[12]

Offshore RMB currency trading started in Hong Kong in July 2010 and reached its peak of RMB500 million (US$70 million) during March–June 2011. It dropped to as low as RMB50 million in September and rebounded to between RMB150 million and RMB200 million in November 2011.[13] Compared to the US$4 trillion daily trading in the global currency market, trading in the offshore RMB is dwarfed by trading in the U.S. dollar, yen and euro. However, the offshore RMB trading is impressive because of its speedy gain in trading volume.

While offshore RMB trading in Hong Kong has been one of the milestones for the internationalization of the RMB, another milestone by way of offshore RMB currency trading was reached in December 2010 when RMB trading took place on the Moscow Interbank Currency Exchange (MICEX). Despite transaction volume was a meager RMB4.92 million (US$738,850) by the end of the first trading day (December 15, 2010) against the ruble, Chinese companies exporting to Russia could buy local currency directly without the need for dollars as a common currency to conduct their business. China is currently the largest consumer of energy and the largest automobile market with a rapid increase in oil consumption, whereas Russia is the second biggest exporter of oil. Thus, if this RMB-ruble market develops further, it could eventually cut the dollar out of a portion of Russian-Chinese trade.[14]

At the beginning of 2011, the Bank of China (BOC), one of China's main state-owned banks, took another important step to internationalize RMB by

---

[10] See Moore (2012b).

[11] See Fung and Yau (2012); Fung, Tzau, and Yau (2013a); and Fung, Wu, and Yau (2013).

[12] See Pang (2011).

[13] See Wei and Chan (2011).

[14] See Fung and Yau (2012).

allowing American firms to trade RMB in the United States. For example, the BOC through its New York branch allows U.S. trading firms and individuals to buy and sell the Chinese currency to the BOC. To fend off speculation in the RMB, the BOC limits the amount of RMB that can be converted by an individual in the United States to US$4,000 a day while there is no limit on the amount that can be converted by businesses, provided that they are engaged in international trade. The RMB is now allowed to move as much as one percent each day in offshore markets.[15] Apparently, China is cautiously pursuing the strategy of making the RMB to become a global reserve currency. With the expanded RMB trading program now, exporters and importers are able to transfer funds in an offshore RMB account more freely than before.[16]

Although New York has the advantage of serving in the same time zone as many of China's largest trading partners, like markets in Latin America, offshore RMB currency trading centers can be developed easily in other world financial centers, such as London and Singapore, which are also major world foreign exchange trading centers. London, which has a comparable infrastructure as New York, is located in a better time zone than New York, since it straddles both the Asian and American time zones. Expansion of the cross-border trade between the Association of Southeast Asian Nations (ASEAN) and China is fueling greater RMB trade settlement activity in Singapore. Besides offshore RMB currency trading, the currency swap market for offshore RMB is still underdeveloped and the capacity of the swap market has been limited. Currency swaps are useful to issuers who want to borrow in RMB and swap it to the preferred currency. Offshore RMB currency swaps used to be only available up to two years, but now longer tenors seem to be more readily available. However, it is still not at the stage where there is an abundance of liquidity and any tenor is open.[17]

1.3.3 Offshore RMB Deposit Center

The growth of RMB deposits in Hong Kong shown in Figure 1.2 reflects the impact of changes of the Chinese government policy on the RMB over time. The pool of RMB deposits has grown from RMB33.4 billion at the end of 2007 to RMB603 billion at the end of 2012, while the number of authorized financial institutions allowed to engage in RMB business has increased from 37 to 139 for the same period (Table 1.1). The growth in RMB deposits is

---

[15] See Wright (2012).

[16] At the time of this writing, China has named the Industrial and Commercial Bank of China (ICBC), which currently offers RMB banking services in Singapore that requires clearing through correspondent banks based in mainland China, or through banks in Hong Kong, as the central clearing bank for RMB funds in Singapore.

[17] See Caiger-Smith (2012).

TABLE 1.1 RMB Deposits (in millions) in Hong Kong (2004–2012)

Year End	Demand & Savings Deposits	Time Deposits	Total	No. of Authorized Institutions Engaged in RMB Business
2004	5,417	6,710	12,127	38
2005	10,620	11,966	22,586	38
2006	12,228	11,175	23,403	38
2007	22,539	10,861	33,400	37
2008	38,118	17,942	56,060	39
2009	40,662	22,056	62,718	60
2010	117,573	197,365	314,938	111
2011	176,398	412,132	588,529	133
2012	123,542	479,453	602,996	139

Source: HKMA

partly attributable to RMB trade settlement. These statistics indicate the phenomenal growth and wide acceptance of this market. The development of this offshore RMB deposit market in Hong Kong results partly from the fact that many Hong Kong residents parked their cash in RMB deposit accounts at local banks in the hope of benefiting from the expected appreciation of the Chinese currency, while Hong Kong dollar deposit rates had been very low since the Hong Kong dollar is pegged to the U.S. dollar.

RMB deposits now are about 10 percent of total deposits in Hong Kong and are expected to grow to 25 percent by 2015 as the offshore currency market develops and more investment opportunities become available as part of the liberalization policy.[18] Such a huge amount of RMB deposits in Hong Kong calls for concern that RMB may be used for speculation. New regulations on RMB currency trading discouraging speculation in RMB trading in Hong Kong was announced at the end of 2010. Banks in Hong Kong face new restrictions on their ability to get access to the RMB through China's foreign exchange market. That is, the limit on net open RMB positions on bank balance sheets in China's currency will be restricted to 10 percent of their assets or liabilities denominated in the currency. Yet, the upward trajectory of RMB deposits in Hong Kong has not been stopped. With this RMB deposit base as the foundation, contributions made by

---

[18] Source: HKMA and "Offshore RMB to Be HK's 2nd Largest Source of Deposits" (2013).

Hong Kong in helping China to internationalize the RMB currency will be unquestionable.

The growth of the dim sum bond market relies heavily on the size of the RMB deposits in the banking system of Hong Kong, which appears to decline in 2012 after peaking in November 2011, and the Chinese government restrictions on the use of the money raised in this market in the mainland. It is certain that the Chinese government will continue to use Hong Kong as the hub for enterprises to issue dim sum bonds while making efforts to develop new offshore RMB bond hubs, such as Taiwan, Singapore, and London.

In July 2012, Taiwan's Financial Supervisory Commission approved the offshore banking unit (OBU) scheme, under which offshore branches of the local Taiwanese banks have received approval to engage in RMB business. In late August 2012, the Taipei branch of the BOC was appointed as the clearing bank for RMB in Taiwan, while the Shanghai branch of the Bank of Taiwan would serve as the clearing bank for the Taiwan dollar in China. Since February 6, 2013, after a cross-strait currency clearing mechanism was established with mainland China, Taiwan's domestic banking sector has been allowed to conduct offshore RMB business, such as deposits, lending, and remittances. With RMB clearing in Taiwan, the CNT market (i.e., offshore CNY deliverable in Taiwan; Taiwan's version of CNH) will accumulate more offshore RMB (CNT) deposits; yet it is still small as compared to the CNH market in Hong Kong. It is expected that the total CNT deposits will be between RMB100 billion and RMB150 billion by the end of 2013.[19]

Singapore has the largest share of global RMB payments, outside China and Hong Kong. Singapore's offshore RMB flows have been buoyed by the healthy growth of trade and financial linkages with China. In 2011, China was Singapore's third-largest trading partner, with trade totaling $101.4 billion or 10.4 percent of the total trade, and an increase of 6.4 percent from 2010. The Monetary Authority of Singapore estimates that the pool of RMB deposits in the city totaled RMB60 billion (US$12 billion), which is about one-tenth of the RMB deposit pool in Hong Kong in early 2012.[20]

On July 6, 2012, China signed an enhanced free trade agreement with Singapore that includes a promise to designate two Chinese banks to clear RMB transactions in Singapore, signifying China's decision to use Singapore as another offshore RMB hub after Hong Kong. The enhanced free trade

---

[19] See Xinhua News, "Taiwan Banks' RMB Deposits Top 60b Yuan," May 17, 2013. At the time of this writing, the outstanding amount of the offshore RMB (CNT) deposits in Taiwan stood at RMB70.1 billion (US$11.42 billion) on June 11, 2013.

[20] See "RMB Internationalization—Singapore Style," July 18, 2012. Retrieved from www.cigionline.org/publications/2012/7/rmb-internationalization-percentE2 percent80 percent94-singapore-style

agreement means greater financial integration between China and Singapore and within the Asian region. The agreement makes it easier for Singapore's leading banks (Development Bank of Singapore, Overseas Chinese Banking Corporation, and United Overseas Bank) to expand in China while making it easier for China's two leading banks to expand in Singapore. Currently operating in Singapore, the BOC and the Industrial and Commercial Bank of China (ICBC), have been granted qualifying full bank (QFB) privileges by the Monetary Authority of Singapore, whereas the China Banking Regulatory Commission (CBRC) will name two Chinese banks as the clearing banks for RMB transactions in Singapore. Apparently, gaining the status of clearing bank means special privileges for the winners. The BOC started operations in Singapore in 1936 and now operates five branches and one remittance center. Since the BOC is a QFB, Beijing would find the advantage in maintaining a single clearing window to track RMB flows and to manage the money supply of the offshore RMB pool since the BOC serves as an RMB clearing bank in Hong Kong. However, the Chinese government is concerned about whether the monopolistic power enjoyed by the BOC would make it less innovative in differentiating the dim sum bond market hub in Singapore from that in Hong Kong. In contrast, the ICBC, which has been operating in the Singaporean market for the past 20 years and the second QFB, would represent a new approach to the evolving regime for RMB internationalization.[21]

The Chinese authorities have remarked that they see a future for the offshore RMB business in London to be developed into an offshore RMB bond hub, although not much progress has been made by the Chinese government since that remark. London as a global financial center offers many advantages over Hong Kong and could eclipse Hong Kong as the center for offshore RMB currency trading (CNL, i.e., London's version of CNH). The City of London Corporation announced that a committee (the CLC committee) composed of Europe-based banks (Barclays, Deutsche Bank, HSBC, and Standard Chartered) and the BOC would work with London city regulators, the Bank of England, the Financial Services Authority, and the U.K. Treasury to develop a plan to strengthen London's CNL capabilities.[22]

While analysis and implementation protocols to facilitate CNL trading and deposits were being drafted, the CLC committee member banks jump-started CNL business by issuing and listing a dim sum bond of their own in London. HSBC's offshore RMB bond issue had received international attention, with European investors accounting for 60 percent of the total issue and the rest sold in Asia. The City of London Corporation announced that

---

[21] At the time of this writing, the ICBC has launched the clearing for RMB transactions in Singapore.

[22] See Davis (2012).

London banks had already taken in deposits of RMB109 billion, which is expected to grow as the city promotes CNL trade settlement. It is doubtful that London banks would soon become clearing banks for RMB settlement since Hong Kong has been acting as London banks' clearing agent.

Regarding how other cities besides Hong Kong (Taiwan, Singapore, and London) would support the offshore RMB markets, Beijing encourages a broader range of borrowers and instrument types to ensure a healthy evolution of these markets.

1.3.4 Implications for the Dim Sum Bond Market: Opportunities and Challenges

Recent Chinese government policies that are explicitly formulated to support the growth of the offshore RMB (CNH) were reviewed in the preceding sections. Next, we sum up the discussion on the impact of these policies on the offshore RMB markets by way of suggesting the implications for the dim sum bond market to foreign investors and domestic issuers in terms of opportunities and challenges.

1.3.4.1 Opportunities   The development of the dim sum bond market offers tremendous opportunity to foreign investors and domestic firms. As capital flows are largely regulated in China, foreign investors and firms are regulated in their investments in China. With the growth of the dim sum bond market, foreign investors and firms can invest directly in these offshore RMB bonds without going through the regulatory red tape for investing in China. At the same time, if foreign firms operating in China need RMB funding, they can raise longer maturity RMB funding through the dim sum bond market instead of relying on shorter-term borrowings from Chinese banks. Usually, it is not easy for foreign firms to obtain loans from Chinese banks. Chinese firms can raise money by issuing dim sum bonds in Hong Kong instead of issuing bonds in the domestic market in which regulations are more restrictive.

As trade volumes increase between China and its trading partners, if the RMB replaces the U.S. dollar as the denomination for trade settlement, the demand for CNH will increase, thus favoring the CNH market since Hong Kong is the conduit of RMB trade settlement. The increasing CNH base will be a source of increasing demand for dim sum bonds. There is also a lot of interest from the European investors, especially private banks. Although dim sum bonds have yet to reach the critical mass to become an asset class in most international portfolios, the potential diversification benefit when they are included in portfolios is evident.

1.3.4.2 Challenges   One notable challenge to dim sum bond issuers includes moving the proceeds from dim sum bonds onshore into mainland China.

On October 14, 2011, market restrictions were once again relaxed when the PBOC and the MOFCOM issued new rules governing foreign investment into China using offshore RMB funds. The new rules opened a new channel for offshore RMB funds to flow back into China's market (including foreign direct investment cross-border financing).[23] Another challenge is competition from the domestic loan market. Although multinational corporations (MNCs) can borrow onshore from the traditional banking and credit channels or via shadow banking channels, it is subject to credit availability and Chinese government's monetary policies. Moreover, some MNCs with operations in mainland China point out that their operations onshore are generating a lot of cash and thus the absolute funding requirements they have in China are not significant and have no immediate need to issue dim sum bonds.[24]

Although the dim sum bond market has provided a channel to investors, investors in Hong Kong have very limited options to invest in the mainland securities markets, such as the A-shares. Responding to rapid developments in the offshore RMB currency, deposit, and bond markets in Hong Kong, the PBOC has sped up the Renminbi Qualified Foreign Institutional Investor (RQFII) program endorsed by the Chinese Vice Premier Li in August 2011. The RQFII program enables funds from the offshore RMB markets to be invested in the domestic A-shares. The RQFII program certainly expands the investment universe for offshore RMB deposits in Hong Kong. The RQFII program differs from the Qualified Foreign Institutional Investor (QFII) program, introduced in China in November 2002, which allows U.S. dollars to be invested in A-shares by one of the 108 foreign institutions approved for the QFII program by the State Administration of Foreign Exchange (SAFE).

The RQFII program was first opened to domestic fund managers and Hong Kong subsidiaries of brokerage firms that were familiar with the A-share market.[25] Thus, the program complements the central government's overall strategy to internationalize the RMB and helps the development of the offshore RMB markets. However, the RQFII program and its future expansion to other cities will take some business from Hong Kong's dim sum bond

---

[23] See www.nortonrosefulbright.com/knowledge/publications/61977/the-market-for-dim-sum-bonds

[24] See Moore (2012a).

[25] At the time of this writing, RQFII has been expanded to Taiwan in June 2013, and to Singapore and London in July 2013. As of July 2013, there have been 37 RQFII licenses granted to institutions, with RMB104.9 billion quota handed out thus far (Muk, 2013b), less than half of the RMB270 billion quota (Tan, 2013).

[26] At the time of this writing, HSBC Global Asset Management has become the first foreign fund house to receive the approval for a RQFII license (Muk, 2013a).

market. The near-monopoly position of Hong Kong will soon be challenged by other cities that have been approved to partake in the RQFII programs.[26]

The RQFII program highlights the challenge that all offshore RMB markets have to deal with: the policy risk. Changes in China's government policy may affect the growth and development of any offshore RMB market considerably because the Chinese government would probably change policies based on considerations at the global level rather than at the individual country's level. With the early success in the internationalization of the RMB, there is a sense of complacency in Hong Kong for its preeminent position in the efforts. Several sources of growth for the dim sum bond market can be attributed to China's favorable policy shift, which provides a huge impetus to this market. Without changes in regulation and policy approved by the Chinese authorities, development in the dim sum bond market would not have taken root so quickly and successfully. In other words, in the development of the offshore RMB market, Hong Kong has played a passive role that has required cooperation and collaboration with the Chinese central government. For that, it might not have to compete directly with Singapore, New York, or London for offshore RMB business. Hong Kong's natural endowment is the competitive niche that other financial centers do not have: the "one country, two systems" basic law that governs Hong Kong as a special administrative region. Under the Basic Law, Hong Kong can maintain its own currency linked to the U.S. dollar. Hong Kong's linked currency system enables China to pursue its RMB internationalization policy as Hong Kong will serve as a testing ground, or better yet, a buffer zone for engaging the rest of the world's financial markets. Thus, even with an expanded RQFII program to future offshore RMB centers, Hong Kong may compete well if the competitive niche can be maintained and reinforced. The development of Hong Kong's RMB offshore market has showcased the role of Hong Kong in the grand scheme of the internationalization of RMB in which it has acted as a buffer zone for China, allowing foreign capital to move in and out of China freely without the adverse impacts of capital flows.[27]

REFERENCES

Caiger-Smith, W. 2012. "Global Banks Rush to Tap Great Renminbi Expansion." *Euroweek: Offshore RMB Bonds: A Maturing Global Market*, June: 53.
Carnevale, Francesca. 2011. "The Game Changer: Dim Sum Market Sets New Pace for RMB Acceptance." *FTSE Global Markets*, October: 6–10.

---

[27] See Fung and Yau (2012).

Davis, Anita. 2012. "Banks to Jumpstart London's Dim Sum Activity." *Asiamoney* 23(4): 73.

Fung, Hung-Gay, and Jot Yau. 2012. "The Chinese Offshore Renminbi Currency and Bond Markets: The Role of Hong Kong." *China and World Economy* 20(3): 107–122.

Fung, Hung-Gay, and Jot Yau. 2013. "The Dim Sum Bond Market and Its Role *in the Internationalization of the Renminbi*." *European Financial Review*, February–March: 64–67.

Fung, Hung-Gay, Jr-Ya Wu, and Jot Yau. 2013. "Recent Policy Changes toward the Internationalization of the Renminbi: A Review." *Chinese Economy*, 46(4): 6–24.

Fung, Hung-Gay, Derrick Tzau, and Jot Yau. 2013a. "A Global Chinese Renminbi Bond Market: The Dim Sum Bond Market," in *Frontiers of Economics and Globalization*, Vol. 13, H.G. Fung and Y. Tse (eds.). Bingley, UK: Emerald Group Publishing Ltd.

Fung, Hung-Gay, Derrick Tzau, and Jot Yau. 2013b. "Offshore Renminbi-Denominated Bonds: Dim Sum Bonds." *Chinese Economy* 46(2): 6–28.

Minikin, R., and K. Lau. 2013. *The Offshore Renminbi: The Rise of the Chinese Currency and Its Global Future.* Singapore: John Wiley & Sons.

Moore, P. 2012a. "Companies Recognize the True Value of Offshore RMB." *Euroweek: Offshore RMB Bonds: A Maturing Global Market*, June: 50–52.

Moore, P. 2012b. "CNH Catches On with Emerging Borrowers." *Euroweek: Offshore RMB Bonds: A Maturing Global Market*, June: 56.

Muk, E. 2013a. "HSBC Global AM Wins RQFII Licence." *AsianInvestor*, July 26.

Muk, E. 2013b. "RQFII Programme Extends to London and Singapore." *AsianInvestor*, July 15.

"Offshore RMB to Be HK's 2nd Largest Source of Deposits." 2013. *China Daily*, February 1. Retrieved from http://chinadaily.com.cn

Pang, P., 2011. "Hong Kong's Expanding Role as an Offshore RMB Center." *Goldman Sachs Global Macro Conference*, February 22, Hong Kong.

Tan, Clement. 2013. "China Plays the Long Game in Latest Investment Quota Expansion." Reuters, July 17.

Wei, Lingling, and Carol Chan. 2011. "Broader Pitch for Dim-Sum Bonds." *Wall Street Journal*, November 17, C3.

Wright, Chris. 2012. "PBOC Loosens Its Grip." *Euroweek: Offshore RMB Bonds: A Maturing Global Market*, June: 30.

CHAPTER 2

Offshore RMB-Denominated Bonds—Dim Sum Bonds

The previous chapter gave an account of the historical developments of the off-shore renminbi (RMB)-denominated bonds as part of China's grand scheme of the internationalization of the renminbi. It highlighted the significance of the government policy as an instrumental directive to the development and growth of this nascent market. From the investor's as well as the issuer's perspective, the future development of this market is very much dependent on the policy stance of the Chinese central government toward its overall policy goal of RMB internationalization. Uncertainty arising from policy risk is largely unhedgeable and can be managed only by careful monitoring of the government policy as well as market conditions, which may in turn force the government to change its course on the internationalization of RMB. In this chapter, we present information and characteristics of the offshore RMB-denominated bonds in Hong Kong, also known as the "dim sum" bonds that are of interest to potential investors and issuers for understanding the details of this new offshore RMB debt market orchestrated by the Chinese government. Systematic presentation of the characteristics of the market enables potential investors and issuers to make informed decisions about whether this market is appropriate for investing or as a funding source. The bond characteristics and trends thereof we present in this chapter include type and form; coupon; tenor; credit ratings; collateral and claim priority; covenants, including financial covenants; credit enhancement such as guarantees, keepwell agreements, and letters of support; and exchange listing.

2.1 DEFINITION

The offshore RMB-denominated bond market, which is a nascent financial market, was developed as part of a multipronged strategy of the Chinese government to internationalize the RMB to become a global reserve currency, to control smooth cross-border capital flows to China so as to harness inflation in mainland China, and to develop offshore RMB markets as a means of tapping foreign capital. The RMB-denominated bonds issued and settled outside mainland China are known as offshore RMB-denominated bonds.

There are two main types of offshore RMB-denominated bonds: dim sum bonds that are issued and settled in Hong Kong based on the *offshore* RMB (CNH) exchange rates; and synthetic RMB bonds that are settled in U.S. dollars based on the *onshore* RMB (CNY) exchange rates.[1] Since the offshore RMB-denominated bonds issued in Hong Kong or dim sum bonds are settled at CNH rates, they are sometimes referred to as CNH bonds. We use the terms *dim sum bonds* and *CNH bonds* interchangeably in this book.

Although the offshore RMB-denominated bond market is at present only a small fraction of the domestic CNY bond markets, its rate of growth has exceeded all expectations and reached many milestones within a very short span of time.[2] There have been opportunities for foreign investors outside Hong Kong to participate in the fast-growing offshore RMB markets. For example, a synthetic RMB bond market emerged in response to changes in the market conditions. Synthetic dim sum bonds are bonds denominated in RMB but settled in U.S. dollars, implying that there is a speculative element in the RMB/USD exchange rate in this type of investment. We discuss this type of RMB bonds in section 2.1.2.

A caveat is in order here. As dim sum bonds refer to a variety of instruments, both short-tenor and long-tenor debt instruments, a proper name for this market should be the dim sum debt market. However, as the term *dim sum debt market* is not commonly used, we continue to refer to this debt market as the dim sum bond market for consistency with the convention.

2.1.1 Dim Sum Bonds

Table 2.1 shows the characteristics of the outright dim sum bond market in terms of the number, amount, average coupon, and average tenor of the issues.[3] For the period June 25, 2007, through December 31, 2012[4], 797 dim

---

[1] Definitions of CNH and CNY exchange rates can be found in Chapter 1, section 1. At the time of this writing, the PBOC has approved clearing and settlement of RMB transactions in Taiwan and in Singapore, thus clearing the way for offshore RMB-denominated bonds to be issued in Taiwan and Singapore (Law, 2013).

[2] Table 6.1 presents the landmark issues of dim sum bonds.

[3] In this chapter and discussions thereafter, we refer only to the outright dim sum bonds, excluding convertible dim sum bonds and synthetic dim sum bonds, which are presented in section 2.1.2

[4] Announcement dates for pricing the bonds according to Bloomberg are used here. Hereafter, we refer to this issuance period as 2007–2012 for brevity.

TABLE 2.1 Number, Amount, Average Coupon, and Average Tenor of Dim Sum Bond Issues by Year (2007–2012)

Year	Number of Issues	Amount RMB(Mln)	Average Amount RMB (Mln)	Average Coupon (% p.a.)	Average Coupon (Exclude Zeros and FRN) (% p.a.)	Average Tenor (Years)
2007	5	10,000.00	2,000.00	3.15	3.15	2.40
2008	5	12,000.00	2,400.00	3.31	3.31	2.40
2009	8	16,000.00	2,000.00	3.21	2.68	2.50
2010	28	35,680.00	1,274.29	2.58	2.52	2.68
2011	290	152,011.50	524.18	2.15	2.19	2.16
2012	461	175,825.40	381.40	3.15	3.25	1.82
Overall	797	401,516.90	503.79	2.77	2.83	1.99

sum bonds with a total amount of RMB401.52 billion were priced to be issued with an average tenor just slightly below two years and an average coupon rate of 2.77 percent, per annum.[5]

The market had experienced significant growth since 2010, when China relaxed some regulations regarding the use of the RMB in trade settlement. In 2011, the growth of the dim sum bond market was further fostered by the relaxation of the use of the proceeds from dim sum bond issues, resulting from the implementation of the Renminbi Qualified Foreign Institutional Investor (RQFII) program in which the RMB raised offshore from the issuance of dim sum bonds can be repatriated back to China as foreign direct investment (FDI).[6]

In 2012, there was a big jump in the market volume, with 461 issues of the dim sum bonds (see Figure 1.1). The average deal size is RMB381.4 million with an average tenor of 1.82 years and an average coupon rate of 3.15 percent, which is greater than the overall average of 2.77 percent, indicating that issuers had been become more responsive to the demand by investors on yield when the appreciation of the Chinese currency slowed down.

2.1.2 Synthetic RMB Bonds

Prior to the debut of dim sum bonds, fixed-income investors could not benefit directly from the anticipated RMB appreciation. Issuers thus came up with

---

[5] Hereafter, all coupon rates are expressed as percent per annum.
[6] See Fung and Yau (2012).

an interim supply of synthetic RMB bonds, which are denominated in RMB, but interest and principal repayments are paid in U.S. dollars. Exchange rates are based on CNY, that is, the onshore exchange rate for settlement purposes. These bonds are structured in such a way that fixed-income investors would benefit from the expected RMB appreciation, while issuers hoping to lower the interest cost but not to risk on the foreign exchange rate would prefer to issue synthetic RMB bonds. Synthetic RMB bonds were therefore issued by corporations before they were approved by the Chinese governments in July 2010 to issue dim sum bonds. Since then, corporations have been allowed to issue dim sum bonds, which replaced synthetic RMB bonds as a one-way bet on the value of RMB appreciation. After dim sum bonds made their debut, synthetic RMB bonds were phased out. Synthetic RMB bonds were issued only within a very narrow time window between December 2010 and March 2011 (see Table 2.2), indicating that synthetic RMB bonds were precursors to dim sum bonds for that interim period. Altogether, seven synthetic dim sum bonds were issued and sold publicly.

2.2 BOND ISSUE CHARACTERISTICS

Dim sum bond issues have similar characteristics as other bond issues. We would not be able to discuss every single characteristic. We select and discuss cross-sectional bond issue characteristics that we find interesting and necessary for understanding the dim sum bond market, including type, form, coupon, tenor, credit ratings, collateral, claim priority, covenants, and exchange listing.

2.2.1 Type

2.2.1.1 Notes, Bonds, and Certificates of Deposit   To classify the types of dim sum bonds is quite a challenge since the conventional terms are not consistently applied to this segment of the Asian debt market. For example, dim sum debt securities with a two-year tenor may be referred to as notes or bonds. Moreover, many dim sum issues are fixed-rate certificates of deposit. Thus, dim sum debt may be known to investors by different appellations. For our purposes, we group the offshore RMB-denominated debt instruments into three categories: notes, bonds, and certificates of deposit. A note is a simple promissory note from one party written as a debt instrument to an investor. Promissory notes are common in many business practices, and types of credit lending, such as car loans and personal loans. A promissory note can be sold just like any other debt instrument.

TABLE 2.2 Synthetic RMB Bonds (2010–2011)

	Coupon (% p.a.)	Amount (RMBbn)	Amount (US$bn)	Issue Date	Maturity Date
Shui On Development (Hong Kong)	6.875	3.0	0.451	December 23, 2010	December 23, 2013
China SCE Property (China)	10.5	2.0	0.303	January 14, 2011	January 14, 2016
Evergrande Real Estate (China)	7.5	5.55	0.841	January 19, 2011	January 19, 2014
Evergrande Real Estate (China)	9.25	3.7	0.561	January 19, 2011	January 19, 2016
Shui On Development (China)	7.625	3.5	0.531	January 26, 2011	January 26, 2015
LDK Solar Co. Ltd (China)	10.0	1.2	0.189	February 28, 2011	February 28, 2014
Powerlong Real Estate	11.50	0.75	0.114	March 9, 2011	March 17, 2014
Total		19.70	2.990		

A dim sum debt issuer can sell medium-term notes (MTNs), which are notes with a tenor typically less than five years. MTNs can be issued under various types of programs, such as the EMTN (Euro MTN) and GMTN (global MTN) programs. These programs give issuers the flexibility to seize an issuance window quickly, without going through the time-consuming and costly route of preparing stand-alone documentation. Issuers can be ready to issue dim sum bonds in an efficient manner in terms of both time and money. McDonald's Corporation was the first issuer that had the first-ever renminbi instrument sold off an EMTN program. The McDonald's issuance has shown great promise for many major corporations, who already have EMTN or GMTN programs in place. Sometimes, an issuer can also issue dim sum MTNs under other debt issuance programs (DIPs).

Certificates of deposit, also referred to as CDs, are short-term debt instruments through which the issuer (such as a bank) and investors may be able to generate interest income on the amount over time. CDs may carry fixed interest rates (denoted as FXCDs) or floating interest rates. Investors in CDs and FXCDs include private banking (PB) clients, who can buy CDs on leverage. Given the generally high credit quality of the CD-issuing banks, PB clients can borrow to buy CDs with a high leverage ratio. The net yield (leveraged yield – funding cost) on leveraged CDs could be good carry trades. Besides PB clients, corporations that generate RMB/CNH funds through daily operations are another type of CD investor. They buy CDs as a safe liquidity tool for treasury management. CD investors who need liquidity prior to maturity could sell the CDs in the secondary market.

Dim sum bonds can carry zero coupons. Zero-coupon dim sum bonds do not pay periodic interest and are bought by investors at a discount, that is, a price lower than the face or par value (e.g., RMB1,000). When the zero-coupon bond matures, the investor will receive the face value. All zero-coupon dim sum bonds issued thus far are short-term instruments with one-year tenor.

2.2.1.2 Registered versus Bearer Bonds   In terms of legal type, dim sum bonds can be registered or in bearer form. Registered bonds are bonds whose owners are registered with the issuer. The owner's name, identity, and contact information are recorded and kept on file with the issuer, allowing the issuer to pay coupon payments to the appropriate person. If the bond is in physical form, the owner's name is printed on the certificate. Most registered bonds are now recorded electronically with the owner's information.

Bearer bonds are unregistered and thus differ from the more common type of investment securities that are registered. That is, there is no record regarding the owner or the transactions involving ownership. Whoever physically holds the paper on which the bond is issued owns the debt instrument. This is useful for investors who wish to remain anonymous.

However, it is not possible to recover the value of a bearer bond in the event of its loss, theft, or destruction. The appeal of bearer bonds is primarily the investor anonymity and probably the tax avoidance on the bond income. Table 2.3 shows that the total number of bearer bonds is 131 (about 16.4 percent of the total number of issues and about 30 percent of the total amount issued) with an average issue value of RMB503.79 million for the period 2007–2012, according to Bloomberg. Also, Bloomberg's record shows that the majority of the dim sum bonds (585, or over 73 percent of the total number of issues, and about 51 percent of the total amount issued) are not stated as either bearer or registered.

2.2.2 Form: Regulation S

Section 5 of the U.S. Securities Act of 1933 requires any offer or sale occurring inside the United States to be subject to registration requirements. This law is meant to protect investors in the United States. However, whether securities issued outside the United States but offered or resold to U.S. investors need registration has not been clear. Regulation S (RegS) is a series of rules clarifying the position of the Securities and Exchange Commission (SEC) that securities offered and sold outside of the United States do not need to be registered with the SEC.[7] RegS stipulates two safe harbor rules, among others, allowing exemption from registration requirements for offers and sales of securities made outside the United States. Thus, securities issuing under RegS can invoke the Issuer and the Resale Safe Harbors to gain exemption from the U.S. registration requirements if they satisfy two general conditions for the Safe Harbors: (1) no securities offer, sale or resale made in an *offshore* transaction is sold directly to any person in the United States); and (2) *no directed selling efforts* (including printing materials) are made in the United States in connection with an offer, sale, or resale.[8]

Table 2.4 reports the number and characteristics of RegS and non-RegS dim sum bonds. One hundred seventy-four dim sum bonds belong to the RegS classification, about 22 percent of the total 797 issues or almost 60 percent of all non-CD dim sum bond issues (296 issues). The average size of RegS dim sum bonds (RMB916.94 million) is larger than that of the non-RegS counterparts (RMB792.82 million). Likewise, the average coupon (3.86 percent) is greater and average tenor (3.52 years) longer than those of the non-RegS issues (3.21 percent and 2.32 years, respectively).

---

[7] See Stroock & Stroock & Lavan LLP (2002).

[8] In Chapter 5, we discuss the difference between RegS and 144A with regard to the issuance regulations in the United States and globally.

TABLE 2.3 Total/Average Amount, Average Coupon, and Average Tenor of Registered and Bearer Bonds

Type	No. of Issues	% Share (No. of Issues)	Total Amount RMB (Mln)	% Share (RMB Amount)	Average Amount RMB (Mln)	Average Coupon (% p.a.)	Average Coupon (Exclude Zeros and FRN)(% p.a.)	Average Tenor (Years)
Bearer	131	16.44	118,245.50	29.45	902.64	2.91	2.87	2.85
Registered	81	10.16	79,911.00	19.90	986.56	4.25	4.25	3.11
Not stated	585	73.40	203,360.40	50.65	347.62	2.53	2.61	1.64
Total	797	100.00	401,516.90	100.00	503.79	2.77	2.83	1.99

TABLE 2.4 Regulation S (RegS)

RegS	No. of Issues	Total Amount in RMB (Mln)	Average Amount in RMB (Mln)	Average Coupon (% p.a.)	Average Coupon (Exclude Zeros and FRN)(% p.a.)	Average Tenor (Years)
Yes	174	159,548.00	916.94	3.86	3.86	3.52
No	122	96,724.55	792.82	3.17	3.21	2.32
CD/FXCD	501	145,244.35	289.91	2.29	2.37	1.37
Total	797	401,516.90	503.79	2.77	2.83	1.99

2.2.3 Bond Coupon

Dim sum bonds can be classified by the type of interest rate on coupon payments: fixed, floating, or zero. Dim sum bonds with fixed-rate coupons are the overwhelming majority, accounting for over 97 percent of all issues in terms of the number of issues and total amount issued (see Table 2.5). Fixed-rate dim sum instruments carry fixed interest rates throughout their tenors. Fixed-rate bonds are welcomed by buy-and-hold investors, which is a major part of the investor base of the nascent dim sum bond market as investors can get rid of interest rate risk if they hold the bonds to maturity.

Floating-rate notes/bonds have coupons tied to a benchmark interest rate, such as the Shanghai Interbank Offered Rate (SHIBOR). The rate on the bond is floating, and coupon payments are adjusted as the benchmark interest rate changes. For example, HSBC (China) sold the first floating-rate bond in the dim sum bond market in June 2009. It was an RMB1 billion, two-year bond priced at SHIBOR + 38 basis points (bp) (i.e., 4.5751 percent). Floating-rate bonds are rare in the dim sum bond market (only three issues; see Table 2.5) since an offshore benchmark yield curve is to be fully established.[9] Subsequently, CDB issued two floating-rate bonds in 2009 and 2010 to help accelerate the development of the dim sum bond market.

Zero-coupon bonds (or zeros) do not pay any coupon during the life of the bond, as they are sold at a discount to the par value. Investors earn a return on their investments as the bond prices move toward the par value over time. Zeros in the dim sum bond market only started to appear in 2011, almost four years after the inception of the market. Five zero-coupon bonds were issued in the dim sum bond market in 2011 and 13 in 2012. Table 2.5 presents the breakdown of dim sum bonds by interest rate type. It is clear that fixed-rate bonds account for the lion share of the market with a total of 776 issues, followed by 18 issues of zeros and 3 issues of floating-rate notes as of the end of 2012. Summary statistics in the table show that fixed-rate dim sum bonds, on average, have a lower coupon rate and a smaller issue size than their floating-rate counterparts. Statistics also indicate that zeros have the shortest tenor among all dim sum bonds. In the first two years since the inception of the dim sum bond market, all issues were in fixed rates. Fixed-rate dim sum bonds are still the prevalent form of issuance.

---

[9] At the time of this writing, the fourth-ever floating-rate dim sum bond since October 2010 was issued by HSBC (China) in January 2013. It was a two-year, RMB1 billion ($160.5 million) issue priced at the three-month SHIBOR−45bps. Retrieved from www.reuters.com/article/2013/01/03/markets-offshore-yuan-idUSL4N0A82JP20130103

TABLE 2.5 Total and Average Amount, Tenor, and Coupon by Interest Rate Type (2007–2012)

Type	No. of Issues	Total Amount RMB (Mln)	Average Amount RMB (Mln)	Average Coupon (% p.a.)	Average Tenor (Years)
Floating rate	3	4,000.00	1,333.33	4.66	2.33
Zero coupon	18	5,591.55	310.64	0.00	1.11
Fixed rate	776	391,925.35	505.06	2.83	2.01
Total	797	401,516.90	503.79	2.77	1.99

2.2.4 Bond Tenor

The tenor of dim sum bonds ranges from 1 to 20 years. As mentioned earlier, dim sum bonds have on average a short tenor of about 2 years. The prevalent short maturity of dim sum bonds can be explained by the demand of risk-averse investors who invest in dim sum bonds as a one-way bet on the RMB appreciation against the U.S. dollar. As such, these investors prefer a short tenor to reduce the uncertainty in the RMB exchange rate fluctuations against the U.S. dollar. This type of bias in investor demand hinders the healthy development of a nascent fixed-income market such as the dim sum bond market when the yield curve is represented only by issues with short maturity. To establish a complete term structure of interest rates for this nascent market, issues with longer maturity must appear in the market. For example, the Asian Development Bank (ADB) issued the first 10-year dim sum bonds in October 2010, while the China Development Bank (CDB) issued the first 15-year dim sum bond in January 2012. It seems that recently issuers have started to issue bonds with relatively longer tenors than earlier years, indicating the issuers' desire to satisfy investors' appetite for longer-tenor dim sum bonds and the market has become more mature.

Table 2.6 reports the total amount and average coupon of dim sum bonds by bond tenor. One-year bonds account for the bulk of all issues in terms of the number of issues (i.e., 465 issues or 58.34 percent of the total number of issues) or the total value of funds raised (RMB117.01 billion or 29.14 percent of the total amount) as of the end of 2012 with the smallest average issue size (RMB251.64 million) and the lowest coupon (averaged 2.28 percent or 2.37 percent excluding floating-rate notes [FRNs] and zeros). The second-largest batch is the three-year bonds with 164 issues (or 20.58 percent of the total issues) for a total amount of RMB140.97 billion (or 35.11 percent) with an average issue size of RMB859.57 million, and

TABLE 2.6 Total and Average Amount, and Average Coupon by Tenor (2007–2012)

Tenor (Years)	No. of Issues	% of Total	Total Amount RMB (Mln)	% of Total	Average Amount RMB (Mln)	Average Coupon (% p.a.)	Average Coupon (Exclude Zeros and FRN) (% p.a.)
1	465	58.34	117,012.85	29.14	251.64	2.28	2.37
2	108	13.55	105,196.00	26.20	974.04	2.92	2.89
2.5	1	0.13	300.00	0.07	300.00	2.90	2.90
2.75	1	0.13	350.00	0.09	350.00	3.25	3.25
3	164	20.58	140,970.00	35.11	859.57	3.72	3.74
5	35	4.39	24,076.50	6.00	687.90	3.48	3.48
5.6	1	0.13	800.00	0.20	800.00	4.00	4.00
7	5	0.63	1,920.00	0.48	384.00	3.88	3.88
8.25	1	0.13	311.55	0.08	311.55	3.65	3.65
9	2	0.25	1,800.00	0.45	900.00	4.73	4.73
10	10	1.25	4,280.00	1.07	428.00	3.92	3.92
15	3	0.38	3,500.00	0.87	1,166.67	4.18	4.18
20	1	0.13	1,000.00	0.25	1,000.00	4.30	4.30
Total	797	100	401,516.90	100	503.79	2.77	2.83

an average coupon rate of 3.72 percent or 3.74 percent (excluding FRNs and zeros). The third largest category is the two-year bonds with 108 issues (or 13.55 percent of the total), RMB105.20 billion (or 26.20 percent of the total amount), an average size of RMB974.04 million and an average coupon rate of 2.92 percent (or 2.89 percent, excluding FRNs and zeros). The tenor distribution of dim sum bonds issued for 2007–2012 is presented in Figure 2.1.

2.2.5 Credit Rating

In the early stage of the dim sum bond market development, given the exuberant expectation of RMB appreciation, limited investment opportunities for CNH holders, and relatively little involvement of institutional investors such as asset managers and hedge funds, dim sum bonds could be issued at less investor-friendly terms and conditions compared with those of Asian USD bonds. That is, issuers could issue dim sum bonds with low coupons and less restrictive covenants compared with Asian USD bonds. They could even issue dim sum bonds without credit ratings; many early issues of dim sum bonds were unrated. We will shed more light on this later.

As the RMB appreciation had started to lose its allure, more investment options for CNH had become available and institutional investors were increasingly involved in the dim sum bond market after gaining access to CNH funds, terms and conditions of dim sum bonds turned more investor friendly. Now, investors pay more attention to credit risk and bond protection, as reflected by the trend that terms and conditions of recent dim

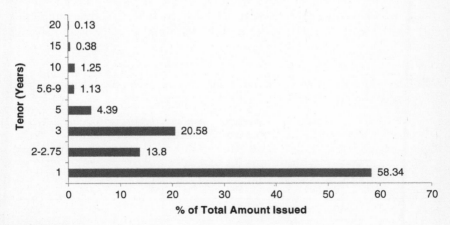

FIGURE 2.1 Tenor distribution of dim sum bonds (2007–2012)

sum bond issues are converging to those of the Asian USD bonds. Yields on dim sum bonds have also been more reflective of issuers' underlying credit-worthiness, while covenants have been changing to align with those of the Asian USD bonds. More important, credit ratings on dim sum bonds have become more common.

Credit ratings of dim sum bonds are typically done by one of the two rating agencies, Moody's or Standard & Poor's (S&P). A few are done by Fitch and Dominion Bond Rating Service (DBRS). Moody's, S&P, and Fitch are well-known credit rating agencies in the United States, whereas DBRS, an independently owned credit rating agency, is based in Toronto, Ontario, Canada. Table 2.7 reports summary statistics of the rated and unrated is-sues of dim sum bonds by the four rating agencies. Of the total 797 is-sues, 149 are rated, suggesting that the majority of bonds are not rated. The average issue size of the rated bonds is larger than that of the unrated bonds (RMB781.03 million vs. RMB440.04 million), the average coupon rate is higher (3.2 percent vs. 2.67 percent), and the average tenor is longer (3.03 years vs. 1.75 years).

If we restrict credit ratings given by the three major agencies (Moody's, S&P, and Fitch), we find some interesting results. Table 2.8 shows that issues with only one rating assigned tend to have the lowest coupon (3.03 percent) and the longest tenor (3.04 years). For issues rated by two or more agencies, the average coupon rate tends to be higher and tenor shorter. This pattern can plausibly be explained by the fact that although investors in general favor rated issues, the marginal benefit for more familiar and solid credits obtaining more than one rating is limited. In contrast, for less familiar and less solid credits, investors are more concerned about their creditworthiness. Investors tend to demand higher coupon, shorter tenor, and more than one rating. Consequently, as we have observed from Table 2.8, dim sum bonds with more credit ratings tend to be those with higher coupon and shorter tenor.

TABLE 2.7   Number of Issues, Total and Average Amount, Average Coupon, and Rated and Unrated Dim Sum Bonds (2007–2012)

Ratings	No. of Issues	Total Amount RMB (Mln)	Average Amount RMB (Mln)	Average Coupon (% p.a.)	Average Coupon (Exclude Zeros and FRN) (% p.a.)	Average Tenor (Years)
Rated*	149	116,373.55	781.03	3.20	3.22	3.03
Unrated	648	285,143.35	440.04	2.67	2.73	1.75
Total	797	401,516.90	503.79	2.77	2.83	1.99

*Rated by at least one of the rating agencies: Moody's, S&P, Fitch, or DBRS.

TABLE 2.8 Number of Issues, Total and Average Amount, Average Coupon, and Average Tenor of Bonds Rated by Moody's, S&P, and/or Fitch

No. of Ratings Given	No. of Issues	Total Amount RMB (Mln)	Average Amount RMB (Mln)	Average Coupon (% p.a.)	Average Coupon (Exclude Zeros and FRN)(% p.a.)	Average Tenor (Years)
1	70	54,645.55	780.65	3.03	3.07	3.04
2	74	59,218.00	800.24	3.35	3.35	2.95
3	1	500.00	500.00	3.75	3.75	2.00
None	652	287,153.35	440.42	2.67	2.74	1.77
Total	797	401,516.90	503.79	2.77	2.83	1.99

2.2.6 Collateral and Claim Priority

The dim sum bond market has evolved from a nascent offshore bond market for Hong Kong investors to become a major thrust in helping China internationalize its currency. Areas that have gone through rapid development include the convergence of covenant and disclosure standards, as reflected by the increasing proportion of issues with bond covenants comparable to the Asian USD bonds and credit ratings as more and more institutional investors involve in the dim sum bond market. Typically, dim sum bonds are issued by the offshore entities such as subsidiaries or overseas branches with limited investors' recourse to the parent company's onshore operating assets in the event of a default.

The majority of dim sum bonds issued to date are unsecured by collateral, and are typically ranked equally, *pari passu*, with all other unsecured and unsubordinated indebtedness, except for creditors whose claims are secured by collaterals or preferred by law to rank ahead of unsecured creditors.[10] Payments to unsecured creditors are effectively subordinated to all secured creditors of the issuer to the extent of the value of the assets securing such debts. Thus, if the issuer becomes insolvent or default on obligations under the unsecured dim sum bonds, investors can only claim against the issuer as unsecured creditors. In other words, the proceeds from liquidation of issuer's secured assets will not be used to pay unsecured creditors until after all secured claims and claims of other creditors preferred by law have been fully paid.

---

[10] *Pari passu*, in legal parlance, means "equal footing." During bankruptcy proceedings, when a verdict is reached, all creditors can be regarded equal, implying that they are *pari passu*. That is, creditors will be repaid at the same time and at the same fractional amount as all other creditors.

For the purpose of ranking claim priority on assets or collateral, dim sum bonds can be ranked into four groups: secured bonds, senior unsecured bonds, unsecured bonds, and subordinated bonds. On top of the claim priority are *secured bonds,* which are backed by assets or collateral to reduce the potential losses resulting from default. Investors holding these dim sum bonds will be paid first from the proceeds of liquidating the collateral in case the issuer defaults on the dim sum bonds. Since the recovery rate of secured bonds will likely be higher, secured bonds typically offer lower coupons/ yields than the unsecured bonds, other things being equal. There are only two secured dim sum bond issues: Jigang Bond Finance (2012), a structured deal secured by proceeds collected from letters of credit issued by the Industrial and Commercial Bank of China (ICBC); and Infrastructure Leasing and Financial Services Transportation Networks (2012), which is secured by the *first lien* on the specified collateral. Issues by Beijing Capital Land Limited (2011), Guangzhou R&F Properties Co. Ltd. (2011), and Gemdale Corporation (2012) are secured by fixed charges over the interest reserve accounts, which are escrow accounts that issuers are committed to deposit amounts equivalent to one to two coupon payments. Since the size of interest reserve accounts is in general relatively small as compared to the principal amount and coupon payables, we believe that a fixed charge over an interest reserve account will have limited impact on the bond recovery ratio in case of default. Thus, it would have limited impact on the pricing of the bond. For the purpose of analysis, we consider these senior unsecured issues, but not secured.

Senior unsecured bonds refer to those dim sum bonds that are only subordinated to debts that are secured or collateralized in terms of claim priority. Since the recovery rates for unsecured bonds could be lower than that of secured bonds in case of liquidation, senior unsecured debt tends to come with a higher yield than the secured debt on an apple-to-apple basis. The majority of dim sum bonds are senior unsecured bonds. *Unsecured bonds* are bonds with no tangible assets on the line as collateral, which can be wiped out by bankruptcy.

Subordinated bonds have the lowest claim priority on the same issuer in case of liquidation, having claim priority behind the liquidator, government tax authorities, and senior debt holders. In the case of liquidation (i.e., when the company winds up its affairs and dissolves), dim sum bondholders would be paid just before stockholders if there are assets left to be distributed after all other liabilities and debts have been paid. Subordinated bonds could be secured or unsecured, but have lower priority than that of any senior debt claims on the same asset. Since subordinated debt is repayable after all other senior debt has been paid, it has a lower recovery rate than other debt classes. The first dim sum subordinated bond was issued by the ICBC (Asia) for RMB1.5 billion in October 2011 with a 10-year tenor, 6 percent coupon, and A– rating from Fitch, which includes a "non-viability loss absorption" clause stipulating that the value of the bonds will be written down to zero if the bank is declared nonviable by the Hong Kong Monetary Authority or if the bank needs an injection of public funds to rescue it.

Table 2.9 reports summary statistics of dim sum bonds by claim priority. The largest category is the senior unsecured bonds, which have 776 issues,[11] followed by 18 issues of unsecured dim sum bonds, 2 secured bonds, and 1 subordinated bond.

2.2.7 Bond Covenants

A protective covenant is a legal contract between the bond issuer and bondholders to protect the interests of bondholders. Protective covenants generally include provisions on financial ratios and imposing performance of the issuer. In general, bonds issued by more reputable banks and corporations with better credit profile will be subject to less restrictive covenants. Hence, we are not surprised to see that dim sum bonds with more restrictive financial covenants will also pay higher coupons.

Bond covenants have become more important in placing dim sum bonds to investors, which is in stark contrast to the earlier period when dim sum bonds were "covenant-lite." Investors have begun to conceive possible consequences of a breach of covenants as the first case emerged. On August 21, 2012, Global Bio-Chem Technology Group announced that it was facing a possible breach of covenants. However, it would buy back 92 percent of its dim sum bonds after bondholders agreed to the market's first tender offer.[12]

2.2.7.1 Financial Covenants   Financial covenants restrict issuers from engaging activities that could increase the credit risk of the issuers. Typical financial covenants include restrictions with regard to the debt service coverage ratio, fixed-charge coverage ratio, liquidity ratio, and tangible-net-worth ratio. With a greater supply of dim sum bonds in the market and increasing institutional investor participation in the dim sum bond market, investors have started looking more closely at bond protections and demanded tighter covenant packages. For example, many of the early issues were not subject to financial covenants, and covenant packages in the early dim sum

---

[11] The number is reduced to 225 if we exclude 501 issues of CDs and FXCDs.

[12] See www.businessweek.com/news/2012-11-30/global-bio-chem-gets-bondholder-nod-for-first-dim-sum-buyback

TABLE 2.9 Number of Issues, Total and Average Amount, Average Coupon, and Average Tenor by Claim Priority

Type of Claim Priority	No. of Issues	Total Amount RMB (Mln)	Average Amount RMB (Mln)	Average Coupon (% p.a.)	Average Coupon (Exclude Zeros and FRN)(% p.a.)	Average Tenor (Years)
Secured	2	780.55	390.28	2.88	5.75	2.00
Senior Unsecured*	3	4,962.00	1,654.00	6.97	6.97	3.00
Senior Unsecured	773	378,299.35	489.39	2.73	2.78	1.92
Unsecured	18	15,975.00	887.50	3.47	3.68	4.33
Subordinated	1	1,500.00	1,500.00	6.00	6.00	10.00
Total	797	401,516.90	503.79	2.77	2.83	1.99

*With a fixed charge over an interest reserve account.

high-yield issuances typically included only a negative pledge, that is, a provision prohibiting the issue from creating any security interests over certain property specified in the provision. Recently, covenants of dim sum high-yield bonds appear to closely resemble the style of U.S. dollar high-yield bond covenants as the dim sum bond market has become more mature. In addition, investment-grade issues are added with new covenant features, such as change-of-control redemptions, restrictions on sale and leaseback, and currency fallback provisions allowing the issuer to repay the bond in another currency if the issuer cannot pay in RMB. For issuers whose credit profiles fall between the investment grade and non–investment grade, we see an "investment grade plus" type of covenant package, including security given by the issuers over an interest reserve bank account and enhanced financial covenants and cross-defaults, in addition to the typical investment-grade covenants.

2.2.7.2 Credit Enhancement: Guarantees, Keepwell Deeds, and Letters of Support   Many offshore RMB bonds are both structurally and legally subordinated to onshore debt of the issuing companies. The legislation in place to protect offshore investors is not always robust because of China's stringent capital controls and the uncertainties in bankruptcy proceedings. While their operating assets and cash flows are mainly onshore, most of the Chinese banks and corporations issue bonds through offshore entities. These offshore entities could be either holding companies that own equity stakes in the onshore operating companies or special purpose vehicles with no material assets and operations. In either case, offshore bonds issued by these entities do not have direct claims on the onshore operating companies or assets. In the case of default, offshore creditors can file bankruptcy claims only against the offshore entities. It remains highly uncertain as to how offshore creditors can enforce their rights against onshore operating companies or assets under the bond indenture. Even if offshore creditors can enforce their rights against the onshore operating companies or assets, offshore creditors are structurally and legally subordinated to onshore creditors, and thus, the recovery rate could be considerably lower. Conceptually, this problem of asymmetric rights between the onshore and offshore creditors can be mitigated by guarantees, keepwell agreements, and letters of support.

The disparity between the rights of onshore and offshore investors can theoretically be minimized if the offshore bonds are guaranteed. The most effective guarantee would be one from the onshore operating company specifying the recourse for the assets of the company, such as in the case of Guangzhou R&F Properties' dim sum bond.

Other forms of credit enhancement include keepwell deeds and letters of support. Keepwell deeds are contractual obligations that keepwell providers will provide financial support in the case of default. Though they are not guarantees, keepwell deeds are legally binding contractual obligations of keepwell providers and can be enforced by the bond trustees (acting on behalf of bondholders) if the issuer defaults on the bond. Since keepwell agreements are not guarantees, they are generally not required to have the State Administration of Foreign Exchange's approval at signing. The regulatory role of the SAFE is presented in Vignette 2.1.

The most commonly used version of the keepwell deed in the dim sum bond market is a keepwell deed with an equity interest purchase undertaking (EIPU), which are used in both dim sum and USD bond issues. This arrangement specifies that keepwell providers will fulfill their obligations under the keepwell deeds through purchases of the bond issuer's equity interests in offshore subsidiaries at agreed prices. In general, the agreed price will be able to cover the principal amounts of the bond and accrued interest. The keepwell deed with EIPU will require approvals from NDRC, SAFE, and/or MOFCOM as well as registration with the State Administration for Industry and Commerce (SAIC). There remains some degree of uncertainties as to whether the required approvals will be obtained and how long the approval process takes.

Letters of support are a less effective protection from the bondholders' perspective because letters of support are not legally binding. They are more of a mere expression of intent to support. Letters of support are not required to be approved by regulators at signing. As for the keepwell deed, regulatory approval may eventually be required when the provider of the letter of support fulfills its commitment, depending on the form of support. Table 2.10 compares and contrasts the different types of credit enhancement.

The presence of credit enhancement structures, such as the keepwell deed and letter of support, which require approval from SAFE, signals to investors that issuers are in earnest and the parent companies have every intention in supporting the operating companies. However, investors have to evaluate the ability and willingness of the provider of credit enhancement in providing support under stress scenarios. This is because the guarantor's credit profile may be closely linked to that of the issuer. If the issuer is in financial distress, the guarantor may also face financial difficulties and therefore may not be able to provide support. Moreover, we can also envisage that the guarantor may provide guarantees to a number of subsidiaries, and the issuer of concern may be one of them. In case of financial distress, the guarantor may choose to save other subsidiaries instead of the issuer of concern.

Table 2.11 details the different types of guarantee in the dim sum bond market. Out of 797 issues, only 70 issues have some kind of guarantees,

VIGNETTE 2.1 THE STATE ADMINISTRATION OF FOREIGN EXCHANGE (SAFE)

SAFE is an administrative agency tasked with drafting rules and regulations governing foreign exchange market activities, and managing the state foreign exchange reserves.

Specifically, the agency is responsible for:

1. Drafting regulations, standards, and policies of the foreign exchange administration system.
2. Managing and monitoring China's balance of payments, external credits, and external debts.
3. Monitoring and managing China's foreign exchange reserves, gold reserves, and other foreign exchange assets.
4. Establishing the renminbi convertibility and exchange rate policy.

while the majority of them (727) do not have any. Guarantees were provided by different entities: parent company, subsidiaries of its own or of its parent company, banks, and local or national governments. The parent companies of 49 issues provided guarantees; 27 issues were *pari passu* with senior unsecured priority claim and three issues of *pari passu* with secured claims. Two issues were guaranteed by subsidiaries; one guarantee was provided by its own offshore subsidiary (outside China or Hong Kong) and the other was guaranteed by other subsidiary of the parent.

Nine issues were guaranteed by multiple subsidiaries, including the issuer's subsidiaries, other subsidiaries of the parent company, and both. One of the issues of multiple subsidiaries guarantee excluded those subsidiaries in the mainland China (China Power New Energy). One issue (Road King Infrastructure Finance [2011] Ltd.) was guaranteed by multiple subsidiaries and the parent company, *pari passu* with senior unsecured priority of claims. It had a record coupon of 6 percent, which was however less than the 8.6 percent coupon of its own issue US$200 million of May 2014 notes yield on February 18, 2012, as well as the 6.45 percent of the onshore three- to five-year money in China.

Banks have provided guarantee to four issues during the period 2007–2012. Bank guarantee plays an important role in providing credit enhancement in this market where most bonds are unrated. For issuers that are not well known to the credit market, bank guarantee provides credit enhancement of the issue and lowers the cost of fund for the issuer. The first credit

TABLE 2.10 Comparison of Guarantee, Keepwell Deed, Equity Interest Purchasing Undertaking Deed, and Letter of Support

	Offshore Guarantee	Keepwell Deed	Keepwell Deed with EIPU	Letter of Support
Legally binding	Yes	Yes	Yes	No
Assumption of repayment in case of default	Yes	No, but commit to provide financial support for issuer to meet payment obligations	No, but commit to provide financial support through acquisitions of equity interests of issuer's offshore subsidiaries at prices sufficient to repay outstanding principal amount plus accrued interest	No
Regulatory approval	Approvals from NDRC, MOFCOM, and SAFE required	No approval required at signing, but approval from regulatory bodies such as NDRC, SAFE, and MOFCOM may be required, depending on ways of fulfilling the keepwell deed	No approval required at signing, but approvals from NDRC, SAFE and MOFCOM and registration with SAIC are required	No

TABLE 2.11 Number of Issues, Total and Average Amount, Average Coupon, and Average Tenor of Dim Sum Bonds by Guarantee Level (2007–2012)

Guarantee Level	No. of Issues	Total Amount RMB (Mln)	Average Amount RMB (Mln)	Average Coupon (% p.a.)	Average Coupon (Exclude Zeros and FRN) (%)	Average Tenor (Years)
Bank	4	2,130.00	532.50	3.80	3.80	3.50
Single; parent	19	19,650.00	1,034.21	3.50	3.50	3.40
Single; parent; *pari passu* with senior secured	3	4,612.00	1,537.33	5.23	5.23	4.33
Single; parent; *pari passu* with senior unsecured	27	29,980.00	1,110.37	3.86	3.86	3.33
Single; other offshore subsidiary	1	1,200.00	1,200.00	9.15	9.15	3.00
Single; other subsidiary of parent; *pari passu* with senior unsecured	1	300.00	300.00	1.15	1.15	3.00
Multiple; subsidiaries	3	2,750.00	916.67	5.46	5.46	3.00
Multiple; subsidiaries, excluding those in the PRC.	1	800.00	800.00	6.50	6.50	5.00
Multiple; subsidiaries; *pari passu* with senior unsecured	4	4,710.00	1,177.50	7.19	7.19	3.00
Multiple; subsidiaries & parent; *pari passu* with senior unsecured	1	1,300.00	1,300.00	6.00	6.00	3.00
Single; local government	1	150.00	150.00	1.65	1.65	5.00
Single; local government; *pari passu* with senior unsecured	3	520.00	173.33	2.75	2.75	4.67
Single; national/sovereign government	1	1,000.00	1,000.00	2.00	2.00	2.00
Single; national/sovereign government; *pari passu* with senior unsecured	1	500.00	500.00	2.00	2.00	2.00
No guarantee	727	331,914.90	456.55	2.65	2.71	1.85
Total	797	401,516.90	503.79	2.77	2.83	1.99

enhancement by bank guarantee was given by the Export-Import Bank of China (Chexim) to an issue of dim sum bonds (RMB400 million, three-year maturity) offered by Hai Chao Trading Co. Ltd. in Hong Kong in July 2011. For the bank guarantee, the parent company, Xiamen IT Group Corp Ltd. from China is the provider of a keepwell agreement.[13] Chexim also provided guarantee to another issue (Pointer Investment HK) in 2012. The other two cases of bank guarantees involved two foreign bank issuers, the Export-Import Bank of India and the Abu Dhabi Commercial Bank PJSC. The Export-Import Bank of India guaranteed an issue of dim sum bonds offered by International Offshore Pte. Ltd., a subsidiary of India's Infrastructure Leasing & Financial Services Transportation Networks Limited. The bonds were secured by the first lien on specific assets. Overall, these four cases of bank guarantees totaled an amount of RMB2.13 billion, an average amount of RMB532.5 million, an average coupon of 3.8 percent, and a tenor of 3.5 years. Six issues were guaranteed by local or national governments.

2.2.8 Exchange Listing

Dim sum bond investors typically participate in the primary market without active trading, holding the bonds till maturity. However, some dim sum bonds have been listed on different exchanges globally to attract investors, who prefer the disclosure requirements and monitoring by the exchanges. Exchange listing also facilitates wider investor participation, particularly some institutional investors can only invest in exchange-listed bonds. Currently, trading of dim sum bonds is limited by the fact that the average deal size of dim sum bonds is small (RMB 503.79 million; see Table 2.1) and bonds are mostly held to maturity by institutional investors, such as commercial banks and insurance companies. Exchange listing also promotes the visibility of the issuer internationally. For example, ANZ Banking Group issued its second dim sum bond in Hong Kong, had it listed in London, and then swapped it into U.S. dollars.[14]

Table 2.12 presents the exchange listings for dim sum bonds. The majority of dim sum bonds are not listed on exchanges. There have been 127 issues (15.9 percent of the total 797 issues) listed on exchanges, including 39 on the Singapore Exchange (SGX-ST), 33 on the Hong Kong exchanges (XHKG), 21 on Luxembourg (XLUX), and 9 on London, which are the top four exchanges with dim sum bond listings. There are 7 issues dually listed on XHKG and SGX-ST; and 3 issues that are listed on four European exchanges (XBER, XFRA, XLUX, and XSTU).

---

[13] We consider this a landmark issue, which will be discussed in Chapter 6.

[14] See Wee (2012).

TABLE 2.12 Number of Issues, Total and Average Amount, Average Coupon, and Average Tenor of Dim Sum Bonds by Exchange Listing (2007–2012)

Exchange	No. of Issues	Total Amount RMB (Mln)	Average Amount RMB (Mln)	Average Coupon (% p.a.)	Average Coupon (Exclude Zeros and FRN)\(%)
Singapore (SGX-ST)	39	40,467.00	1,037.62	4.66	4.66
Hong Kong (HK)	33	45,211.00	1,370.03	3.98	3.98
Luxembourg (XLUX)	21	12,145.00	578.33	3.23	3.23
London	9	4,414.00	490.44	3.45	3.45
HK; SGX-ST	7	7,500.00	1,071.43	3.69	3.69
Euronext-Paris	4	2,250.00	562.50	5.34	5.34
Berlin (XBER); Frankfurt (XFRA); XLUX; Stuttgart (XSTU)	3	1,650.00	550.00	2.25	2.25
Dublin	2	2,000.00	1,000.00	3.73	3.73
XBER; XFRA	2	1,100.00	550.00	3.35	3.35
XBER; Dusseldorf; XFRA; Munich; XSTU	1	1,000.00	1,000.00	3.80	3.80
EMTF (EuroMTF) and XLUX	1	1,000.00	1,000.00	3.50	3.50
Bursa Malaysia (XKLS); SGX-ST	1	1,000.00	1,000.00	3.75	3.75
XBER; XFRA; SGX-ST	1	500.00	500.00	4.90	4.90
Euronext-Amsterdam	1	500.00	500.00	3.50	3.50
XKLS; Labuan Int'l Fin	1	500.00	500.00	2.90	2.90
XBER; XLUX; XSTU	1	250.00	250.00	2.25	2.25
Subtotal—listed	127	121,487.00	956.59	3.97	3.97
Not listed	670	280,029.90	417.96	2.54	2.60
Overall Total/Weighted Average	797	401,516.90	503.79	2.77	2.83

Further breakdown of the 39 bonds listed solely on the SGX-ST indicates that 16 were issued by issuers from China, 9 from Hong Kong, 7 from Korea, 3 from India, 2 from Singapore, 1 from Taiwan, and 1 from the United States. Moreover, among the 33 bonds solely listed on the XHKG, 21 were issued by issuers from China, 7 from Hong Kong, and 1 each from Taiwan, India, Korea, the United Kingdom, and a supranational agency. It is clear that Asian issuers tend to have the dim sum bonds listed on an Asian exchange, whereas European issuers tend to list dim sum bonds on the European exchanges, such as the XLUX and XFRA. While listing bonds on exchanges could cost issuers a lot, exchange listing attracts the interests of investors and helps marketing the bonds to institutional investors that can only trade the exchange listed bonds. This suggests that exchange listing could potentially reduce the funding cost (cost of capital) because it broadens the investor base of dim sum bonds. While listed dim sum bonds may not be traded frequently on the exchanges, the purpose of listing the bonds is to ensure that they and their issuers are subject to monitoring and disclosure requirements by exchanges.

2.3 CONCLUSION

This chapter presents information on the pertinent characteristics of dim sum bonds in terms of type, form, coupon, tenor, credit ratings, collateral and claim priority, covenants, credit enhancement, and exchange listing. We discussed the development of two types of offshore RMB bonds: the dim sum bonds and synthetic RMB bonds. The synthetic RMB bonds were later replaced by the dim sum bonds after most restrictions on the issuance of dim sum bonds and remittance of funds into the mainland were lifted in July 2010.

In terms of the type, dim sum debt instruments can be issued as certificates of deposit, notes, and bonds, although strict classification by the length of maturity as in other debt markets is not being followed in this market. Dim sum bonds can be registered or in bearer form. Most registered bonds are now recorded electronically with owners' information, while the appeal of bearer bonds is primarily investor anonymity and probably the tax avoidance on the bond income. In the dim sum bond market, most of the reported deals are bearer bonds as compared to registered bonds. Likewise, dim sum bonds (excluding CDs) are largely issued under Regulation S.

In terms of the nature of interest rate, the vast majority of dim sum bonds are fixed-rate instruments, while there are a few issues of floating-rate bonds. Only three zero-coupon dim sum bonds have been issued since the inception of the market. Most of the fixed-rate dim sum debt instruments are fixed-rate certificates of deposit with short tenors. Although issuers have issued medium-term notes and longer-term bonds in the dim sum bond market, the depth of this market segment is still yet to improve. The trend of having longer-tenor bonds is expected, and long-tenor bonds will provide useful benchmark rates for future issues of dim sum bonds.

The increasing number of dim sum bonds having credit ratings and credit enhancement structures (keepwell deeds and letters of support) is a positive market development, reflecting the dim sum bond market's growth toward maturity as investors demand more credit protection. Specifically, we discussed bond protection as well as various credit enhancement mechanisms used in the dim sum bond market. Credit enhancement in general signals to investors that the issuer has every intention in supporting the operating company, although investors have to evaluate the information independently on their own to assess the credibility of the credit enhancement.

Most dim sum bonds are not listed on exchanges, but there are over 120 dim sum bonds listed on different exchanges around the world, such as Hong Kong, Singapore, Luxembourg, and London, among others. As the market begins to take root, more dim sum bonds would be listed on exchanges around the world. Listing of bonds on exchanges would subject the issuers to exchanges' monitoring and disclosure requirements. Liquidity in the secondary market may eventually improve. While listing of dim sum bonds on exchanges could cost issuers more, it helps attract more investors and promote the bonds to institutional investors that can only trade the exchange listed bonds. In addition, improved secondary liquidity with exchange listing could potentially reduce the funding cost as it broadens the investor base of dim sum bonds.

Throughout this chapter, we introduce to readers the details of the new offshore RMB market, which has been orchestrated by the Chinese government since its inception. The chapter should help market participants, especially those who are looking for investment options for CNH or exploring to see if the dim sum bond market is a feasible and sustainable funding channel, to better understand the characteristics of this new bond market in terms of available type, coupon, tenor, credit rating, and credit enhancement structure of the dim sum bonds. Discussions in this chapter provide market participants a wide scope of the issues to be considered in participating in this market, enabling them to make informed decisions.

REFERENCES

Fung, Hung-Gay, and Jot Yau. 2012. "The Chinese Offshore Renminbi Currency and Bond Markets: The Role of Hong Kong." *China and World Economy* 20(3): 107–122.

Law, Fiona. 2013. "U.K. Banks Sell $245 Million Dim Sum Bonds in Singapore."
   Wall Street Journal, May 26. Retrieved at http://online.wsj.com/news/articles/
   SB10001424127887323855804578508141867207184.
Stroock & Stroock & Lavan, LLP. *Regulation S*, 2002. Retrieved from the Web site
   www.stroock.com
Wee, Denise. 2012. "ANZ Taps Arbitrage Opportunity with London Dim Sum."
   FinanceAsia, August 10.

CHAPTER 3

Issuers

In Chapters 1 and 2, we presented the origin of the dim sum bond market and a historical account of its development from the perspective of the Chinese government policy and market characteristics of dim sum bonds. These chapters give a macro view of this nascent market. In this chapter, we present and discuss the characteristics of issuers who play a pivotal role in this emerging debt capital market. Issuers may elect to issue dim sum bonds with different choices with regard to bond attributes (amount, coupon, tenor, credit ratings, and bond protection) that are appropriate to their funding needs. We take the approach to understand the issuers' motivations behind this funding option and the dim sum bond market by way of exploring the profile characteristics of issuers. We classify issuers by type of organization, industry, issuer's domicile, and deal nationality. More important, we explore and discuss the rationales of different groups of issuers. For some issuers, they may simply consider it from an economic perspective (i.e., weighing the benefits of issuing dim sum bonds against the funding costs from alternative sources), while others may consider it from a strategic perspective, which could either be forging the long-term business relationship with China by supporting China's government efforts in anticipation of greater business relationship with the Chinese government in the future once the market matures, engaging its own existing investors in a new market, or broadening the investor base.

Issuers of dim sum bonds include financial institutions and corporations from all over the world, which have operations in mainland China. Supranational organizations and agencies are also interested in issuing dim sum bonds. Sovereign and subsovereign entities (e.g., state government) are also issuers of dim sum bonds for different reasons. Chinese financial institutions and corporations issue dim sum bonds after obtaining approval from the authorities or issuing dim sum bonds through special purpose vehicles incorporated offshore.[1] Issuers that intend to repatriate the bond proceeds raised through the dim sum bond market to China will need to obtain approval from the relevant regulatory bodies such as the National Development and Reform Commission (NDRC), State Administration of Foreign Exchange (SAFE), and Ministry of Commerce (MOFCOM), for such repatriation, which are obtained on a case-by-case basis and could take time to obtain. Issuers of dim sum bonds may choose to leave the CNH funds offshore and acquire assets onshore through buying offshore holding companies, as Guangzhou R&F Properties Co. Ltd., a Chinese property developer, did.

3.1 ISSUERS

At the debut of the dim sum bond market in 2007, dim sum bonds were all issued by Chinese financial institutions that had received approval from the government to issue dim sum bonds. In June 2009, HSBC (China) Limited and the Bank of East Asia (China) Limited, locally incorporated subsidiaries of non-Chinese banks were allowed to issue dim sum bonds. Since July 2010, policy restrictions were relaxed further allowing foreign and mainland Chinese entities to issue dim sum bonds. To date, although issuers still primarily come from certain groups, issuers have become more diverse as the nascent market matures.

The contrast can be seen in Figure 3.1, in which the year 2010 is used as the demarcation line since the Chinese government liberalized its policy in July 2010, inducing an influx of non-Chinese-bank issuers to the dim sum bond market. The pre-2010 period refers to July 2007 to the end of 2010, whereas the post-2010 period refers to January 2, 2011, to the end of 2012. Figure 3.1 clearly shows that in the pre-2010 period, Chinese issuers dominated the market when only the Chinese banks were allowed to issue dim sum bonds along with the central government. Two years later, two non-Chinese bank entities allowed to issue dim sum bonds were the mainland entities of the Bank of East Asia (of Hong Kong) and HSBC (of the United Kingdom) to join mainland borrowers in the market. In contrast, in the post-2010 period, there were issuers from many more countries from different regions, including Asia-Pacific, the Middle East, Europe, and North and Latin Americas.

---

[1] A special purpose vehicle (SPV) is a legal entity created to fulfill narrow, specific, or temporary objectives. Normally, a company will transfer assets to the SPV for management or use the SPV to finance a large project, thereby achieving a narrow set of goals without putting the entire firm at risk.

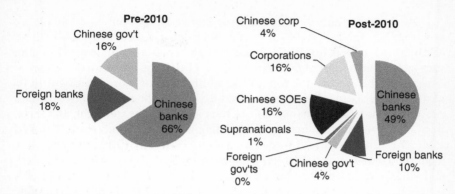

FIGURE 3.1 Dim sum bond issues by total RMB amount for pre-2010 and post-2010 periods.
*Notes:
1. Pre-2010 refers to mid-2007 to end of 2010; post-2010 refers to 2011 to end of 2012.
2. Foreign banks in the pre-2010 period are China-incorporated subsidiaries of foreign banks.

For the period 2007–2012, there have been 176 names issuing 797 dim sum bonds for a total amount of RMB401.52 billion.[2] These 176 unique issuers come from different industries, types of organization, and geographic locales. Many are subsidiaries and overseas branches of Chinese banks and corporations. Deals from these 176 unique issuers if rolled up and combined with their parents would reduce the list of issuers to 150. For example, besides itself, the Bank of China (BOC) has bonds issued by its branches from Hong Kong, Singapore, Macau, and Sydney, while the Industrial and Commercial Bank of China (ICBC) has bonds issued by its subsidiary, ICBC (Asia), and branches from Macau, Sydney, and Tokyo. Likewise, corporations have issued dim sum bonds in the names of their subsidiaries from Hong Kong or offshore locations. Other examples include BYD Co. Ltd., a Chinese hybrid automobile manufacturer, issued dim sum bonds via its Hong Kong subsidiary, BYD HK Co. Ltd. Similarly, Ping An Insurance Group Company issued dim sum bonds via Victor Soar Ltd., a British Virgin Islands company and a subsidiary of a Hong Kong subsidiary of the parent, whereas Shangdong Iron & Steel issued a bond via Jigang Bond Finance incorporated in the Cayman Islands. Many factors determining which branch or subsidiary would issue the bonds include the tax implications, internal capital control, internal use of RMB funds, and exchange rate and cross-border capital flow control considerations.

---

[2] Based on information compiled from Bloomberg.

The top 25 dim sum bond issuers for the period 2007–2012 are presented in Table 3.1.[3] As a group, they have issued a total worth of RMB288.71 billion (or 71.91 percent of the total amount issued) of dim sum bonds and a total of 605 issues (or 75.91 percent of the total number of issues). In other words, the top 25 issuers account for more than two-thirds of the market share in terms of the total RMB amount and number of issues. Among them, 19 are from mainland China including the top eight, and seven from places outside the mainland including, two from South Korea (ranked 17th and 22nd), and two from Hong Kong (9th and 13th), and one each from the United States (12th), the United Kingdom (15th), Germany (21st), and Singapore (24th). The largest issuer is the BOC, which issued 151 dim sum bonds for a total amount of RMB49.83 billion. Closely behind the BOC is China Construction Bank (CCB), which has sold a total of 152 issues for RMB47.42 billion. Together, the BOC and CCB account for about 24 percent of the market in terms of the total RMB amount issued.

Another major issuer is the China Development Bank (CDB), which has sold 44 issues of dim sum bonds for a total of RMB32.90 billion, accounting for an 8.19 percent of the market share. The distant fourth ranked issuer is ICBC, which issued 59 dim sum bonds for a total amount of almost RMB20 billion, accounting for a 4.98 percent of the market share. The Chinese Ministry of Finance (MOF) issuing dim sum bonds on behalf of the People's Bank of China (PBOC) is ranked fifth in Table 3.1, closely behind ICBC in terms of the total RMB amount with only six issues. As such, the average size for ICBC issues (approximately RMB338.97 million) is much smaller than that of ministry issues (RMB3.25 billion).

Next, we classify issuers of dim sum bonds by type of organization, industry, issuer domicile, and deal nationality for analytical purposes. Understanding different types of issuers and the motivations behind their dim sum bond issuance, one can infer the future trends in terms of the supply of dim sum bonds as government policies and the economy evolve.

3.2 CLASSIFICATION OF ISSUERS BY TYPE OF ORGANIZATION

Issuers are grouped into five types of organization:

1. Government (sovereign and subsovereign)
2. Banks

---

[3] For issuer ranking, we rolled up all deals to the issuers' parents based on data from Bloomberg. We then ranked the issuers based on the total amount of dim sum bond issues. The list actually has 27 names since both the 23rd and 25th ranks are tied.

TABLE 3.1   Top 25 Issuers Ranked by Total RMB Amount (2007–2012)*

Ranked by RMB Amount	Name	Issuer Nationality	Total Amount (RMB Mln)	Market Share (%)	No. of Issues	Market Share (%)
1	Bank of China	China	49,827.30	12.41	151	18.95
2	China Construction Bank	China	47,417.00	11.81	152	19.07
3	China Development Bank Corp.	China	32,902.55	8.19	44	5.52
4	Industrial & Commercial Bank of China Ltd.	China	19,999.50	4.98	59	7.40
5	People's Republic of China	China	19,500.00	4.86	6	0.75
6	Export-Import Bank of China	China	12,000.00	2.99	7	0.88
7	Bank of Communications Co. Ltd.	China	11,811.50	2.94	21	2.63
8	Agricultural Bank of China Ltd.	China	10,798.50	2.69	26	3.26
9	Bank of East Asia Ltd.	Hong Kong SAR, China	7,825.50	1.95	18	2.26
10	Shanghai Baosteel Group Corp.	China	6,500.00	1.62	6	0.75
11	Agricultural Development Bank of China	China	6,000.00	1.49	6	0.75
12	Caterpillar Inc.	US	5,560.00	1.38	4	0.50
13	New World Development Co. Ltd.	Hong Kong SAR, China	5,300.00	1.32	2	0.25
14	China CITIC Bank Corp. Ltd.	China	5,234.50	1.30	22	2.76
15	HSBC Holdings PLC	UK	5,000.00	1.25	3	0.38
16	China Merchants Bank Co. Ltd.	China	4,985.00	1.24	25	3.14
17	Export-Import Bank of Korea	South Korea	4,615.00	1.15	17	2.13

(*continued*)

TABLE 3.1 (*Continued*)

Ranked by RMB Amount	Name	Issuer Nationality	Total Amount (RMB Mln)	Market Share (%)	No. of Issues	Market Share (%)
18	China National Heavy Duty Truck Group Co.	China	4,500.00	1.12	2	0.25
19	China Merchants Group Ltd.	China	3,700.00	0.92	3	0.38
20	Sinochem Group	China	3,500.00	0.87	1	0.13
21	BSH Bosch und Siemens Hausgeraete GmbH	Germany	3,250.00	0.81	6	0.75
22	Korea Finance Corp.	South Korea	3,187.00	0.79	12	1.51
23	Beijing Enterprises Water Group Ltd.	China	3,150.00	0.78	5	0.63
23	Beijing Capital Land Ltd.	China	3,150.00	0.78	2	0.25
25	Global Logistic Properties	Singapore	3,000.00	0.75	2	0.25
25	China National Petroleum Corp.	China	3,000.00	0.75	2	0.25
25	COFCO Corp.	China	3,000.00	0.75	1	0.13
	Total for Top 25 Issuers		288,713.35	71.91	605	75.91
	Total for all 150 Issuers		401,516.90	100.00	797	100.00

*Deals are rolled up and combined to the parent company's total.

3. State-owned enterprises (SOEs)[4]

4. Corporations (Chinese, Hong Kong, and multinationals [MNCs])

5. Supranational agencies

---

[4] SOEs refer to nonbank state-owned enterprises; state-owned banks are grouped under banks.

3.2.1 Government (Sovereign and Subsovereign)

The first sovereign dim sum bonds were issued in 2007 by the People's Republic of China, which were conducted under the MOF in three tranches.[5] Two tranches were allocated to retail investors for a total amount of RMB5.5 billion and one to institutional investors for RMB500 million. Subsequently, the MOF had issued three more dim sum bonds in 2010, 2011, and 2012 on behalf of the central government for a total of RMB19.5 billion. MOF is ranked fourth among all issuers for a market share of 4.86 percent of the total amount raised from this market (Table 3.1). The MOF's issues provide the risk-free benchmark for the market and are useful to the development of the market.

The subsovereign government category has only one issuer, the Swedish government's export credit agency, Svensk Exportkredit AB, which has issued three bonds for a total RMB amount of RMB0.85 billion.[6]

3.2.2. Banks

As a group, banks are the largest issuer of dim sum bonds. Chinese banks, in particular, are the predominant issuers, accounting for just over 50 percent of the total RMB amount (RMB201.70 billion) with 520 issues.[7] Chinese banks issuing dim sum bonds include state-owned banks, which comprise:

- Three policy banks:
  - China Development Bank, ranked 3rd with 44 issues for a total of RMB32.90 billion, as shown in Table 3.1.
  - Agricultural Development Bank of China, ranked 11th with 6 issues for a total of RMB6 billion.
  - Export-Import Bank of China, ranked 6th with 7 issues for a total of RMB12 billion.
- Eight commercial banks:
  - Bank of China, ranked 1st, 151 issues for RMB49.83 billion.
  - China Construction Bank, ranked 2nd, 152 issues for RMB47.42 billion.
  - Agricultural Bank of China, ranked 8th, 26 issues for RMB10.8 billion.
  - ICBC, ranked 4th, 59 issues for RMB20 billion.

---

[5] For details of this landmark case, see Chapter 6.

[6] The Export-Import Bank of China and the Export-Import Bank of Korea are also responsible for export credits for their respective countries. However, they provide a full banking services include import financing and the like, and thus are classified under the banks category.

[7] We rolled up the bond issues done by the branches and subsidiaries of the Chinese banks to the parent organization.

- Bank of Communications, ranked 7th, 21 issues for RMB11.8 billion.
- China Merchants Bank, ranked 16th, 25 issues for RMB4.99 billion.
- China CITIC Bank International, ranked 14th, 22 issues for RMB5.23 billion.
- Shanghai Pudong Development Bank, ranked 91st, 7 issues for RMB727 million.

Three Hong Kong banks issued 26 issues for about RMB9 billion, whereas 28 foreign banks have issued 93 issues for RMB33.28 billion. Among the foreign banks, HSBC (China) Limited and the Bank of East Asia (China) Limited[8] incorporated in mainland China were approved to issue dim sum bonds in 2009 before other non-Chinese financial institutions outside mainland China were allowed to do so.

3.2.3 China's State-Owned Enterprises (SOEs)

Table 3.2 shows that as a group, 30 SOEs from mainland China have issued a total of 49 issues (6.15 percent of the total number of issues) of dim sum bonds for a total amount of RMB58.60 billion (14.59 percent of the total RMB amount issued).

Many SOEs sold dim sum bonds through their Hong Kong subsidiaries or offshore holding companies (mostly in tax-haven countries such as the British Virgin Islands, Cayman Islands, and Bermuda) to spare the regulatory approvals required for issuances by onshore entities. For example, the first red-chip financial institution issue was from China CITIC Bank International Ltd. (July 2010) and the first nonfinancial red-chip issue was from Sinotruk (Hong Kong) Ltd. (October 2010), a subsidiary of China National Heavy Duty Truck Group Co. Baosteel is the first China-based nonfinancial company to sell dim sum bonds directly by itself after receiving permission from the NDRC in October 2011. Some bonds were issued through a special purpose vehicle (SPV); for example, Sinochem issued the dim sum bonds via Sinochem Offshore Capital Ltd., an SPV 100 percent owned by Sinochem Hong Kong in January 2011. These issuers may find it advantageous to issue dim sum bonds for arbitraging interest rates or for tax purposes.

3.2.4 Corporations

Chinese and foreign corporations together have issued 95 issues (11.92 percent of the total number of issues) of dim sum bonds for a total

---

[8] Their parent companies HSBC Plc and Bank of East Asia are ranked 15th and 9th, respectively, among all issuers.

TABLE 3.2 Dim Sum Bond Amount and Number of Issuers and Issues by Issuer's Type of Organization (2007–2012)

Type of Organization of Issuer	Issuer Nationality	No. of Issuers	Amount RMB (Mln)	Market Share — Amount (%)	No. of Issues	Market Share — No. of issues (%)
Government	China	1	19,500.00	4.86	6	0.75
	Foreign	1	850.00	0.21	3	0.38
	Subtotal	2	20,350.00	5.07	9	1.13
Bank	China	11	201,702.85	50.24	520	65.24
	Hong Kong	3	8,997.50	2.24	26	3.26
	Foreign	28	33,281.00	8.29	93	11.67
	Subtotal	42	243,981.35	60.76	639	80.18
State-Owned Enterprise	China	30	58,600.55	14.59	49	6.15
	Subtotal	30	58,600.55	14.59	49	6.15
Corporation	China	19	16,372.00	4.08	21	2.63
	Hong Kong	14	18,920.00	4.71	18	2.26
	Macau	1	2,300.00	0.57	1	0.13
	Taiwan	5	2,561.00	0.64	6	0.75
	Foreign	34	35,482.00	8.84	49	6.15
	Subtotal	73	75,635.00	18.84	95	11.92
Supranational Agency	Supranational	3	2,950.00	0.73	5	0.63
	Subtotal	3	2,950.00	0.73	5	0.63
	Total	150	401,516.90	100.00	797.00	100.00

amount of RMB75.64 billion (18.84 percent of the total RMB amount issued), as shown in Table 3.2. The breakdown of the 73 corporations that have issued dim sum bonds by issuer's domicile is as follows:

- 19 corporations from China
- 14 from Hong Kong
- 1 from Macau
- 5 from Taiwan
- 34 from other countries

Foreign corporations, that is, corporations from countries outside Greater China (mainland China, Hong Kong, Macau, and Taiwan), account for 8.84 percent of the total RMB amount issued and 6.15 percent of the number of issues. Corporations from Greater China have a little bigger market share in terms of the total RMB amount issued but smaller in terms of the number of issues than foreign corporations.

3.2.4.1 Chinese Companies   Among the Chinese corporations that have issued dim sum bonds, 19 corporations are non-state-owned companies from China (e.g., PCD Stores Group Ltd., Guangzhou R&F Properties Co. Ltd., Gemdale Corporation, and Intime Retail Group Co. Ltd.) in contrast to state-owned enterprises. These non-state-owned companies are relatively smaller than the SOEs and may not have access to local banks or the capital market for financing. They were not allowed to issue dim sum bonds until the liberalization policy was announced in July 2010. As a group, Chinese companies account for 21 issues (2.63 percent of the total number of issues) for a total RMB amount of RMB16.37 billion (4.08 percent of the total RMB amount).

3.2.4.2 Hong Kong Companies   Since Hong Kong is home to the dim sum bond market, it is natural that Hong Kong companies have keen interest in issuing dim sum bonds. These companies have significant operations in mainland China and hence genuine RMB requirements to fund these operations. The first Hong Kong company that issued the dim sum bond in July 2010 is Hopewell Holdings. The company utilized Hopewell Highway Infrastructure, a Cayman Islands subsidiary of Anber Investments which is a wholly owned subsidiary of Hopewell Holdings to issue the bonds. This offshore SPV structure is common in bond issuance for the advantage of capital control in addition to possible tax benefits and less stringent governance requirements. As a group, Hong Kong companies account for 18 issues (2.26 percent of the total number of issues) for a total RMB amount of RMB18.92 billion (4.71 percent of the total RMB amount).

3.2.4.3 Macau and Taiwan Companies   Macau has only one issuer that accounts for only one issue (0.13 percent of the total number of issues) for a total amount of RMB2.3 billion (0.57 percent of the total RMB amount). Five Taiwanese companies account for six issues of dim sum bonds (0.75 percent of the total number of issues) for a total RMB amount of RMB2.56 billion (0.64 percent of the total RMB amount).

3.2.4.4 Foreign Corporations   Since July 2010, foreign corporations have been allowed to issue dim sum bonds and remit funds into the mainland with prior approval. Among them, McDonald's Corporation issued the first dim sum bonds in August 2010.[9] Subsequently, corporations from the United States, such as Caterpillar and Ford Motor Company, as well as from Europe, such as Unilever, BSH Bosch, and Siemens, have issued dim sum bonds in Hong Kong. América Móvil, a Mexican telecommunications provider, was the first Latin American corporation to issue a dim sum bond (2012). It is also the first dim sum bond offering executed under the U.S. shelf registration, opening up a new investor base in the process. This issue was a good indicator of the interest of the U.S. investors, since not too many issuers from the Americas have issued dim sum bonds. With a strong investor demand on this issue, it encourages other issuers to consider issuing dim sum bonds. Although the bond was not specifically targeted at U.S. investors, more than 25 percent of the demand came from the United States.[10] As a group, foreign corporations account for 49 issues (6.15 percent of the total number of issues) for a total RMB amount of RMB35.48 billion (8.84 percent of the total RMB amount).

3.2.5 Supranational Agencies

Supranational agencies that have issued dim sum bonds include the Asian Development Bank (ADB) and United Nations organizations including the World Bank and International Finance Corporation (IFC). ADB is the first supranational agency that issued dim sum bonds in 2010 for an amount of RMB1.2 billion, which is an issue characterized by many "firsts."[11] The World Bank and IFC have issued three issues of dim sum bonds for a total amount of RMB1.15 billion in 2011 and 2012. Corporacion Andina de Fomento (CAF), the Latin American development bank headquartered in Caracas, Venezuela, is the other supranational agency that has issued dim sum bonds. CAF aims at stimulating sustainable development and regional

---

[9] For details of this landmark case, see Chapter 6.

[10] See Moore (2012b).

[11] For details of this landmark case, see Chapter 6.

integration by financing projects in the public and private sectors, and providing technical cooperation and other specialized services. As a group, the three supranational agencies have issued five issues of dim sum bonds for a total of RMB2.95 billion (Table 3.2).

3.3 CLASSIFICATION OF ISSUERS BY INDUSTRY

Companies that issue dim sum bonds come from different economic and industrial sectors, including banking, real estate/property development, transportation, automobile and truck manufacturers, and chemicals. Issuers come from an array of 25 industries as of the end of 2012.[12] The vast majority of issues were CDs and bonds from banks and financial institutions, including commercial and savings banks, development banks, and export-import banks, and the central government of China.

Table 3.3 presents the ranking of issuers in terms of the total RMB amount raised, total number of issues, and average RMB amount issued by industry. In terms of the total RMB amount raised, the top three issuing industries include banks, sovereign government, and real estate/property development. At the top of the list, 44 unique bank issuers account for 57.61 percent of the total RMB amount raised and 621 or 77.92 percent of the total number of issues. The sovereign government is ranked second and had issued six bonds for a total amount of RMB19.5 billion. Real estate/property development industry is ranked third by total RMB amount and sixth by number of issues. Finance-export credit is ranked fourth, and the auto/truck industry is ranked fifth by both total RMB amount issued and number of issues. Utility and energy, transportation, finance, metal and steel, and food and beverage are in the top 10 in terms of the total RMB amount issued. The finance sector includes different types of financial institutions, such as leasing companies, credit agencies, investment banks, and finance captive subsidiaries.

It is worth noting that the average coupon rate and average tenor vary among the industries. For example, the average tenor and average coupon of the dim sum bonds from the banking industry, which is the top-ranked industry in terms of the total RMB amount issued are 1.67 years, and 2.47 percent, respectively, whereas the averages for all industries are 1.99 years and 2.77 percent, respectively.[13] The third-ranked industry, the real estate/property development industry, has a higher average tenor (4.12 years) with a higher coupon rate (5.3 percent) than the averages for all industries and much higher than

---

[12] We segregated the export-import banks from the bank or finance sector to highlight the importance of trade credit in this debt capital market.

[13] These are computed as weighted averages.

TABLE 3.3 Dim Sum Bond Issues by Industry (2007–2012).

Rank by Total Amount Issued	Rank by No. of Issues	Rank by Average Amount	Industry	No. of Issuers	Total Amount RMB (Mln)	Market Share (%)	No. of Issues	Market Share (%)	Average Amount RMB (Mln)	Average Coupon (%)	Average Coupon (Exclude Zeros and FRN)(%)	Average Tenor (Years)
1	1	23	Bank	44	231,316.35	57.61	621	77.92	372.49	2.47	2.53	1.67
2	12	1	Sovereign Government	1	19,500.00	4.86	6	0.75	3,250.00	2.31	2.31	2.67
3	6	6	Real Estate/Property Development	8	18,212.00	4.54	13	1.63	1,400.92	5.30	5.30	4.12
4	2	18	Finance-Export Credit	3	17,465.00	4.35	27	3.39	646.85	2.62	2.62	2.33
5	5	13	Auto/Truck	10	14,100.00	3.51	14	1.76	1,007.14	4.08	4.08	2.64
6	3	17	Utility & Energy	12	13,610.00	3.39	19	2.38	716.32	4.31	4.31	4.11
7	7	8	Transportation	9	12,160.00	3.03	10	1.25	1,216.00	4.77	4.77	2.90
8	4	20	Finance	12	9,487.00	2.36	17	2.13	558.06	4.36	4.36	2.71
9	8	15	Metal & Steel	4	7,425.55	1.85	10	1.25	825.06	3.43	3.85	3.11
10	10	10	Food & Beverage	7	7,350.00	1.83	7	0.88	1,050.00	3.23	3.23	3.00
11	11	12	Construction/Building Products	6	7,066.00	1.76	7	0.88	1,009.43	5.04	5.04	2.86
12	14	5	Chemicals	4	7,050.00	1.76	5	0.63	1,410.00	3.94	3.94	4.20
13	13	11	Holding Companies—Conglomerates	4	6,300.00	1.57	6	0.75	1,050.00	3.46	3.46	3.17

(continued)

TABLE 3.3 (Continued)

Rank by Total Amount Issued	Rank by No. of Issues	Rank by Average Amount	Industry	No. of Issuers	Total Amount RMB (Mln)	Market Share (%)	No. of Issues	Market Share (%)	Average Amount RMB (Mln)	Average Coupon (%)	Average Coupon (Exclude Zeros and FRN)(%)	Average Tenor (Years)
14	15	9	Machinery	2	6,060.00	1.51	5	0.63	1,212.00	2.77	2.77	2.20
15	9	19	Consumer Products	3	4,550.00	1.13	8	1.00	568.75	3.32	3.32	4.81
16	17	7	Oil & Gas	2	3,700.00	0.92	3	0.38	1,233.33	2.40	2.40	2.67
17	20	3	Leisure & Recreation	2	3,680.00	0.92	2	0.25	1,840.00	4.19	4.19	2.50
18	18	14	Telecommunications	3	3,000.00	0.75	3	0.38	1,000.00	4.18	4.18	2.67
19	19	16	Retail	3	2,475.00	0.62	3	0.38	825.00	3.88	3.88	3.00
20	23	2	Insurance	1	2,000.00	0.50	1	0.13	2,000.00	2.08	2.08	3.00
21	16	22	Computers & Electronics	4	1,950.00	0.49	5	0.63	390.00	4.03	4.03	3.40
22	24	4	Aerospace	1	1,500.00	0.37	1	0.13	1,500.00	4.80	4.80	3.00
23	21	21	Forestry & Paper	2	800.00	0.20	2	0.25	400.00	3.03	3.03	3.00
24	22	24	Dining & Lodging	2	550.00	0.14	2	0.25	275.00	2.69	2.69	3.00
25	25	25	Software	1	210.00	0.05	1	0.13	210.00	10.00	10.00	3.00
			Overall Total/ Weighted Average	150	401,516.90	100.00	797	100.00	503.79	2.77	2.83	1.99

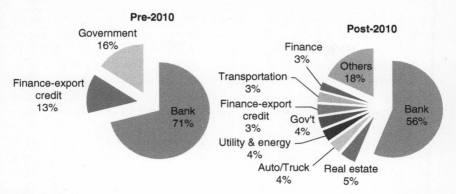

FIGURE 3.2   Dim Sum Bond Issues by Industry for Pre-2010 and Post-2010 Periods
Notes:
1. Pre-2010 refers to mid-2007 to end of 2010; post-2010 refers to 2011 to end of 2012.
2. Others refer to 17 industries that each accounts for less than 2.5 percent of the total amount of dim sum bonds issued.

the banking industry. Statistics in Table 3.3 clearly indicate that issuers from the banking and finance-export credit sectors prefer to issue short tenor (and hence a lower coupon rate), while real estate, utility and energy, transportation, metal and steel, food and beverages, and finance-leasing/credit companies prefer to borrow for a longer duration for a higher coupon rate. It should be noted that since banks have been the predominant issuers of FXCDs, which tend to be short-dated, the overall averages tend to be lowered by those issues.

Figure 3.2 shows the contrasting changes in the total RMB amount issued by industry for the pre- and post-2010 periods. In the pre-2010 period, issuers came from only three industry sectors: bank, government, and finance-export credit, where bank issuers accounted for 71 percent of the total RMB amount issued. In contrast, in the post-2010 period, issuers came from 25 industry sectors, with bank issuers still the predominant issuers, albeit with a lower percentage of the total (56 percent).

3.4 CLASSIFICATION OF ISSUERS BY DOMICILE AND BY DEAL NATIONALITY

There have been 150 issuers of dim sum bonds using 176 unique names in issuing dim sum bonds for the period 2007–2012. Among them, three supranational agencies using four unique names issued five dim sum bonds;

the remaining 147 issuers from 25 nations and cities using 172 unique names had issued a total of 797 issues. Forty-nine of the unique names belong to companies domiciled in Hong Kong and 14 in China (Table 3.4). Issuers issuing dim sum bonds via their affiliates incorporated in tax haven countries, namely, Bermuda, the British Virgin Islands (BVI) and the Cayman Islands together accounted for 56 issues using 44 unique names. In the rest of the chapter, we treat these three domiciles as a single group: the "tax-haven trio."

In terms of the total amount, Hong Kong ranked first (RMB175.5 billion), followed by China (RMB95.0 billion), BVI, Cayman Islands, and South Korea. In terms of the number of issues, the top five in order are Hong Kong, China, South Korea, Cayman Islands, and BVI. It is interesting to note that because Hong Kong ranked high in both the number of issues and total amount, the average amount becomes relatively small (RMB339.36 million), which is below the overall weighted average (RMB503.79 million) for all issues. For issuers that have issued more than five issues, China, the United States, and the tax-haven trio have averaged bigger deal size on the top.

In terms of tenor, issuers from Hong Kong, South Korea, Macau, the United Arab Emirates, and Australia tend to issue bonds on average with a tenor shorter than the overall average (1.99 years).

In terms of the geographical distribution of issuers, the mainland Chinese and Hong Kong issuers have been very active since the inception (see the pre-2010 period in Figure 3.3). As mainland Chinese issuers have slowed down since 2011 due to easing of borrowing costs in the mainland and investors pushing for higher yields, more ratings, and stricter covenants, this reduction in supply from mainland issuers is easily replaced by foreign issuers, particularly the Asia-Pacific and European issuers. Deals from the Middle East and Latin America have now been successfully closed (see the post-2010 period in Figure 3.3).

Table 3.5 presents the type of issuers by deal nationality. Comparing the results in Tables 3.4 and 3.5, some interesting patterns are observed. First, there are 44 issuers from the tax-haven trio issuing 56 dim sum bonds in Table 3.4 compared to no deals originated from the tax-haven trio in Table 3.5. This result suggests that many firms do not issue dim sum bonds directly in their home countries but prefer to issue them through their SPVs or offshore subsidiaries in the tax-haven trio, likely for tax purposes and/ or better firm capital control. Second, China has issued the most dim sum bonds, that is, a total of 594 issues (Table 3.5), but China's dim sum bond deals totaled 56 (Table 3.4), implying that the majority of the dim sum bonds issued by Chinese entities placed their issuing units offshore. Similarly, Taiwanese firms have issued six bonds (Table 3.5) but no listing in the

TABLE 3.4 Issuer and Issues by Issuer Domicile (2007–2012)

Rank by Total Amount	Rank by No. of Issues	Issuer Domicile	No. of Unique Name Issuer	No. of Issues	Total Amount RMB (Mln)	Average Amount RMB (Mln)	Average Coupon (%)	Average Coupon (Exclude Zeros and FRN)(%)	Average Tenor (Years)
1	1	Hong Kong	49	517	175,449.40	339.36	2.42	2.49	1.52
2	2	China	14	56	95,006.05	1,696.54	3.25	3.17	3.83
3	5	British Virgin Islands	16	18	26,737.00	1,485.39	4.34	4.34	2.94
4	4	Cayman Islands	20	25	18,148.55	725.94	4.66	4.86	2.76
5	3	South Korea	6	33	9,687.00	293.55	2.78	2.78	1.45
6	9	Bermuda	8	13	9,180.00	706.15	4.94	4.94	3.92
7	8	Singapore	6	14	7,692.00	549.43	3.84	3.84	3.00
8	15	United States	5	8	7,610.00	951.25	2.68	2.68	2.50
9	12	France	6	10	6,650.00	665.00	4.25	4.25	3.20
10	6	United Kingdom	6	17	6,080.00	357.65	3.32	3.32	2.94
11	7	Macau	2	15	6,064.00	404.27	2.89	2.89	1.27
12	11	Germany	3	12	5,420.00	451.67	2.89	2.89	4.63
13	16	Netherlands	5	7	4,800.00	685.71	3.00	3.00	3.39
14	9	Japan	8	13	4,530.00	348.46	2.50	2.96	2.69
15	17	Supranational	4	5	2,950.00	590.00	2.21	2.21	4.40
16	21	Panama	1	1	2,600.00	2,600.00	3.30	3.30	3.00
17	14	United Arab Emirates	3	9	2,560.00	284.44	3.76	3.76	1.67

(continued)

TABLE 3.4 (*Continued*)

Rank by Total Amount	Rank by No. of Issues	Issuer Domicile	No. of Unique Name Issuer	No. of Issues	Total Amount RMB (Mln)	Average Amount RMB (Mln)	Average Coupon (%)	Average Coupon (Exclude Zeros and FRN)(%)	Average Tenor (Years)
18	12	Australia	3	10	2,132.90	213.29	2.67	2.97	1.00
19	17	Sweden	3	5	2,020.00	404.00	2.47	2.47	2.80
20	19	Luxembourg	1	2	2,000.00	1,000.00	3.73	3.73	3.00
21	19	Malaysia	2	2	1,500.00	750.00	3.33	3.33	2.50
22	21	Mexico	1	1	1,000.00	1,000.00	3.50	3.50	3.00
23	21	Austria	1	1	750.00	750.00	4.55	4.55	2.00
24	21	Chile	1	1	500.00	500.00	3.75	3.75	2.00
25	21	New Zealand	1	1	300.00	300.00	1.10	1.10	3.00
26	21	Brazil	1	1	150.00	150.00	4.05	4.05	2.00
Overall Total/Wt. Average			176	797	401,516.90	503.79	2.77	2.83	1.99

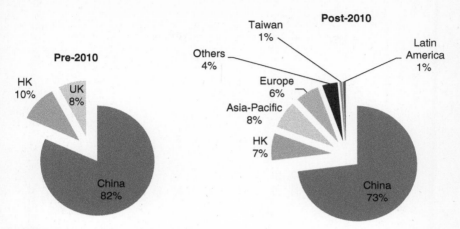

FIGURE 3.3   Deal nationality of dim sum bond issues by geography for the pre- and post-2010 periods.

Notes:

1. Pre-2010 refers to mid-2007 to end of 2010; post-2010 refers to 2011 to end of 2012.

2. In pre-2010, the Hong Kong and U.K. bonds were actually issued by the two China-incorporated banks of a U.K. bank (HSBC [China]) and a Hong Kong bank (BEA [China]).

3. In the post-2010 period, Asia-Pacific includes eight countries/cities; Europe include the United Kingdom and six other countries; Latin America includes two countries; and Others include the United States, supranationals, Russian Federation, and United Arab Emirates.

issuer domicile category (Table 3.4), implying that these Taiwanese firms use shell companies in the tax-haven trio to issue the bonds.

3.5 MOTIVATIONS BEHIND ISSUERS

Now, we know who the issuers of dim sum bonds are. But what makes these different types of organization issue dim sum bonds? What are the rationales, economic or otherwise, for issuing bonds in this offshore market? Understanding the issuer's motivations is useful in figuring out the trend(s) of the supply of dim sum bonds. Broadly speaking, there are several main reasons why different types of organization, Chinese or otherwise, issue dim sum bonds:

1. Supporting the government's RMB policy.
2. Cross-border funding arbitrage

TABLE 3.5 Dim Sum Issues by Nationality of Deal (2007–2012).

Rank by Total Amount	Rank by No. of Issues	Rank by Average Amount	Nationality of Deal	Total Amount RMB (Mln)	Market Share of Total Amount (%)	No. of Issues	Market Share of No. of Issues (%)	Average Amount RMB (Mln)	Average Coupon (%)	Average Coupon (Exclude Zeros and FRN)(%)	Average Tenor (Years)
1	1	14	China	293,175.40	73.02	594	74.53	493.56	2.6	2.7	1.8
2	2	9	Hong Kong	30,917.50	7.70	46	5.77	672.12	3.2	3.2	2.2
3	3	20	Korea	11,537.00	2.87	35	4.39	329.63	2.8	2.8	1.5
4	4	12	Germany	9,495.00	2.36	17	2.13	558.53	2.9	2.9	4.2
5	7	8	France	8,150.00	2.03	11	1.38	740.91	4.7	4.7	3.2
6	9	4	United States	7,610.00	1.90	8	1.00	951.25	2.7	2.7	2.5
7	5	13	United Kingdom	7,214.00	1.80	14	1.76	515.29	3.3	3.2	3.0
8	6	19	Japan	4,220.00	1.05	12	1.51	351.67	2.9	2.9	2.8
9	13	5	Singapore	3,879.00	0.97	5	0.63	775.80	2.9	2.9	3.0
10	13	11	Supranational	2,950.00	0.73	5	0.63	590.00	2.2	2.2	4.4
11	11	16	India	2,590.00	0.65	6	0.75	431.67	4.9	4.9	3.0
12	11	17	Taiwan	2,561.00	0.64	6	0.75	426.83	3.8	3.8	3.2
13	21	1	Macau	2,300.00	0.57	1	0.13	2,300.00	3.8	3.8	2.0
14	8	23	United Arab Emirates	2,210.00	0.55	10	1.25	221.00	3.7	3.7	2.2
15	13	18	Sweden	2,020.00	0.50	5	0.63	404.00	2.5	2.5	2.8

Rank by Total Amount	Rank by No. of Issues	Rank by Average Amount	Nationality of Deal	Total Amount RMB (Mln)	Market Share of Total Amount (%)	No. of Issues	Market Share of No. of Issues (%)	Average Amount RMB (Mln)	Average Coupon (%)	Average Coupon (Exclude Zeros and FRN)(%)	Average Tenor (Years)
16	17	2	Russian Federation	2,000.00	0.50	2	0.25	1,000.00	3.7	3.7	3.0
17	16	15	Netherlands	1,800.00	0.45	4	0.50	450.00	2.8	2.8	2.7
18	17	6	Malaysia	1,500.00	0.37	2	0.25	750.00	3.3	3.3	2.5
19	10	24	Brazil	1,488.00	0.37	7	0.88	212.57	3.7	3.7	2.0
20	17	10	Australia	1,200.00	0.30	2	0.25	600.00	2.2	2.2	2.5
21	21	2	Mexico	1,000.00	0.25	1	0.13	1,000.00	3.5	3.5	3.0
22	21	7	Austria	750.00	0.19	1	0.13	750.00	4.6	4.6	2.0
23	17	21	Spain	650.00	0.16	2	0.25	325.00	3.9	3.9	2.0
24	21	22	New Zealand	300.00	0.07	1	0.13	300.00	1.1	1.1	3.0
			Overall Total/ Wt. Average	401,516.90	100.00	797	100.00	503.79	2.8	2.8	2.0

3. Hedging RMB operating expenses
4. Lower cost of debt
5. Supporting client needs.

3.5.1 Supporting the Government's RMB Policy

The Chinese government formally established a policy to internationalize the RMB in 2009. Hong Kong was the first offshore market to launch the RMB business as far back as in 2004. Soon after, the offshore RMB deposit center in Hong Kong was then set up as a precursor to the offshore RMB bond market. In 2007, Hong Kong launched the dim sum bond market as a complement to the overall RMB internationalization efforts.[14] As part of the grand scheme, the Chinese policy banks, state-owned commercial banks and corporations helped kick start the development of dim sum bond market by issuing dim sum bonds with landmark issues.[15] This can be demonstrated by the mandates of dim sum bond issues by the MOF of the People's Republic of China. As stated in the MOF's dim sum bond prospectus, the bond offering

> ... aims at ... promoting the development of the offshore renminbi business in Hong Kong, and promoting the settlement for and circulation of RMB in the surrounding countries and regions. The issuance of the bonds will also provide a pricing benchmark for future offerings of dim sum bonds in Hong Kong by institutions from the mainland, and pave the way for more mainland institutions to offer dim sum bonds in Hong Kong so as to promote the development of the dim sum bond market in Hong Kong.[16]

Moreover, the Export-Import Bank of China has also facilitated the issuance of dim sum bonds as well as providing trade credit to Chinese trading companies.[17] From the national policy perspective, these financial institutions issue dim sum bonds as a policy target.

3.5.2 Cross-Border Funding Arbitrage

At present foreign and domestic companies can get access to the RMB debt markets in both Hong Kong and mainland China through the issuance

---

[14] See Fung and Yau (2012); Fung and Yau (2013); and Fung, Tzau, and Yau (2013a, 2013b).

[15] We discuss these in more detail in Chapter 6.

[16] See The Central People's Government of the People's Republic of China (2009), p. 21.

[17] See The Export-Import Bank of China (2010).

of dim sum and panda bonds respectively. They can also conduct cross-border transactions, and they can trade in RMB offshore with minimum restrictions. So how come there are two different RMB markets with separate quotations? Again, the issue relates back to China's stringent capital controls. Corporations have a natural incentive to buy RMB in the cheapest market and sell them in the priciest, which will limit the divergence between the domestic, onshore RMB (CNY) and the offshore RMB (CNH). However, as transactions can only be conducted against the background of approved corporate activity, there is no clean-cut arbitrage relationship between the two markets. Thus, as long as the cross-border arbitrage can be based on current account items such as trade and profit repatriation, companies can move RMB relatively easily across the Chinese border and potentially take advantage of the spread between the two markets.

However, the cross-border funding arbitrage becomes difficult to implement when transaction relates to China's capital account. Under normal circumstances it takes two or three months for a foreign company to inject new capital into a mainland China foreign-invested entity and the process may potentially be extended by another month when the capital to be injected comes in the form of offshore RMB. Investors have to undergo a similarly cumbersome process when funds are transferred through the Renminbi Qualified Foreign Institutional Investor (RQFII), Qualified Foreign Institutional Investor (QFII), and Qualified Domestic Institutional Investor (QDII) schemes. Thus, for non-Chinese companies and individuals the capital controls do not put severe restrictions on the currency flow out of the country; the problem is rather getting capital into the country.[18]

3.5.3 Hedging against Currency Risk

Borrowing in RMB enables the borrower to hedge against the exposure in RMB if they have significant operations in mainland China. This type of balance sheet hedging is attractive to companies, particularly MNCs, which may find it difficult to finance their mainland China's operations in RMB. For MNCs that have significant operations in mainland, this market offers the chance to raise money in RMB to fund operations or expansion plans, mitigating a large portion of the currency risk. For example, McDonald's sold RMB200 million (US$32 million) of 3 percent dim sum notes with a three-year tenor on September 16, 2010, to fund its operations and expansion in mainland China. It is McDonald's target that cash flow from operations and financing activities, plus cash on hand of its foreign operations will sufficiently cover its operating expenses, capital expenditure, and other funding requirements of its foreign operations.

---

[18] See Guo and Huang (2010).

3.5.4 Lower Cost of Debt

For corporations, whether Chinese or foreign, a commonly cited reason for borrowing in the dim sum bond market is that dim sum bonds offer a lower cost to borrowers (issuers) as compared to alternative financing sources such as the domestic, onshore borrowing or the Asian U.S. dollar bond market. For mainland Chinese companies and agencies, issuing dim sum bonds is another way to raise capital, outside of traditional methods such as bank borrowings (which has come under increasing pressure after successive rises in local banks' reserve requirement ratio as Beijing tries to put a lid on inflation) or the domestic corporate bond market which requires regulatory approval for access. For multinational corporations, some have not encountered difficulty in getting local bank financing,[19] although some admitted that they had the access to 'shadow banking'.[20]

Judging from the average yield of bonds issued, there are also significant cost savings for issuers in the dim sum bond market, as compared to the onshore bond market. The average yield differential between the onshore and offshore bond markets exceeds 2 percent. Offshore investors are willing to give up this yield to the issuers' benefit because they believe CNH bonds allow them to capture the currency appreciation rate in the future. For example, Baosteel Group Corp, China's second-largest steelmaker, issued the largest corporate RMB-denominated bond in Hong Kong in 2011. The total issue size was RMB3.6 billion ($565 million) with tranches due in two, three, and five years. The yield on the three-year tranche was 3.5 percent, compared favorably with 4.9 percent on outstanding notes due in 2014 sold three years earlier by the company's Shanghai-listed unit, Baoshan Iron & Steel Co.[21]

The strong demand allowed Ford to fix the issue size at RMB1 billion (US$156 million) and yield at 4.875 percent. Ford's financing was the first in the Chinese currency from an entirely foreign company with a sub-investment-grade rating. The issuer, Ford Motor Credit, has ratings of Ba1 (positive) from Moody's, BB+ (stable) from S&P, and BB+ (positive) from Fitch. Ford lost its investment-grade rating in 2005 and narrowly escaped bankruptcy in the wake of the 2008 crisis. The low yield relative to non-investment-grade ratings reflects the strong appeal of currency appreciation to dim sum bond investors despite the high credit risk. However, expectations for RMB appreciation have

---

[19] See Moore (2012b), p. 51.

[20] Standard & Poor's defines shadow banking as "credit intermediation involving entities and activities outside the regular banking system," where the regular banking system includes the central bank and all depository institutions in China (Standard & Poor's, 2013).

[21] See Evans, Angerer, and Yuan (2011).

changed since the Ford issue. Investors are increasingly willing to look beyond top-rated Chinese names in search of higher returns. At 4.875 percent, Ford had saved at least 200 basis points (bp) versus an onshore bank loan. China's onshore benchmark lending rate is at 6.9 percent for loans of three to five years.[22]

Another way to illustrate the cost savings is to compare the cost of funding in the offshore dim sum bond market versus the cost of funding of its own recent past transactions. For example, in June 2012, although onshore yields had been falling and offshore dim sum yields rising, the Export-Import Bank of China (Chexim) was still able to reap some savings from tapping the dim sum bond market, albeit much less than what was offered in the past. Chexim's onshore five-year bond was yielding 3.58 percent, suggesting a saving about 20 bp for the five-year bond.[23]

In many deals, foreign issuers were motivated by the opportunity to arbitrage the cost of fund differential in two different markets. Foreign issuers would tap the dim sum bond market when they could lower the cost of funding by doing a currency swap after issuing dim sum bonds in RMB. Sometimes, the issuer may even have to swap the dim sum bond deal in and out of, say, the U.S. dollar. For example, the basis in the cross-currency swap, which in the dim sum bond market refers to the cost of converting fixed-rate offshore RMB to floating-rate U.S. dollars, would favor the issuer of dim sum bonds if the basis goes up and makes it favorable for a borrower to issue in offshore RMB and swap to U.S. dollars. For example, in August 2012, ANZ Banking Group had tapped the offshore RMB market with a RMB1 billion offshore bond listed on the London exchange, which yielded 2.9 percent and swapped to the London Interbank Offered Rate (LIBOR) plus 90 bp. The swap rate was almost flat with the RMB. Thus, it was possible to get lower-cost funding by issuing in RMB and swapping it into U.S. dollar.[24]

There are other swap cases. Axiata, a Malaysian telecommunications company issued a dim sum bond issue for RMB1 billion (US$157 million) with a two-year tenor and 3.75 percent coupon in September 2012. It was the second *sukuk* in the dim sum bond market after Khazanah Nasional's (Danga Capital) RMB500 million *sukuk* dim sum bond priced in October 2011.[25] Although *sukuk* bonds have increased its popularity among global

---

[22] See Wong (2012).

[23] See Wee (2012a).

[24] See Wee (2012b).

[25] *Sukuk* is an Islamic financial certificate (like a bond) that complies with Sharia, Islamic religious law. The traditional Western interest-paying bond structure is not allowed under the Islamic law; the issuer of a *sukuk* sells the certificate to an investor group, who then rents it back to the issuer for a predetermined rental fee. The issuer also makes a contractual promise to buy back the certificate at a future date at par value.

investors, especially those from the Islamic countries, the limited amount of issuance may suggest that the *sukuk* structure has not exactly found favor with dim sum investors.[26] Axiata had to pay up 85 bp compared to the 2.9 percent pricing that Khazanah Nasional achieved for its RMB500 million three-year bond even Axiata's bonds are one year shorter in maturity.[27] This partly reflects Khazanah's closer link to the Malaysian government and hence the probability of default is lower. This also partly reflects that expectations of RMB appreciation had waned. It was reported that the deal was probably swapped out as Axiata did not have RMB requirements.[28] Likewise, Shinhan Bank, a South Korean bank, also priced its oversubscribed RMB600 million dim sum bond at a yield of 3.5 percent at around the same time as Axiata's issue. It was reported that the bank swapped the proceeds.[29]

An issuer who actually does not have renminbi requirements in their operations may actually swap the dim sum bond proceeds into U.S. dollar and then swap the U.S. dollars for the currency it prefers. This way, the dim sum bond issuance is simply an arbitrage to lower the cost of borrowing. For example, Hyundai Capital tapped the dim sum bond market in August 2012 for an 18-month senior unsecured offshore RMB bond for a RMB500 million bond (US$78 million) with a yield of 3.45 percent taking advantage of the arbitrage opportunity while swaps were in their favor. Hyundai Capital swapped the proceeds back to Korean won but it would first have to swap to U.S. dollars. It swapped to three-month LIBOR plus 105 bp in U.S. dollars and 3 percent in Korean won.[30] Another example is the dim sum bond deal done by Lloyds TSB Bank. The bank did not have onshore demand for RMB, and so anything it did raise was swapped back to dollars, euros, or sterling.[31]

The preceding cases indicate that the dim sum bond market provides another conduit from which corporations with or without operations in mainland China could obtain alternative financing at a reduced cost of debt,

---

[26] Wee (2012b) reports that Axiata's *sukuk* had a *wakala* structure, in which the underlying asset was airtime vouchers (representing an entitlement to a specified number of airtime minutes) from Celcom Axiata, which holds Malaysian wireless operations, and a wholly owned subsidiary of Axiata Group. She also suggests that the structure was unusual, as typically the underlying asset is a property, and is not very commonly used in the Middle Eastern *sukuk* bonds.

[27] See Wee (2012c).

[28] Ibid.

[29] Ibid.

[30] See Wee (2012b).

[31] See Caiger-Smith (2012).

which may, however, entail a currency swap to achieve that. The RMB swap market is yet to be fully developed. As internationalization of RMB continues, it is expected that the RMB swap markets will grow.

3.5.5 Supporting Client Needs

Foreign banks would like to issue dim sum bonds to raise RMB funds so that they can support the funding requirements of their clients who have operations in China. For example, IDBI, a state-controlled bank of India, was quoted that they issued dim sum bonds specifically "to give loans to our existing corporate clients, who have operations abroad."[32] Likewise, Lloyds TSB Bank did a few dim sum bond deals not for the RMB funding needs but to engage investors, existing or new, from the very beginning when a new market is being established. China CITIC Bank International tapped the dim sum bond market to get funding there with no intention to repatriate the funding across the border. Their strategic goal was to grow the balance sheet in Hong Kong so that they could have a much larger share of the offshore RMB market to provide trade loans to its own clientele and participate in the growing settlement of trade onshore.[33]

3.6 CONCLUSION

This chapter presents detailed information on the characteristics of issuers in the dim sum bond market. In general, there are five groups of issuers, including (1) government, (2) banks, (3) state-owned enterprises, (4) corporations, and (5) supranational agencies. Of the five groups, banks are the largest group of issuers of dim sum bonds in terms of the number of issues as well as the total RMB amount issued. Apparently, in terms of industry type, banks play a predominant role in issuing dim sum bonds. Real estate/property development firms and financial institutions other than banks are also major issuers in this market.

In analyzing the country of origin of issuers of dim sum bonds, we find that many issuers from China and other economies set up entities offshore to issue the bonds. Using offshore special investment vehicles to issue dim sum bonds may attribute to different reasons for different companies. It could be related to tax, capital control, and/or default considerations as the parent firm may not have legal obligations to bail out the offshore shell subsidiaries if they fail.

---

[32] See Unnikrishnan (2011).

[33] See Moore (2012a).

We discussed the various reasons for issuers raising funds in the dim sum bond market. Reasons include the strategic push by the Chinese government in the effort in internationalizing RMB, cross-border arbitrage, lowering the cost of borrowing, hedging RMB operating expenses, and supporting client needs offshore. In addition, considering growing liquidity in the CNH market, further RMB appreciation potential, and improving protection on bondholders with stricter covenants, increasing demand from global investors who look for an alternative investment asset class may encourage more issuers to tap the dim sum bond market, which will be discussed further in Chapter 5.

In the next couple of years, a good number of dim sum bonds will mature. It is expected that more issues of dim sum bonds will be offered to the market to refinance the maturing bonds. Issuers who plan to go to the dim sum bond market frequently in the future would like to see greater liquidity in the secondary market for the bonds they will issue, so that they do not have to pay a premium for refinancing the maturing issues. They will also face the refinancing risk, which is a recurrent risk, if they cannot issue long-dated bonds to finance capital expenditure since the liquidity in the dim sum bond market is limited.

Moreover, Chinese issuers, in particular, will face a more demanding investor base that is now calling for more ratings, strict covenants, and better pricing. Not all Chinese issuers are being forced to stray far from the liberal covenant policy of their domestic market. And, for foreign issuers, there are still big hurdles to overcome before they can expect the market to develop into a truly reliable source of funding. Foreign issuers are also concerned about swap liquidity since they swap back to other currencies for they do not necessarily have onshore demand for RMB. For some foreign issuers who have genuine need for onshore liquidity, the transparency and certainty of the approval process to remit the money onshore holds them back. Hence, some argue that currently more foreign issuers are interested in raising money for onshore needs than simply looking for a funding arbitrage. Overall, there are a lot of potential issuers but they have to pay up with higher yields because investors are now more demanding.

Finally, the Chinese government has committed to further develop the offshore RMB-denominated bond market. A different policy mix will be implemented to promote this market further, for example, the recent setup of the RMB clearing centers in Taiwan and Singapore.

REFERENCES

Caiger-Smith, Will. 2012. "Global Banks Rush to Tap Great Renminbi Expansion." *Euroweek: Offshore RMB Bonds: A Maturing Global Market,* June, 53.

Central People's Government of the People's Republic of China. 2009. *Offering Circular,* September 28: 21.

Export-Import Bank of China. 2010. *Offering Circular,* November 5: 3.

Evans, Rachel, Tanya Angerer, and Helen Yuan. 2011. "Baosteel Sells Dim Sum Bonds." *China Daily*, November 29.

Fung, Hung-Gay, and Jot Yau. 2012. "The Chinese Offshore Renminbi Currency and Bond Markets: The Role of Hong Kong." *China and World Economy* 20(3): 107–122.

Fung, Hung-Gay, and Jot Yau. 2013. "The Dim Sum Bond Market and Its Role in the Internationalization of the Renminbi." *European Financial Review*, February–March: 64–67.

Fung, Hung-Gay, Derrick Tzau, and Jot Yau. 2013a. "A Global Chinese Renminbi Bond Market: The Dim Sum Bond Market," in *Frontiers of Economics and Globalization*, Vol. 13, H. G. Fung and Y. Tse (eds.). Bingley, UK: Emerald Group Publishing Ltd.

Fung, Hung-Gay, Derrick Tzau, and Jot Yau. 2013b. "Offshore Renminbi-Denominated Bonds: Dim Sum Bonds." *Chinese Economy* 46(2): 6–28.

Guo, Feng, and Ying Huang. 2010. "Hot Money and Business Cycle Volatility: Evidence from China." *China and World Economy* 18: 73–89.

Moore, P. 2012a. "Companies Recognize the True Value of Offshore RMB." *Euroweek: Offshore RMB Bonds: A Maturing Global Market,* June: 50–52.

Moore, P. 2012b. "CNH Catches On with Emerging Borrowers." *Euroweek: Offshore RMB Bonds: A Maturing Global Market,* June: 56.

Standard & Poor's. 2013. "Will Shadow Banking Destabilise China's Financial System?" *FinanceAsia*, April 10.

Unnikrishnan, Dinesh. 2011. "IDBI Taps Dim Sum Bonds: Raises $102mn." *HT Media,* November 17.

Wee, Denise. 2012a. "Taiwanese Lifers Pull Weight on Chexim 15-Year Bond." *FinanceAsia*, June 13.

Wee, Denise. 2012b. "Dim Sum Bonds Offer Borrowers Arbitrage Opportunity." *FinanceAsia*, August 24.

Wee, Denise. 2012c. "Dim Sums Keep Pace as Axiata and Shinhan Print Deals." *FinanceAsia*, September 12.

Wong, Nethelie. 2012. "Ford Proves Dim Sum Draw." *IFR Asia*, March 17: 738.

CHAPTER 4

Investors

In previous chapters, we suggested that early dim sum bond investors were interested in the renminbi (RMB) appreciation instead of the low yield in dim sum bonds. They did not even mind that many of the dim sum bonds were unrated and without much bond protection. As the dim sum bond market continues to grow, the demand for dim sum bonds increases from investors seeking to gain from China's economic growth as an alternative to uncertainties posed by developed markets, as we discussed in previous chapters. As RMB appreciation is expected to subside, investors are more concerned about the RMB's value, and issuers' creditworthiness need to be addressed to sustain the market's long-term growth. Investors have started to push the issuers to adopt ratings, accept stricter covenants, and increase bond yields.

Generally, investors are concerned about the risk and return trade-off of alternative assets in a global market. Thus, we analyze various aspects of risk and return on dim sum bonds so that readers can get a better feel for the analysis required for this "new" asset class. In this chapter, we provide the investor perspective on dim sum bonds by analyzing the mix of investors and their motivation and risk preference for these dim sum bonds.

To understand the investor perspective, we first identify the type of investors—are they retail or institutional investors outside the mainland who have access to RMB funds? Or are they investors who wish to participate in the expected growth in the People's Republic of China's economy and appreciation of the RMB against the U.S. dollar? Are they local or international investors? Moreover, we want to understand how dim sum bond investors' perspectives are different from investors of other asset classes, in particular their counterparts, such as the Asian USD bonds.

4.1 INVESTOR TYPE AND MIX

As mentioned in Chapter 2, the dim sum bond market is an offshore RMB-denominated debt market including a myriad of products such as the short-term floating rate and zero-coupon notes, fixed-rate certificates of deposit (FXCDs), medium-term notes (MTNs), and long-term bonds. Investors of FXCDs are mainly private and retail banking clients. Investors also include life insurance companies, banks, and corporations. Since most of the FXCDs are short-dated (typically with a one-year tenor) and held to maturity, we focus our discussion on risk and return with regard to investors of other types of dim sum debt securities.

Like those of the Asian USD bonds, investors of dim sum bonds (i.e., collectively for MTNs, floating-rate notes [FRNs], and bonds) comprise mainly the "real money" funds, hedge funds, corporations, commercial banks, and private banks. Private banks refer to a wide array of financial services entities ranging from global family offices, of which the size and daily operations management are comparable to mid-sized funds and wealth management companies that serve high-net-worth individuals.

However, as dim sum bonds are effectively local-currency bonds and the dim sum bond market is in a relatively early stage of development, the investor mix of dim sum bonds is somewhat different from that of the Asian USD bonds. The investor mix varies largely from bond to bond, depending on the issuer profile, bond structure, and issuer's access to capital markets, among other things. When dim sum bonds were launched a few years back, many of them were either unrated or rated by only one international credit rating agency, whereas many of the Asian USD bonds are conventionally rated by two or more. Comparing to those of the Asian USD bonds, the earlier dim sum bond issues were "covenant-lite" with few restrictive covenants to protect the bondholders, and their coupon rates were on average lower as investors were more accommodating given the expectation of the RMB appreciation and lack of investment options for CNH funds. In general, the more investor friendly the bond structure (e.g., bonds rated by international credit rating agencies and having bondholder protection such as bond covenants), the more established the track record of the issuer, the more appealing the issue is to the institutional investors, such as the "real money" funds and hedge funds, and the higher will be their participation. However, the less investor friendly the bond structure, the less established the track record of the issuer in capital market (i.e., if bank loans are the major source of the issuer's funding), the more likely the bonds end up in the books of commercial and private banks.

The deal statistics of dim sum bonds are not as readily available as those of Asian USD bonds; as such, the full picture of bond allocation to different investor types is not as transparent. However, from the limited deal statistics available, as well as our observations and numerous discussions with market participants, we believe that there is a higher proportion of bonds allocated to commercial banks and private banks, especially for earlier issues, compared with that of Asian USD bonds. For example, commercial banks and private banks account for a total of 52 percent of the total allocation, or 26 percent each, as indicated by order books (see Figure 4.1).

Investors based in Asia are major holders of dim sum bonds since Hong Kong and Singapore, especially the former, are the key CNH markets and major sources of CNH liquidity. As indicated by order books in Figure 4.2, more than 45 percent of investors (37 percent from Hong Kong, 4.68 percent from China, and 3.6 percent from Taiwan) come from Greater China, 15.88 percent from Singapore, and 25.06 percent from Asia. As the offshore RMB markets and RMB currency trading are expanding to Taiwan, Singapore, and London, we see more foreign corporations and banks tap the dim sum bond market, which will raise the awareness of the dim sum bond market among global investors and help geographically diversify the investor base of dim sum bonds.

Furthermore, as the dim sum bond and CNH markets grow to a critical mass, there will be more RMB funds for investing in dim sum bonds. The investor base of dim sum bonds is expanding and the mix is diversifying. As such, we notice that institutional investors ("real money" funds and hedge funds) are getting more involved, accounting for an increasing proportion of dim sum bond allocations for new issues. These, coupled with fading

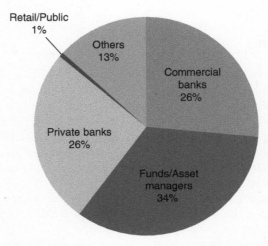

FIGURE 4.1 Dim sum bond investors by type as indicated by order books

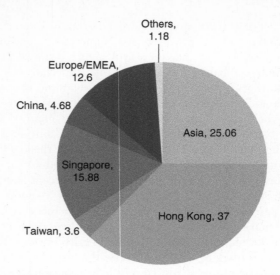

FIGURE 4.2   Dim sum bond investor mix (%) by geography as indicated by order books

expectations of RMB appreciation, lead to convergence of terms and conditions for dim sum bond issues with those of the Asian USD bonds. For example, coupons of dim sum bonds are now more in line with the issuers' credit quality; a higher proportion of issues is rated by international credit rating agencies; and bond covenants are more in line with the Asian USD bond issues. We expect this converging trend to continue.

4.2 MOTIVATION

Investors worldwide are interested in dim sum bonds for several reasons. First, they anticipate gains on the RMB appreciation in spite of the relatively low yield on dim sum bonds. Dim sum bonds may serve as a currency hedge for investors who have liabilities denominated in RMB, and thus dim sum bond investing represents a proxy play on RMB appreciation. Second, the liquidity of dim sum bonds is significantly enhanced and greater than other RMB-denominated assets because many of the dim sum bonds are listed on exchanges around the world. Third, these bonds offer a new opportunity to invest in China, particularly for financial institutions, which need new conduits for investing the offshore RMB deposits in RMB-denominated assets. RMB-denominated assets may represent a new asset class for those who want to diversify into the growing Chinese economy.

Given the persistent trend of appreciating RMB in the past few years, dim sum bonds have become a favorite asset class among investors in the local market. Recently, as RMB appreciation has started to subside, investors in the dim sum bond market appear to have paid more attention to the credit quality of these investments as applications for credit rating on the dim sum bonds have become more ubiquitous. This shift would enhance the appeal of dim sum bonds to investors who are interested in RMB-denominated assets.

4.2.1 Expected Currency Appreciation and Yield

As mentioned before, in the first few years since its inception, when RMB appreciation was envisaged and alternatives for CNH investments were scarce, dim sum bonds were sold at unrealistic yields without standard covenants of the Asian USD bonds. However, as the much anticipated RMB appreciation subsides, more investment options are now available to CNH investors, and increasing participation of institutional investments, terms and conditions of recent dim sum bond issues have started to converge with those of the Asian USD bond issues, rendering dim sum bonds a competitive asset class for investors. As we pointed out earlier, coupon rates of dim sum bonds are getting more in line with credit quality, a higher proportion of issues is rated by international credit rating agencies, and bond covenants are more in line with the Asian USD bond issues.

While the yield of dim sum bonds may not be particularly attractive compared with other asset classes such as the Asian USD bonds, especially if the expectation of RMB appreciation subsides, investors may still be interested in dim sum bonds since investment options for CNH are quite limited at this stage. Dim sum bonds offer investors higher return than bank deposits. The dim sum bond market remains a treasury investment option for investors who obtain CNH funds in the course of their business operations. Dim sum bonds also have their appeal to investors who are familiar with the operations of small and medium enterprises in China, such as the China-focused funds and private banking clients, and to investors who have access to low-cost CNH funding, such as Chinese commercial banks.

4.2.2 Liquidity

Because the issue size of dim sum bonds is, in general, smaller and a relatively large proportion of bonds (specifically the FXCDs) are in the hands of the buy-and-hold investors, dim sum bond investors typically participate in the primary market. Trading of dim sum bonds in the secondary market is relatively thin. Hence, the bid-ask spreads of dim sum bonds are generally wider and the liquidity lower.[1]

A few of dim sum bonds have been listed on different world exchanges to attract investors that prefer disclosure requirements and monitoring by exchanges. Exchange listing also fosters wider participation by investors, particularly institutional investors that can trade only exchange-listed bonds. Thus, exchange listing of dim sum bonds helps promote a liquid secondary market. Currently, trading of dim sum bonds is limited by the fact that the average deal size of dim sum bonds is small (RMB503.79 million; see Table 2.1) and bonds are mostly held to maturity by institutional investors, such as commercial banks and insurance companies. Exchange listing also enhances the visibility of issuer internationally. For example, ANZ Banking Group issued its second dim sum bond in Hong Kong, had it listed in London, and then swapped it into U.S. dollars.[2] (See Table 2.12 for the exchanges listing dim sum bonds.)

4.2.3 Diversification

Investors may be interested in using dim sum bonds as an asset class in their global portfolio diversification. Whether dim sum bonds are considered to be an asset class depends on whether dim sum bonds pass the test for being an asset class over time.[3] At present, the dim sum bond market is still growing, and it will take some time before we can affirm whether dim sum bonds play an efficient diversification role in portfolios. To illustrate the potential benefits of diversification of dim sum bonds in portfolios, we ran correlations of the Bank of China (Hong Kong) (BOCHK) Dim Sum Bond Index monthly returns with selected fixed income and equity indices, and exchange rates. The indices can be seen as diversified portfolios of fixed income and equity assets in U.S. dollars, whereas exchange rates can be considered as exposures in those currencies against the U.S. dollar. Table 4.1 shows that correlations of dim sum bonds with other assets are in general low; the highest correlation (0.86) is with the JP Morgan Asia Credit (China) Index, which is a subindex of the JP Morgan Asia Credit Index that includes only Chinese credits. Other correlations are either low positive or, in a few cases, negative, for example, with

---

[1] Liu (2010) reports that the bid-ask spread was in the range of 20-40 bp, as compared to 10 bp for onshore government bonds and 15 bp for corporate bonds.

[2] See Wee (2012).

[3] For a discussion of the definition of an asset class, see Kritzman (1999).

JPM Global Aggregate and Barclays U.S. Aggregate in bonds, Nikkei 225 in equities, and the Japanese yen, Brazilian real, and British pound sterling in exchange rates. These results suggest that dim sum bonds are potentially good diversifiers in many types of asset portfolios. In other words, dim sum bonds, if included in other asset portfolios, could potentially reduce the risk of the portfolios.

TABLE 4.1   Correlation of BOCHK Dim Sum Bond Index with Selected Bond Indices, Equity Indices, and Exchange Rates (2011–2013)

	Monthly Correlation with BOCHK
Bond Indices	
JPM Global Aggregate Bond Index (Total Return (US$))	.36
Barclays U.S. Aggregate Bond Index (Total Return (US$))	−.03
JP Morgan Asia Credit Index	.78
JP Morgan Asia Credit (China) Index	.86
Equity Indices	
Hang Seng Index (Hong Kong)	.81
Nikkei 225 (Japan)	.39
S&P 500 (U.S.)	.67
MSCI AC Asia ex Japan	.78
MSCI World	.71
MSCI Europe	.61
MSCI RM Latin America	.74
Currencies	
CNH/USD	.59
Japanese Yen/USD	−.31
Euro/USD	.61
Korean Won/USD	.73
British Pound Sterling/USD	.50
Brazilian Real/USD	.19
Mexican Peso/USD	.72
Russian Ruble/USD	.73

4.3 RISK/RETURN ANALYSIS

From the investor perspective, the risk and return analysis on an investment provides a rational justification for the investment decision. For a nascent market like the dim sum bond market, which is still growing and evolving every day. Results from the analysis must be interpreted cautiously and applied carefully for future decisions. The analysis could only be done on a relatively short period of time. The usual caveat that past results do not guarantee future performance applies. We present the historical performance and various types of risk in dim sum bonds, namely, the country risk, currency risk, credit risk, interest rate risk, and liquidity risk in the following section.

4.3.1 Historical Performance

At inception in mid-2007, investors invested in dim sum bonds for the coupon yield when interest rates were low for the U.S. dollar or Hong Kong dollar deposits. As the RMB appreciated against the U.S. dollar, dim sum bond investors bet on the currency appreciation by holding RMB-denominated assets. Dim sum bonds came into being at the right time. Since most dim sum bonds were priced at par and most were held to maturity, the total yield to bondholders was basically the stated coupon rate on the bond. The average coupon rate of all dim sum bonds for the five-and-a-half-year period (July 2007 to the end of 2012) is 2.77 percent (see Table 2.1). The average coupon rate for dim sum bonds had declined since 2008 to its low in 2011 at 2.15 percent. It went back up in 2012 and averaged 3.15 percent for the year.

Table 4.2 breaks down the average coupon rates of dim sum bonds with fixed coupons by tenor and by year. It shows that the average coupon ranges from 2.37 percent for 1-year tenor, 3.48 percent for 5-year, 3.92 percent for 10-year, and 4.18 percent for 15-year, to 4.30 percent for 20-year tenor. Bonds with 2-year and 3-year tenors had been issued since 2007, and the trend of the changes of the average coupon rate indicates the volatility in the coupon rate for dim sum bonds over time. It is noted that, in general, the coupon rate reached a peak just one year after it was launched. In 2009, the average coupon rates for the 2-year tenor bonds started to decline until it picked up again in 2012, whereas for the 3-year tenor bonds, the average coupon had a similar trend but picked up in 2011. In general, the coupon rates for all tenors have risen.

A caveat on the average coupon rate of all dim sum bond issues described here is in order. The above analysis of the average coupon rate is based on the relatively short history of the dim sum bond market, during

TABLE 4.2 Average Coupon (No. of Issues) of Dim Sum Bonds Excluding Zeros and FRNs by Tenor and by Year (2007–2012)

Tenor (Years)	2007	2008	2009	2010	2011	2012	Overall
1				1.95 (4)	1.36 (154)	2.91 (290)	2.37 (448)
2	3.07 (3)	3.25 (3)	2.53 (4)	2.14 (12)	2.08 (31)	3.53 (53)	2.89 (106)
2.5						2.90 (2)	2.90 (2)
2.75						3.25 (1)	3.25 (1)
3	3.28 (2)		2.70 (1)	3.08 (8)	3.48 (69)	4.08 (79)	3.74 (161)
5		3.40 (2)	3.30 (1)	3.48 (2)	3.33 (20)	3.75 (12)	3.48 (35)
5.6						4.00 (1)	4.00 (1)
7					3.80 (4)	4.20 (1)	3.88 (5)
8.25						3.65 (1)	3.65 (1)
9				2.85 (1)	3.30 (1)	6.15 (1)	4.73 (2)
10					3.93 (6)	4.26 (3)	3.92 (10)
15						4.18 (3)	4.18 (3)
20						4.30 (1)	4.30 (1)
Overall Average (no. of issues)	3.15 (5)	3.31 (5)	2.68 (6)	2.52 (27)	2.19 (285)	3.25 (448)	2.83 (776)

which the coupon rate of the dim sum bonds was primarily driven by the expectation of RMB appreciation. However, in the future, the pricing of a dim sum bond or the determination of its coupon rate will be determined by a myriad of factors, such as the expected value of the RMB against the U.S. dollar, market sentiment, and credit quality.

Table 4.3 presents the average coupon rates of the rated (first line) and unrated (second line) dim sum bonds. It is worth noting that among the 14 cases where averages for both the rated and unrated bonds are available for the same tenor (pairs shaded in Table 4.3), the average coupon rates for the unrated bonds are higher than the rated bonds in seven cases (2-year tenor: 2010, 2011, 2012; 3-year tenor: 2010, 2011, 2012; 5-year tenor: 2011) (in bold italics); the other seven cases have equal or lower coupon rates than those of the rated bonds. Intuitively, we would expect bonds without ratings would need to offer a higher coupon to attract investors as investors would be less comfortable with unrated issues, which would not be subject to the scrutiny of rating agencies and the investor base could be smaller as some institutional investors might only invest in rated issues. This is true for the seven cases cited earlier.

However, the other seven cases have rated bonds offering higher or equal coupons. As we discussed in Chapter 2, we believe some of the counterintuitive cases can be attributable to the credit quality of issuers. For issuers with less solid credit profiles or lesser known to fixed-income investors, they may be more inclined to obtain one or more ratings from international credit rating agencies in order to market the bonds to investors. Hence, even if the bonds are rated, the yields are higher, reflecting the lower credit quality or less established track record in debt capital market. We note that out of these seven counterintuitive cases, that is, rated bonds offering higher/equal coupons, five of them have tenors with five years or longer. Issuers of them are mainly government entities, large commercial large banks, and state-owned enterprises (SOEs). These issuers have good credit quality and are well known to the debt capital market. They will be able to market their bonds even without credit ratings.

We present the further breakdown statistics of the rated and unrated bonds by Moody's rating in Table 4.4. It is clear that the majority of rated bonds are of high quality, investment grade (Aaa, Aa, and A), with 21 issues of medium quality (Baa) and 3 issues of speculative grade (Ba).

For investors who do not hold the bonds to maturity, their total return on dim sum bond investments depends on the selling price when they sell the bonds. To present a general picture on the average total return on dim sum bonds, we use the BOCHK Offshore RMB Bonds Index yield (BOCHK Dim Sum Bond Index), a popular dim sum bond index, from its inception to the end

TABLE 4.3 Average Coupon (No. of Issues) of Rated/Unrated [second line] Dim Sum Bonds Excluding Zeros and FRNs by Tenor and by Year (2007–2012)

Tenor (Years)	2007	2008	2009	2010	2011	2012
1				1.95 (4)	1.84 (12) 1.32 (146)	3.07 (15) 2.90 (288)
2	3.07 (3)	3.25 (1) 3.25 (2)		2.08 (3) 2.16 (9)	1.73 (9) 2.23 (22)	3.51 (23) 3.54 (30)
2.5			2.53 (6)			
2.75						2.90 (1)
3	3.28 (2)	3.4 (2)	2.70 (1)	2.85 (6) 3.76 (3)	2.96 (17) 3.65 (53)	3.25 (1) 4.04 (35) 4.11 (44)
5			3.30 (1)	3.75 (1) 3.20 (1)	2.65 (9) 3.89 (11)	3.99 (6) 3.50 (6)
5.6						
7					3.80 (4)	4.00 (1)
8.25						4.20 (1)
9						3.65 (1)
10				2.85 (1)	3.30 (1) 6.00 (1)	6.15 (1) 4.38 (1)
15					3.52 (5)	4.21 (2) 4.20 (2) 4.15 (1)
20						4.30 (1)

TABLE 4.4 Dim Sum Bonds by Moody's Rating (2007–2012)

Moody's Rating	# of Issues	Amount RMB (Mln)	Average Coupon (%)	Average Tenor (Years)
Aaa	8	3,870	2.20	4.38
Aa1	5	2,450	1.78	2.40
Aa2	3	1,820	2.52	2.67
Aa3	12	10,715	3.08	2.33
A1	25	10,995	2.35	1.64
A1 (P)	1	1,000	3.20	3.00
A2	16	11,443	3.10	2.19
A3	14	12,750	3.62	3.36
Baa1	6	4,225	3.49	3.17
Baa2	12	8,690	4.21	2.83
Baa3	3	1,067	3.31	2.33
Ba1	1	750	5.63	2.00
Ba3 (P)	2	3,200	8.38	3.00
Not Rated by Moody's	689	328,542	2.71	1.90
Total	797	401,517	2.77	1.99

(P)—Moody's provisional ratings in advance of the final sale of the securities. The ratings, however, only represent Moody's preliminary opinion. Moody's will assign a definite rating to the securities upon conclusive review of the transactions and associated documents.

of 2012.[4] Figure 4.3 shows that the per annum (p.a.) yield of the BOCHK Dim Sum Bond Index commenced with a 2.06 percent p.a. yield on December 31, 2010, bottomed at 1.74 percent on January 20, 2011, and peaked at 6.27 percent on October 10, 2011. At the end of 2012, it stood at 4.63 percent. The average daily yield of the BOCHK Dim Sum Bond Index is 4.71 percent p.a. with a standard deviation of 0.97 percent for the period 2011–2012.

---

[4] The index tracks the total return performance of RMB-denominated bonds with a minimum outstanding face value of RMB50 million issued outside the mainland Hong Kong). It also includes RMB-denominated bonds with settlements, coupon payments and principal repayments paid in another currency (i.e., including synthetic dim sum bonds). The base date of the index is December 31, 2010. The index yield is the average of the total returns on the bonds in the index. Other dim sum bond indices include those from HSBC, Citigroup, and Deutsche Bank.

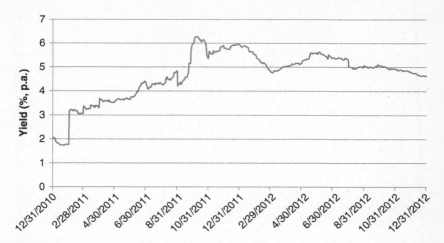

FIGURE 4.3 The yield on the BOCHK Dim Sum Bond Index (December 31, 2010, through December 31, 2012)

Table 4.5 presents the average monthly total return of the BOCHK Dim Sum Bond Index adjusted for exchange rate (vs. USD bond return based on JP Morgan Asia Credit [China] Index) for the period, January 2, 2011 through January 3, 2013—0.37 percent (0.77 percent) with a standard deviation of 1.98 percent (4.87 percent). The annualized mean return of the BOCHK Dim Sum Bond Index (vs. JP Morgan Asia Credit [China] Index) for the period is 4.48 percent (9.28 percent) with an annualized standard deviation of 6.85 percent (16.86 percent). Despite a lower mean return than the Asian USD bonds, the dim sum bonds have a lower volatility. However, the return/standard deviation ratio (0.65) for dim sum bonds is worse than that for the Asian USD bonds (0.55). The dim sum bonds have underperformed the Asian USD bonds in the risk-return trade-off from January 2, 2011 through January 3, 2013. We discuss various risks that are present in the dim sum bond market in the following section.

4.3.2 Risks

As alluded to in Chapter 2, the dim sum bond market is actually an offshore RMB-denominated debt market including products, such as the short-term FRNs, FXCDs, MTNs, and long-term bonds. Most of the short-term products are FXCDs, placed by commercial banks. However, FXCDs are not equivalent to a time deposit and are not protected under the Hong Kong Deposit Protection Scheme nor guaranteed by the Hong Kong SAR Government's

TABLE 4.5 Mean Return and Standard Deviation of BOCHK Dim Sum Bond Index and Asian USD Bond Index for January 2, 2011 through January 3, 2013

	BOCHK Return (%)	Currency Return (%)	Total Return in USD (%)	USD Bond Return* (%)
Mean (monthly)	0.13	0.23	0.37	0.77
Std Dev (monthly)	1.48	0.71	1.98	4.87
Annualized Mean	1.57	2.77	4.48	9.28
Annualized Std Dev	5.13	2.48	6.85	16.86
Annualized Mean/ Annualized Std Dev	0.6169	1.12	0.65	0.55

*Based on JPMorgan Asia Credit (China) Index.

Exchange Fund. Moreover, if the dim sum debt product is not listed on organized exchanges, investors are not protected by the local investor protection scheme, such as the Investor Compensation Fund in Hong Kong.[5]

Furthermore, the issuers may not be governed and enforced by the laws of where the issuing entities domiciled since most of the operating assets of dim sum bond issuers are in mainland China, offshore bondholders are legally and structurally subordinated to onshore creditors, recoverability of onshore operating assets in case of bankruptcy remains untested. Thus, the risks in dim sum bonds are analogous to Eurobonds, which are issued in a currency other than the local currency. Many risk issues pertaining to dim sum bonds require legal interpretation and they are beyond the scope of this book.[6] We consider dim sum bonds as investment products rather than bank products. The major risks we discuss next include country risk, currency risk, credit risk, interest rate risk, and liquidity risk.

4.3.2.1 Country Risk   Country risk refers to the risks emitted from the country of the issuer that affect the value of the bond. It includes economic, social, cultural, and political risks. The majority of dim sum bond issuers are

---

[5] The Investor Compensation Fund in Hong Kong SAR has been established to pay compensation to retail investors of any nationality who suffer pecuniary losses, as a result of a default of a licensed intermediary or authorized financial institution, in relation to exchange-traded products in Hong Kong SAR. If the bond is not listed on the Hong Kong Stock Exchange, investors will not be covered by the investor compensation fund if the placing bank or any other intermediary defaults.

[6] For a roundtable discussion on the risks pertaining to the dim sum bond markets from the institutional investor's perspective, see Euroweek (2012, pp. 35–42).

entities from Greater China, either mainland China or Hong Kong (together they account for more than 80 percent of the number of issues and total amount issued), while a few come from Macau and Taiwan. The largest group of issuers outside Greater China in terms of both number of issues and the total amount issued is from Korea. Korean issuers tend to issue dim sum bonds with short tenor, averaging 1.54 years, which is the lowest among all issuers. Table 4.6 reports the number, total amount, and average size of the dim sum bond issues by issuer's country/economy of risk.

Because most issuers are from mainland China, country risk is more relevant to the changes in China's policy. The risks involved in the government policy changes include the following policy areas:

■ *Cross-border transfer of funds.* China has changed the policy on cross-border transfer of funds since the inception of the dim sum bond market a few times. Thus far, each of the changes allows easier transfer of funds raised in the dim sum bond market back to the mainland. The RQFII program allows the RMB funds from the dim sum bond issuance to fund direct investment in China and the Chinese government has encouraged the use of RMB for trade settlement. However, an abrupt change in the policy may adversely tighten the flows and thus affect the issuers' ability to repay the bond.

■ *Rule of law.* Since dim sum bonds are issued in Hong Kong, the governing law for the majority of dim sum bonds are the laws of Hong Kong, which is a special administrative region (SAR) of China, having its own rule of law under "one country, two systems" as stated in the Basic Law of Hong Kong. Thus, it may be difficult to enforce judgments in Hong Kong against Chinese issuers and their management, even though the statutory financial institutions (like the Export-Import Bank of China or CDB) organized under the laws of China and substantially all of its assets and operations are located in mainland China. There is uncertainty regarding the recognition and enforcement in mainland China of judgments given by the Hong Kong SAR courts of law.

■ *Tax laws.* Currently, any gains realized on the transfer of the bonds by nonresident enterprise holders are not subject to the enterprise income tax since such gain is not regarded as income derived from sources within China.[7] According to the arrangement between China and Hong Kong, residents of Hong Kong, including enterprise and individual holders of dim sum bonds, will not be subject to the People's Republic of China

---

[7] The applicable tax law is the PRC Enterprise Income Tax Law, which took effect on January 1, 2008, and is currently at a 10 percent rate on capital gains.

TABLE 4.6 Number, Total Amount, and Average Size of Dim Sum Bond Issues by Issuer's Country/Economy of Risk (2007–2012)

Country/Economy	No. of Issues	Market Share (%)	Amount RMB (Mln)	% Amount	Average Size (RMB (Mln))	Average Coupon (%)	Average Tenor (Years)
Australia	2	0.25	1,200.00	0.30	600.00	2.18	2.50
Austria	1	0.13	750.00	0.19	750.00	4.55	2.00
Brazil	7	0.88	1,488.00	0.37	212.57	3.74	2.00
China	594	74.53	293,175.40	73.02	493.56	2.62	1.79
France	11	1.38	8,150.00	2.03	740.91	4.68	3.18
Germany	17	2.13	9,495.00	2.36	558.53	2.86	4.21
Hong Kong	46	5.77	30,917.50	7.70	672.12	3.19	2.17
India	6	0.75	2,590.00	0.65	431.67	4.90	3.00
Japan	12	1.51	4,220.00	1.05	351.67	2.88	2.83
Korea	35	4.39	11,537.00	2.87	329.63	2.80	1.54
Macau	1	0.13	2,300.00	0.57	2,300.00	3.75	2.00
Malaysia	2	0.25	1,500.00	0.37	750.00	3.33	2.50
Mexico	1	0.13	1,000.00	0.25	1,000.00	3.50	3.00
Netherlands	4	0.50	1,800.00	0.45	450.00	2.79	2.69
New Zealand	1	0.13	300.00	0.07	300.00	1.10	3.00

Russian Federation	2	0.25	2,000.00	0.50	1,000.00	3.73	3.00
Singapore	5	0.63	3,879.00	0.97	775.80	2.94	3.00
Supranational	5	0.63	2,950.00	0.73	590.00	2.21	4.40
Spain	2	0.25	650.00	0.16	325.00	3.90	2.00
Sweden	5	0.63	2,020.00	0.50	404.00	2.47	2.80
Taiwan	6	0.75	2,561.00	0.64	426.83	3.82	3.17
United Kingdom	14	1.76	7,214.00	1.80	515.29	3.26	3.00
United Arab Emirates	10	1.25	2,210.00	0.55	221.00	3.72	2.20
United States	8	1.00	7,610.00	1.90	951.25	2.68	2.50
Total	797	100.00	401,516.90	100.00	503.79	2.77	1.99

(PRC) tax on any capital gains derived from a sale or exchange of the bonds. However, should the PRC tax authorities reinterpret that gains on the transfer of the dim sum bonds are considered income derived from sources within China, capital gains on dim sum bonds may become subject to PRC income taxes and will adversely affect the value of the bonds.

4.3.2.2 Currency Risk For the past several years, the value of the Chinese currency has appreciated against the U.S. dollar. Figure 1.3 shows the value of one U.S. dollar in terms of RMB since 2007, the year the internationalization of the Chinese currency commenced. As shown in the figure, the RMB had risen in the past several years until it started to stall in early 2012. Appreciation of the RMB was attributed to a number of factors: the growth of the Chinese economy, the weakening of the U.S. dollar, and the ongoing pressure from the United States and other countries to push up the value of the RMB.

However, the RMB may take an about turn because of the slowdown in economic growth, rising domestic inflation rate, higher labor costs resulted from the newly implemented labor law, high taxes imposed on domestic business operations, and difficulty in securing financing by Chinese firms from banks and other financial institutions. These explain the recent slowdown of the RMB appreciation. At any rate, dim sum bonds have become an investment vehicle that enables investors to settle differences in opinion in the future prospect of the RMB movements.

4.3.2.3 Credit Risk Like investors of any other bonds, dim sum bond investors are exposed to the creditworthiness of the issuer, that is, the issuer's ability as well as willingness to repay, even for bonds issued by policy banks of China, such as the CDB and the Export-Import Bank of China, and the default risk is considered to be minimal. In the early stage of development, many of the investors consider dim sum bond a proxy play on RMB appreciation; as such, credit risk, to a large extent, was not investors' number one concern. For investors seeking to diversify their currency holdings into the RMB, the dim sum bond market in Hong Kong has been one of the few investment options. Investors were therefore willing to sacrifice covenant protection to gain exposure to the RMB. Many of the early dim sum bonds were unrated and "covenant-lite." However, as the RMB appreciation loses its allure, investors are paying more attention to credit risk and bond protection. In other words, investors are concerned about the paucity of covenant protection structured on dim sum bonds, as well as the poor level of operational disclosure compared with a typical U.S. dollar high-yield bond. Bond covenants become more important in placing the bonds to investors, which is in stark contrast to the earlier period when dim sum bonds were "covenant-lite." Investors began to conceive possible consequences of a breach of covenants as the first case emerged. On August 21, 2012, Global Bio-Chem Technology Group (Global Bio-Chem) announced that it was facing a possible breach of covenants, and bought back 92 percent of its dim sum bonds after bondholders agreed to the market's first tender offer.[8] In our opinion, this incident revealed the importance of bond covenants. The way Global Bio-Chem handled the incident gave investors some more confidence in the nascent dim sum bond market.

4.3.2.4 Interest Rate Risk   Dim sum debt products carry a fixed interest rate, with a few exceptions (i.e., FRNs and zero-coupon bonds). Consequently, the value of most dim sum debt products in the secondary market will vary inversely with the RMB interest rate. If the RMB interest rate increases significantly, the market value of these instruments may be adversely affected. In light of the recent trend of gradual interest rate liberalization by the Chinese government, the risk of increasing interest rate volatility is imminent and hence the increasing mark-to-market risk in dim sum bonds. The interest rate risk will be even more relevant as the market becomes more mature. The average tenor as well as the duration of dim sum bonds will likely get longer.

Since dim sum bonds have short tenors, averaging about two years, the maturity profile does not cover all the needs of investors who might have an appetite for longer tenor for their exposures. Thus, dim sum bonds have to extend their maturity profile since the absence of maturities longer than three years is apparent. Despite the fact that benchmark issues for 10-, 15-, and 20-year tenors have been issued as part of the national policy to establish the term structure of interest rates in this market, numbers of issues with long tenor are quite limited. As indicated in Table 2.6, there are 35, 10, 3, and 1 outstanding issues of dim sum bonds for 5-, 10-, 15-, and 20-year tenor, respectively, as of the end of 2012. For investors who need long-tenor bonds, the market is yet to come up with more long-dated issues. However, long bonds typically have greater volatility, and the interest rate risk may be a concern to investors.

4.3.2.5 Liquidity Risk   Only a few dim sum bonds are traded with limited liquidity on securities exchanges at this time. In other words, there is no liquid secondary market for dim sum bonds, although the trading liquidity

---

[8] See www.businessweek.com/news/2012-11-30/global-bio-chem-gets-bondholder-nod-for-first-dim-sum-buyback

is gradually improving as more institutional investors are getting involved in the market. In general, the investment banks that help bring the bonds to the market will make a market for the bonds over the counter. However, the relatively thin trading liquidity has led to wider gap between the bid and the ask prices. The thin trading liquidity will have the most impact in times of market downturn when investors may not able to sell the bonds without materially lowering the selling price.

In addition, the Chinese government continues to regulate the conversion between the RMB and foreign currencies, including the Hong Kong dollar. Despite the significant reduction over the years by the Chinese government of its control over routine foreign exchange transactions under current accounts, the liquidity of dim sum bonds may still be adversely affected.

4.4 CONCLUSION

The dim sum bond market has shown rapid development, thanks partly to the RMB appreciation over the past few years. The recent slowdown in development is likely to have come from both the supply and demand sides. On the demand side, since the potential of currency appreciation is getting less, investors have less incentive to buy dim sum bonds unless issuers are willing to pay higher coupons. On the supply side, many issuers simply consider dim sum bonds as a lower cost, short-dated, smaller-size funding alternative. They tap the dim sum bond market only if they can raise fund at a lower cost and/or terms and disclosure requirements are less stringent than those of the Asian USD bond market.

To make dim sum bonds a viable and logical investment beyond the short-term currency speculation, the dim sum bond has to provide investors a risk-return profile comparable to those of other asset classes. Dim sum bonds need to compete directly with the Asian USD bonds on coupon, disclosure, and information (such as financials, sell-side research coverage, and credit ratings), and investor protection (such as bond covenants). In our opinion, valuation has to be more reflective of the credit risk of issuers, information flow must be more transparent, and terms and conditions, such as credit rating requirements and covenants must be more in line with those of the Asian USD bonds in the future. These are key factors to the future development of the dim sum bond market.

Overall, we remain optimistic on the development of the dim sum bond market. China's long-run national policy for internationalizing the RMB to become a global reserve currency provides a sustainable impetus to the growth and development of the dim sum bond market. In the past few years, the Chinese government has strived hard to develop the dim sum bond market into a global capital market. Indeed, new rules have been implemented to promote this market, including the easing of the transfer of RMB funds into mainland China and a trial program to allow the RMB funds raised from this dim sum bond market to be invested in the Chinese domestic financial and good markets. These new policy mandates could stimulate the demand for RMB and RMB-denominated bonds, helping to sustain the market in the future. The dim sum bond market will likely grow and thrive to offer investors in the United States and throughout the world a new asset class.

REFERENCES

Euroweek. 2012. "Investors Still Hungry for Dim Sum but Getting Pickier." *Offshore RMB Bonds: A Maturing Global Market*, June.

Kritzman, Mark. 1999. "Toward Defining an Asset Class." *Journal of Alternative Investments*, 2(1): 79–82.

Liu, Becky. 2010. "RMB Offshore Bonds: Developments, Dynamics and Outlook." HSBC Global Research, Hong Kong and Shanghai Banking Corporation Limited, December 13.

Wee, Denise. 2012. "Dim Sum Bonds Offer Borrowers Arbitrage Opportunity." *FinanceAsia*, August 10.

CHAPTER 5

Investment Banks and the Dim Sum Bond Issuing Process

Investment banks are one of the major players in the offshore renminbi (RMB) bond market. They act as go-betweeners, liaising between issuers and investors. They help to close deals by coordinating all processes related to the bond issues. As it happens in other capital markets, the demand and wishes of both issuers and investors are to be negotiated and agreed by both parties with the help of the mediator: investment banks.[1] This chapter aims at providing a distinct perspective to prospective issuers and investors with regard to the bond issuing process in the dim sum bond market.

5.1 DIM SUM BOND ISSUING PROCESS

In this chapter, we present the issuing process in the offshore RMB market in general and the dim sum bond origination process in particular. We first discuss the rationale for issuing dim sum bonds from the issuer perspective and investing in dim sum bonds from investor perspective. By way of discussing the steps of the bond origination process in detail, we highlight the peculiar characteristics in the dim sum bond market as compared to the traditional investment banking process such as that of the USD bond market in the region of Asia-Pacific ex Japan and Australasia.

5.1.1 Rationale for Dim Sum Bonds: Issuer and Investor Perspectives

The bond origination process begins with the matching of bond issuers and investors through the help of investment banks, which act as global

---

[1] See Mehta and Fung (2004), Chapter 11, and Stowell (2010), Chapter 3.

coordinators, bookrunners, and lead managers (see Vignette 5.1). The matching process is largely the same for both the dim sum and Asian USD bonds. In the rest of this and subsequent chapters, we refer to various dim sum bond issuance processes as dim sum bond origination for simplicity. However, as dim sum bonds are by definition denominated in RMB, which has yet to be fully internationalized, issuers are mostly entities with genuine RMB requirements in their daily operations. Dim sum bonds have some similarities, such as short tenor and small issue size, with local-currency bonds. These characteristics, coupled with the dim sum bond market's nascent stage of

VIGNETTE 5.1 THE ROLES OF GLOBAL COORDINATORS, BOOKRUNNERS, AND LEAD MANAGERS

Global coordinators are responsible for the entire bond issuance process, carrying out the execution strategy, managing the timetable, and coordinating the due diligence process. Global coordinators are automatically bookrunners of the issue (but not vice versa) and receive a larger share of fees than other bookrunners who are not global coordinators.

In general, only issues of larger size that have a wider investor base geographically, will have global coordinators assigned. In the absence of global coordinators, joint bookrunners will assume the roles of global coordinators, as well as arranging roadshow presentations, investors' meetings, bookbuilding, pricing, and settlement. Each bookrunner will be awarded league table credit.

If the bond issues are underwritten, each joint bookrunner will have to underwrite an equal share of the issue. By underwriting, joint bookrunners agree to subscribe to an equal share of the issue regardless of the orders they receive from prospective investors. Underwriting is a major role of investment banks in other capital markets, including the Asian USD bond market. That said, "hard" underwriting bond issues are rare in dim sum bond issues as most of them are marketed on a best-effort basis. We present this in more detail in Vignette 5.3.

Bookrunners can also be the lead managers who do not play an active role in marketing and selling bond issues and will not be awarded league table credit; that is, bookrunner ranking does not include deals in which bookrunners do not have an active role. Lead managers are more relationship managers, liaising and engaging the issuers and potential investors.

development, suggest that the profiles of issuers and investors of dim sum bonds are somewhat different from those of the Asian USD bonds affecting the supply and demand of dim sum bonds.

From the issuer perspective, the dim sum bond market once offered a funding channel of which the funding costs were lower and requirements for issuance such as credit ratings and covenants were less demanding. Although the bond indenture terms of dim sum bonds are converging toward those of the Asian USD bonds, the dim sum bond market will continue to play an important role as an alternative channel for raising RMB funds in the offshore market. The dim sum bond market will help diversify funding channels for established issuers as well as for issuers trying to tap smaller size and shorter tenor funding. The dim sum bond market provides a lower-cost funding option for smaller issuers who are lesser known to international capital markets, their funding costs will be higher if issuing Asian USD bonds.

From the investor perspective, the dim sum bond offers an investment option. Although the yield may not be very attractive, especially if the envisaged RMB appreciation dissipates, investors may still be interested in dim sum bonds since there are limited investment options as CNH is still in early stage of development. Dim sum bonds offer investors return higher than the CNH deposit rate. The dim sum bond market could remain a viable investment option, especially for treasury management of investors who obtain CNH from their business operations.

Given thin trading in the secondary dim sum bond market as issue size is smaller with a higher proportion of unrated issues, dim sum bonds have less appeal to large foreign institutional investors. In contrast, for investors, such as China-focused funds and private banking clients that may be more familiar with the operations of certain small and medium corporations in China, and for investors that have access to low-cost CNH funding, such as the Chinese commercial banks, dim sum bonds still maintain its allure.

Nonetheless, we note that institutional investors' participation in the dim sum bond market has been increasing. As issue and disclosure standards of dim sum bonds have been converging with those of the Asian USD bonds, dim sum bonds are becoming an increasingly competitive asset class especially from the institutional investors' perspective. This trend of growing interest from institutional investors, coupled with a growing CNH deposit base (see Table 1.1), will continue to generate demand for dim sum bonds. The recurring cash flows from coupon and redemption of maturing dim sum bonds will also add to the CNH deposit base creating the "technical" demand for dim sum bonds. Since most dim sum bond issues are held to maturity, particularly the short-term ones, the potential amount of near future issuance of dim sum bonds can be estimated by the number of outstanding, unmatured bonds. The potential rollovers of dim sum bonds maturing in the next five years as of the end of 2012 will be presented in Table 7.1. It is noted that not all maturing dim sum bonds will be rolled over in the dim sum bond market. However, it provides a means to assessing one of the potential sources for the demand for dim sum bonds. As indicated in Table 7.1, as of the end of 2012, 553 bonds would mature, with a total amount of about RMB270 billion (about 77 percent of all bonds remain outstanding) during the period 2013–2015. The average coupon rate (and roughly the average yield as well) for the bonds maturing in 2013 is 2.73 percent, whereas the average tenor is 1.14 years.

5.2 PRIMARY ISSUES

Primary issues refer to bond offerings from issuers to investors through which issuers raise funds in the bond market to fund capital expenditure and daily operations, as well as to refinance the maturing bonds. A primary bond issuance begins with a series of meetings between issuers and investment banks discussing a variety of financing solutions, taking into consideration an array of factors such as the funding cost, issue cost, size of funding requirement, duration, and regulatory requirements.[2] Investment banks compete for the mandate of the appropriate financing solutions (e.g., equity vs. bonds, dim sum vs. Asian U.S. dollar bonds, and convertible vs. nonconvertible bonds) via a "beauty contest." If the dim sum bond is considered to be the most appropriate funding option, issuers would choose the investment bank(s) after considering all relevant factors pertaining to the dim sum bond issue.

The origination process will formally begin after a potential issuer gives a mandate to an investment bank/investment banks for the issuance of dim sum bonds. The process can be broadly divided into five steps (Figure 5.1):

1. *Documentation and due diligence.* This first step is to be done by investment banks, auditors, and legal counsels. They need to develop a thorough understanding of the issuer's background including the financial information, in order to prepare marketing materials and the offering circular as well as to avoid any exposure to legal risk.
2. *Premarketing campaign.* Typically, this step is actually done concurrently with Step 1. The purpose of the premarketing campaign is to identify the investor base and "soft-sound" the forthcoming issue to potential investors on a confidential basis to gauge their interest in the issue. Also, some investment banks may have their credit research team start

---

[2] The bond issuance process is in general similar to those for stock issues. See Fung (2009).

preparing investor education research reports for the first-time issuers. The premarketing campaign provides a channel for the syndication, sales, and research desks to obtain the initial feedback from investors prior to the formal announcement of the bond issue.

3. *Marketing campaign, roadshows, and bookbuilding.* After the formal announcement of the issue is made, a marketing campaign including roadshow presentations is formally launched to introduce the issuer to investors through one-on-one meetings, small group meetings, conference calls, and roadshows on the Internet ("net roadshows"). Investment banks will also disseminate marketing materials such as the preliminary offering circular and investor presentation. Internally, the syndication desk and research team of the investment banks will conduct sales teach-ins (i.e., the general educational forum) to bring salespeople up to speed on the structure of the issue and the credit profile of the issuer, helping salespersons answer questions from investors. Through roadshows, investment banks will also obtain feedback from a wider investor base.

4. *Pricing and allocation.* In the final step, the investment banks will help the issuer determine the final offer size, price, and allocation to different investors. In determining the final offer price, investment banks will try to optimize the funding cost and issue size for the issuer while protecting the bond price stability in the secondary market. In other words, the investment bank will try to get a price as high as it could from investors (i.e., by paying a yield as low as it could to investors) with large orders, provided that the resulting allocation would not cause too much volatility in the bond prices in the secondary market. Hence, allocation priority will be generally given to investors whose order size is larger and the pricing requirement of the order is more favorable from the issuer's perspective. In addition, priority is given to buy-and-hold investors and investors who have participated in previous issues since their investment objectives and their aftermarket trading behavior are more aligned with the investment bank's price stabilization objective. In other words, allocation priority depends, to some extent, on the past relationship with the investment banks.

5. *Aftermarket support and trading in the secondary market.* In the final step, the investment banks will help stabilize the bond prices after the bond is offered and starts trading in the secondary market. The investment banks will provide liquidity for the bond issue in the secondary market. The most commonly used price support mechanism is over-allotment, which creates pressure on investment banks to cover its short position and hence support bond price. Nonetheless, the price support mechanism is less relevant for dim sum bonds, as issue size is relatively small and secondary trading is thin; investors mostly adopt a buy-and-hold approach.

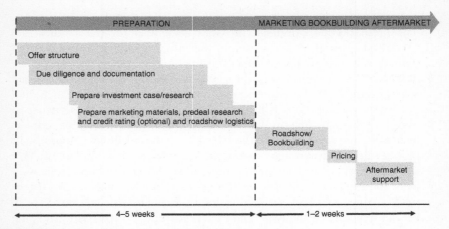

FIGURE 5.1 Timeline for the bond origination process

Depending on market conditions, the entire process generally lasts five to seven weeks. The documentation and due diligence step takes four to five weeks, while marketing and pricing take one to two weeks. The major difference of the primary issue origination process between dim sum bonds and USD bonds lies in the *premarketing efforts* given the differences in the issuer and investor profiles. We discuss in detail each step of the process below.

5.2.1 Documentation/Due Diligence

Documentation/due diligence is a fact-finding step in the process involving parties such as the issuer, investment banks, auditors, and legal counsels. For these involved parties, the purpose of this step is to develop a comprehensive and thorough understanding of all business aspects of the issuer. This step is crucial to the preparation of the required documentation for regulatory filing purposes and marketing materials, such as the offering circular (see Vignette 5.2) and marketing teasers for presentations to investors.

During the due diligence step, investment banks will have numerous meetings, phone calls, and site visits with the issuer in order to have a clear understanding of the issuer's history, business model, management strategy and expansion plan, background of the major shareholders, and corporate governance. The due diligence process is not only important for preparing the necessary documentations, but also for the investment banks to scrutinize the background of the majority shareholders and senior management to avoid future scandals.

In addition, auditors need to conduct an audit and a review of the company's financials. The issuer will also provide management accounts for the period since the last financial reporting period. Meanwhile, lawyers will conduct documentation due diligence to review the issuer's pertinent documents such as the certificates of incorporation, legal titles of assets, and other business agreements and contracts.

5.2.2 Premarketing Campaign

Different investment banks may have different bond origination strategies, and different issuers will require different origination strategies, depending on factors such as their credit quality, size of operations, and track record and reputation in capital markets. For example, investment banks may turn to commercial banks that have a banking relationship with the issuer to "anchor" a dim sum bond issue offered by a small/medium enterprise (SME) that is unfamiliar in the capital markets.

Prior to the formal bookbuilding process, investment banks will, in the parlance of investment banking, "sound out softly" the preliminary terms and structure of the bond issue to selected investors such as asset managers, funds, and commercial banks on a confidential basis to gauge their interests of the bond deal. The feedback from the investors may sway the issuer and investment banks to adjust the terms and structure of the proposed bond issue accordingly.

VIGNETTE 5.2 BOND-OFFERING CIRCULAR

A bond-offering circular offers potential investors detailed information regarding (1) terms and condition of the bond, (2) risks related to the bond and issuer, (3) use of proceeds, and (4) business and financial information of the issuer. Additional information in a bond-offering circular/prospectus include the early redemption feature; description of collateral of credit enhancement, if any; details of settlement; and the tax status of the bond. An investor can thus determine the true value of the investment and risks of the bond. At times, firms issue a blanket prospectus for all the bonds to be issued, including dim sum bonds. With such a blanket prospectus, there will be no specific prospectus for every issue. In fact, many of the dim sum bonds do not have a prospectus. However, they have a term sheet summarizing the terms of the issue.

For investor education, some investment banks, especially those with stronger franchise in credit research, will publish investor education research reports for debut issuers prior to the formal announcement of bond issues. Investor education research reports provide investors with information on the background of the issuers and their majority shareholders, as well as an in-depth analysis on the business, financial, and liquidity profiles of the issuers. The content of investor education research is more restrictive compared with other research reports published by investment banks, and thus these reports do not provide any investment recommendation so as to avoid the conflict of interests and potential legal liabilities in relation to the bond issues. Also, these reports do not contain any forecast or projection.

The premarketing campaign provides a channel for the syndication, sales, and research desks of investment banks to obtain the initial feedback from investors in terms of demand, pricing, and key credit concerns prior to the formal announcement of the bond issues. As mentioned before in this chapter, since the dim sum bond market is still in the nascent stage of development, the issue size is relatively small compared with those of the Asian USD bonds. Since commercial banks with a CNH deposit base are the major source of the CNH liquidity in Hong Kong, investment banks turn to them for "anchoring" the dim sum bond issues from issuers who are cost-conscious or not well known in the capital markets. Commercial banks that have banking relationships with the issuer are generally willing to participate in the deal as they are comfortable with the credit profile of the issuer in the first place. Besides, dim sum bonds are normally priced more attractive than bank loans to attract interests from commercial banks. To date, commercial banks have accounted for a significant portion of distribution for dim sum bonds issued. We discuss this in the next section.

5.2.2.1 Participation of Commercial Banks As discussed before, investment banks may turn to commercial banks to "anchor" a dim sum bond issue offered by an SME that has an unfamiliar name in the capital markets. Investment banks will sound out the preliminary terms and structure of the bond issue to selected commercial banks on a confidential basis to gauge their interests to anchor the bond deal. According to our own estimate, commercial banks account for about one-fourth of the order books (Figure 4.1).

The early involvement by commercial banks also allows themselves to have more time to go through their own internal credit approval process for investments. By the time that the deals are publicly announced and the bookbuilding process is formally started, the commercial banks may already have the internal credit approval process completed and their participation in the deals confirmed. The involvement of commercial banks does not only help create traction in the bookbuilding process, but also bring down the overall funding cost of the issue. We observe that the lesser known the issuer to the bond market but the stronger the issuer's banking relationship with commercial banks, the more likely it is that the deal will be anchored by commercial banks and the higher the percentage of bonds distributed to commercial banks. Thus, getting commercial banks involved early in the bookbuilding process is especially important to issuers who have well-established commercial banking relationships but are not well known to bond investors.

Thus far, we stress the importance of the participation of commercial banks in a dim sum bond deal to issuers who are less well known in the capital markets. To investors, commercial banks also play an important intermediary role in the capital markets—providing credit endorsement to the bond issue. This encourages other investors who are not familiar with the issuer to invest in the bond. The greater involvement of commercial banks and less participation of institutional investors in the early days explain the early credit protection feature of dim sum bonds. That is, covenants for dim sum bonds are more similar to those of commercial loans rather than the standard covenants for the Asian USD bonds.

5.2.2.2 Dim Sum Bond Covenants   Early dim sum bond issues were considered "covenant-lite." However, as more institutional investors get involved and more investment options for CNH are available, covenants on dim sum bonds have become more in line with those for the Asian USD bonds. In addition, a notable difference between the covenants of dim sum bonds and USD bonds is that maintenance covenants are more common in dim sum bonds. To illustrate, standard financial covenants for the USD high-yield bonds include the minimum fixed charge coverage ratio and the maximum debt/EBITDA ratio. These covenants are generally "incurrence covenants"; that is, issuers only need to test compliance with these covenants if they incur additional debts. Failure to meet the covenanted ratios does not constitute an event of default. However, we note that many of the existing dim sum bond issues do not have any financial covenants (see Chapter 2, section 2.2.7.1, for discussion). For bond issues with financial covenants, the covenants resemble those of the bank loans. For example, some typical financial covenants of dim sum bond issues include the minimum tangible-net-worth amount and the maximum consolidated total debt to consolidated total asset ratio. These are "maintenance covenants," meaning that issuers have to comply with the ratios from time to time, and failure to do so will trigger an event of default. Inclusion of maintenance covenants is typical when a significant portion of the dim sum bonds is distributed to commercial banks.

5.2.3 Roadshow/Marketing

Roadshows allow issuers to engage investors in different regions. The roadshow can be in the form of one-on-one meetings, small group meetings, conference calls, or roadshow on the Internet ("net roadshow"). Investment banks will also disseminate marketing materials, such as preliminary offering circulars and investor presentations. Issuers will discuss their business models, market positions, regulatory environment, industry outlook, financials, expansion plans, and others with potential investors and address investors' key concerns on the credit fundamentals of issuers. Within investment banks, syndication desks and research will conduct internal sales teach-in to bring salespeople up to speed on the structure of the issues and credit profile of issuers, so that salespersons can address questions from investors. Roadshows and marketing are particularly important for the first-time dim sum bond issuers to introduce themselves to as many investors as possible. Since many of the dim sum bond issues are not rated by credit rating agencies, roadshows are even more important for issuers to address investors' credit concerns. Through roadshows and marketing, investment banks will also obtain more detailed feedback from a wider investor base on the structure and pricing of the issues, as well as key credit concerns of the issuers.

Considering various factors such as the issue size, issuing cost, disclosure, and due diligence requirements, issuers and investment banks will decide whether the dim sum bond will be issued under Regulation S (RegS) only or a combination of both RegS and Rule 144A. To illustrate, the disclosure requirements and costs related to the issues are lower for RegS issues and higher for 144A issues. Specifically, 144A issues are subject to the so-called 135-day rule, whereas RegS issues are not. Under the 135-day rule, auditors may choose to convey a negative assurance by stating that they have inquired of the issuer and are not aware of specific changes in the financial statements up to a date that is less than 135 days from the end of the most recent financial period such as December 31 of the previous year. In other words, without the updated financial statements, issuers will not be able to issue bonds 135 days after the most recent financial period. Given the more stringent requirements of 144A issues, bonds qualified for 144A issues will generally qualify for RegS issues, but not vice versa. In Asia, most of the bonds intended to be distributed and marketed under 144A will also be distributed and marketed under RegS. Put another way, global issues are typically marketed under RegS/144A.

Since many dim sum bond investors are mainly based in Asia and on average the size of dim sum bond issues is smaller, it makes sense from a cost-benefit perspective to issue dim sum bonds under RegS. Thus far, except for dim sum bonds of multinational corporations and Chinese state-owned entities, an overwhelming majority of dim sum bonds are issued under RegS, which can only be distributed to investors outside the United States (see Chapter 2, section 2.2.2 and Stroock & Stroock & Lavan, LLP (2002)). If bond issues are intended to be distributed and marketed in the United States to "qualified institutional buyers" (QIBs), that is, the large, sophisticated investors, issuers must fulfill the disclosure and other requirements of Rule 144A under the Securities Act. Please refer to Table 5.1 for the comparison of major differences between the RegS and 144A/RegS issues.

TABLE 5.1 Comparison of Major Differences between RegS and 144A/RegS Issues

	RegS only	144A/RegS
Distribution/ Investor Base	Located outside the United States (including U.S. investors who have offshore affiliates or offices).	The U.S. portion is limited to QIBs; non-U.S. portion is to the same investor base as a RegS offering.
Disclosure and Due Diligence Requirements	No legal requirement Market practice is generally at a lower level than for 144A or U.S. registered offerings. The offering document may not include a "management's discussion and analysis of financial conditions and results of operations," referred to as the "MD&A." The exchange that the securities are to be listed may require certain type of disclosure.	No legal requirement, but because securities are being sold in the United States, the market practice is to have a level of disclosure in the offering document and due diligence similar to those for U.S. registered offerings. Includes an MD&A and "Risk Factors" similar to those in U.S. registered offerings. The exchange that the securities are to be listed may require certain type of disclosure.
Financial Statements	Primarily determined by the exchange on which the securities are listed. Market practice is to require same type of financial statements in 144A offerings, with occasional exceptions depending on situation. The 135-day rule is not applicable.	Market practice is to include in the offering document the same type of financial statements in U.S. registered offerings. Requirements of the exchange that the securities are listed must also be satisfied. The 135-day rule is applicable.

(continued)

TABLE 5.1   *Continued*

	RegS only	144A/RegS
Costs	Lower legal and marketing costs.	Higher legal and marketing costs.
Time required for origination process	Shorter time for preparation, roadshow, and marketing.	Longer time to fulfill the disclosure and due diligence requirements of Rule 144A. No need to roadshow in the United States.
Issue size	US$500 million equivalent or lower.	Larger than US$500 million equivalent.
Maturity	5 years or shorter.	Longer than 5 years.

5.2.4. Bookbuilding, Pricing, and Allocation

After the roadshows, investment banks will "build" the order books for the issue. Investment banks will solicit indications of demand from investors and provide them with information such as the pricing guidance and size of order books.

Dim sum bond issues, like those of the Asian USD bonds, are mostly marketed through a book-building process. There are few "hard" underwriting mandates (see Vignette 5.3) nowadays for dim sum or Asian USD bond issues because investment banks are increasingly reluctant to commit their balance sheets to the underwriting business and take risk. Investment banks will sell bond issues on a best-effort basis, where the final offer size and pricing of the issue will depend on the bookbuilding process.

Based on the pricing of comparable bonds and feedback from investors after the roadshows, investment banks provide investors with the preliminary range for the offer price. Investors will then place orders. In some cases, investors will place "limit orders" to indicate how much they are willing to buy at certain price/yield levels. Depending on the bookbuilding momentum, the price guidance, that is, the range of the yield of the issue, will be revised during the bookbuilding process.

When investment banks have the final order books completed, they will discuss the final terms, size, and pricing of the issue with the issuer. Depending on the size of the order book, indications of investor demand and issuer's funding requirements (in terms of size and tenor), the issuer and investment banks may choose to pay a higher coupon rate in exchange for a larger issue size or a longer tenor, or alternatively, they may choose to limit the funding

VIGNETTE 5.3 "HARD" UNDERWRITING

In a "hard" underwriting deal, investment banks underwrite the amount of an issue at an agreed level and thus the issuer will know for certain how much money can be raised at an agreed funding cost. If the issue is not fully subscribed, investment banks will make up the shortfall, carrying the risk on their balance sheets. Thus, investment banks will only enter into "hard" underwriting agreements with issuers who have solid financial and business profiles, as well as close relationship with investment banks. Given the increased capital requirements for financial institutions, investment banks are more reluctant to commit their own balance sheets to underwrite deals and thus "hard" underwriting is getting increasingly rare.

Instead, investment banks will generally enter into subscription agreements with issuers after the bonds are priced and allocated. The subscription agreement will stipulate the size and offer price the investment banks will receive from the issuers. The investment banks then reoffer the bonds to investors who have been assigned certain allocations. Investment banks will therefore not be exposed to "hard" underwriting risk but to settlement risk as newly issued bonds will generally be settled five days after pricing.

cost by having a smaller issue or a shorter tenor. Figure 5.2 illustrates how the balancing is achieved with a target allocation, say, just below 5 percent.

In the case that the bookbuilding momentum is weak, investment banks and issuers may price the deal at the wide end of the price guidance, or even widen the price guidance in some rare cases. They may also downsize the issue. Some issues may eventually be canceled as issuers are reluctant to pay a higher coupon or investors are simply not comfortable with the credit profile of the issuer. In the latter case, investor demand may remain anemic, leading to the cancellation of the issue even if the issuer is willing to pay a higher coupon.

Once the final terms and pricing are determined, the investment banks will allocate the bond issue to investors according to the size and pricing requirements of the orders, investment track records, and, to some extent, the relationship with the investment banks. Allocation is not an easy task as investment banks have to strike a balance between bond price stability and trading liquidity. In general, investment banks will build an investor base comprising long-term buy-and-hold investors to ensure a higher proportion

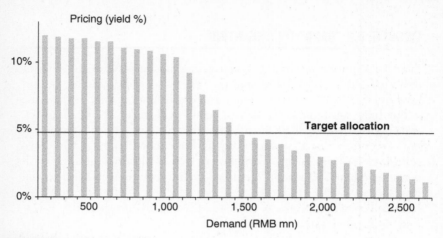

FIGURE 5.2   Illustration of allocation

of bonds allocated to stable hands for sustaining price stability. Investors who obtain bonds through primary issues can trade the bonds immediately in the secondary market without a lockup period. Hence, the "real money" investors, such as long-only funds, sovereign wealth funds, and insurance companies are the preferred long-term investors in bond allocations. However, the "fast money" investors, such as certain hedge funds which tend to trade more frequently to take advantage of price movements, will also be allocated to improve the trading liquidity of the bonds. "Real money" investors who place large orders and are less demanding on pricing (i.e., they demand a lower required yield) are usually given priority in allocation. Thus, investment banks favor a larger allocation of the bond issue to the "real money" investors. Investment banks would also favor investors who provide constructive suggestions as to the structure, size, and pricing of an issue during the premarketing and roadshow phase.

That said, the makeup of the investor base will vary with credit quality of the issuer, size of the issue, pricing target of the issuer, and market sentiment.

5.2.5 Aftermarket Support and Trading in the Secondary Market

Aftermarket support is as important as the previous steps in the issuing process. Investment banks may use the overallotment technique to support bond prices in the aftermarket. As the dim sum bond market is still at an early stage of development with very thin secondary trading, investors of dim sum bonds may face greater than usual liquidity risk should they want to sell their dim sum bonds prior to maturity.

5.2.5.1 Aftermarket Support   As mentioned before, bondholders who obtained bonds through primary issues are not subject to a lockup period. Therefore, "reasonable" pricing of the bond (i.e., not far too expensive given the issuer's credit quality), structure of the bond and the underlying market condition, and placing a higher proportion of the bonds to "stable hands" are keys to providing stability to bond prices. Additionally, investment banks may support bond prices through an overallotment mechanism, a practice also used as a price support mechanism in an equity issue. For issues that can eventually be priced, investment banks should in general be able to build books with a varying degree of oversubscription. Oversubscribed order books give investment banks room for overallotting bonds to investors so that investment banks could have short positions in the bonds. The pressure to cover these short positions will help support the bond price.

To illustrate, suppose the issue size is fixed at RMB1 billion, but investment banks allot a total of RMB1.2 billion to investors, intentionally creating a short position of RMB200 million on investment banks' books. The need to cover the short position will force investment banks to purchase the bonds from sellers in the secondary market, thereby creating a positive market sentiment and bond performance in the secondary market. That said, because of the small issue size and less liquidity in the secondary dim sum bond market, the use of overallotment to maintain price stability in the dim sum bond market is not as ubiquitous as in the Asian USD bond market.

In general, the weaker the market sentiment, the more demanding the bond pricing (i.e., bonds are priced at a lower yield), and the more likely the bonds will underperform in the secondary market. Hence, the larger the requirement for price support,[3] the larger is the overallotment amount, that is, the larger the short positions held by investment banks. There is no hard-and-fast rule on the size of overallotment and the timing for investment banks to cover their short positions. However, any losses resulting from the aftermarket price support will be charged against the fees the investment banks are going to receive from the issue. From a risk management perspective, investment banks will undoubtedly limit their exposure to the market risk in a fee-based business. Hence, the size of overallotment is usually small, say, for up to 5 percent of the issue size,

---

[3] The requirement for price support refers to the dollar amount required for price support, which is normally measured by a percentage of the issue size.

and investment banks tend to cover the short positions from overallot-ment as soon as possible to avoid losses resulting from unfavorable bond price movements.

5.2.5.2 Trading in the Secondary Market   Like the Asian USD bonds, trading of dim sum bonds is conducted over the counter even though many of the bonds are listed on exchanges, such as the Hong Kong Stock Exchange and the Singapore Exchange. Exchange listing of bonds aims primar-ily to provide comfort to investors that bonds and issuers are subject to monitoring and disclosure requirements of the exchange. Exchange listing does not help facilitate trading or improve liquidity of the bonds but instead help secure a wider investor base for the bonds because some institutional investors are mandated to only buy listed bonds.[4] Since the issue size of dim sum bonds is generally smaller and a relatively large proportion of bonds are in the hands of commercial banks, which tend to be the buy-and-hold investors, trading of dim sum bonds in the sec-ondary market is relatively thin. Hence, the bid-ask spread of dim sum bonds is wider, while the loan-to-value ratio for dim sum bonds is lower; that is, brokers or banks are more reluctant to lend to dim sum bond investors to trade on leverage given that the liquidity of dim sum bonds is generally weaker.

While many of the major investment banks trade dim sum bonds in the secondary market, not too many of them have dedicated dim sum bond traders given the absence of a critical mass in the dim sum bond market thus far. Currently, trading of dim sum bonds are either covered by the Asian USD bond traders or traders who cover interest rate or other CNH prod-ucts. Major market makers of dim sum bonds include the Bank of China (BOC), HSBC, and Standard Chartered Bank (SCB). All of their investment banking divisions are also the major players in the primary issuance of dim sum bonds.

5.3 BOOKRUNNER/MANAGER RANKINGS

Issuers choose bookrunners based on their ability to distribute the bonds at the lowest cost and their relationship with bookrunners, among oth-er factors. As such, investment banks with a larger CNH deposit base which represents a larger potential investor base and a long banking relationship with the issuers are in a better position in securing dim sum

---

[4] Table 2.12 in Chapter 2 provides summary statistics of dim sum bonds since its inception by exchange listing.

bond mandates. Major bookrunners of dim sum bonds include BOC, HSBC, and SCB. They rank high by the amount raised and by the number of issues in Table 5.2.

TABLE 5.2   Top 25 Bookrunners/Managers Ranked by RMB Amount Issued (2007–2012)

Rank by Amount	Bookrunner/Manager	Amount RMB (Mln)	Mkt Share (%)	No. of Issues
1	HSBC Bank PLC	92,897.45	23.14	232
2	Bank of China	55,456.67	13.81	78
3	Standard Chartered Bank	46,690.54	11.63	151
4	BNP Paribas Group	24,011.62	5.98	80
5	Deutsche Bank AG	22,278.72	5.55	65
6	RBS	17,751.71	4.42	54
7	Barclays	14,617.67	3.64	56
8	UBS	12,906.33	3.21	79
9	Industrial & Comm Bank of China	12,682.74	3.16	41
10	Bank of Communications	9,099.40	2.27	19
11	JPMorgan	8,279.50	2.06	13
12	Agricultural Bank of China Ltd.	8,226.83	2.05	24
13	Goldman Sachs & Co.	7,300.02	1.82	23
14	Citi	5,856.83	1.46	24
15	China Construction Bank	5,668.19	1.41	15
16	Morgan Stanley	5,300.67	1.32	22
17	CITIC Securities Co. Ltd.	5,283.33	1.32	12
18	ANZ Banking Group	4,779.00	1.19	17
19	Oversea-Chinese Banking Corp.	4,410.00	1.10	13
20	Bank of America Merrill Lynch	4,408.33	1.10	12
21	DBS Group Holdings Ltd.	4,305.17	1.07	19
22	National Australia Bank Ltd.	4,161.00	1.04	18
23	China International Capital Corp.	3,676.52	0.92	10
24	China Merchants Bank	2,571.17	0.64	12
25	Bank of East Asia Ltd.	2,100.00	0.52	2

Note: The total amount issued for the period is RMB401,516.89 million; Total number of issues is 797; Total number of bookrunners/underwriters is 55.

5.4 BOND ISSUING FEES

The fees charged by investment banks on the dim sum issues depend on the credit quality/credit rating of the issuer and the structure of the issue. In general, the lower the credit quality of the issuer and the more complicated the issue structure, the higher will be the issuing fee. Issuing fees are not usually disclosed, except for a few cases. The issuing fee ranges from 30 basis points (bp) to 50 bp of the issue amount for investment-grade issuers and 150 bp to 250 bp for non-investment-grade issuers. These fees, as a percentage of the issue size, are comparable to those of the Asian USD bonds. However, because the issue size of dim sum bonds is smaller on average, the total fees received by investment banks are thus smaller for dim sum bond issues. In addition, commercial banks that come in as "anchors" in dim sum bond issues will likely request to share the issue fees (income) based on the amount of the issue in which they participate. For example, if 30 percent of the issue is distributed to commercial banks, investment banks will likely have to share 30 percent of the fees with participating commercial banks. Therefore, the absolute size of the issue fee for a dim sum bond deal could be considerably lower than that of an Asian USD bond issue, although the amount of work involved may not be materially different. Furthermore, the trading volume of dim sum bonds is much lower than that of the Asian USD bonds given the smaller issue size, the income from sales and trading of dim sum bonds is also considerably lower. The profitability of a single dim sum bond issue is less attractive as compared to that of an Asian USD bond issue for investment banks. However, the dim sum bond market is potentially lucrative for investment banks as the market is gaining awareness and a critical mass of investors, as well as improvements in institutional and infrastructural framework. We believe dim sum bonds will eventually grow into an important funding channel too big to ignore for issuers and investment banks alike.

5.5 RETAIL VERSUS INSTITUTIONAL TRANCHES

For retail dim sum bonds, such as the first dim sum bonds issued by the China Development Bank and Export-Import Bank of China in 2007, the issuer makes arrangements with the "placing banks," which are commercial banks with branch networks in Hong Kong to take orders from retail investors. These orders are placed through the banks' branches. The issuer will pay the placing banks a commission of 0.15 percent to 0.18 percent of the principal amount of bonds they sell. In addition to offering and selling the bonds to retail investors in Hong Kong, the issuer may also offer and sell the bonds to institutional or other investors in different tranches, whether in Hong Kong or abroad, under separate arrangements that are not usually set out in the offering circular to retail investors. Bonds offered to institutional or other investors from the institutional tranche could be made at a lower issue price, or on other terms, than are available to retail investors who buy the bonds from the retail tranche through a placing bank specified in this offering circular. Typically, there are no soft commission or rebate arrangements between the issuer and any of the placing banks. The retail bonds are sold to investors directly from the issuer by subscription.

5.6 CONCLUSION

The bond issuance process is largely the same for both dim sum and Asian USD bonds. They both comprise five major steps: (1) documentation and due diligence; (2) premarketing campaign; (3) marketing campaign, roadshows, and bookbuilding; (4) pricing and allocation; and (5) aftermarket support and trading in the secondary market. The major difference of the primary issue origination process between the dim sum bonds and Asian USD bonds lies in the premarketing efforts due to the differences in the issuer and investor profiles.

As we discussed in this chapter, the dim sum bond market is still at the nascent stage of development and is effectively a local currency bond market. The dim sum bond market offers issuers requiring RMB for their daily operations a funding channel, where the funding costs are lower and the requirements for issuance such as credit rating and covenants are less demanding.

However, dim sum bond issues thus far have less appeal to institutional investors including the long-only funds and hedge funds, which are the major participants in Asian USD bonds. To date, dim sum bonds are generally smaller in size, and hence trading is thin in the secondary market as compared with those of the Asian USD bonds. The coupon rates of dim sum bonds are on average lower and not indicative of the credit quality of the issuers as options for CNH investment have been scanty.

Moreover, many of the dim sum bonds were either unrated or rated by only one international credit agency, whereas many Asian USD bonds are conventionally rated by two or more international credit rating agencies. The earlier dim sum bond issues are "covenant-lite" with few restrictive covenants to bondholders, compared those of the Asian USD bonds. Institutional investors are therefore less involved in dim sum bond issues.

As a result, investment banks more often turn to commercial banks which have a CNH deposit base for "anchoring" the dim sum bond issue during the premarketing campaign. While the issuers may be more cost-conscious and/or not well known in the debt capital markets, commercial banks that have banking relationships with the issuer are generally willing to participate in the deal as they are comfortable with issuers' credit profile in the first place. Besides, dim sum bonds are normally priced more attractively than bank loans to lure the interests from commercial banks. As such, commercial banks have accounted for a significant portion of distribution for dim sum bonds.

The dim sum bond market has developed rapidly over the past few years, as such profiles of investors and issuers have also evolved. As the RMB appreciation has no longer been a one-way bet, more CNH investment options are now available, and an increasing rate of participation by institutional investors as the dim sum bond marketing is gaining critical mass, terms of recent dim sum bond issues, as well as the dim sum bond issuing process, have started to converge with those of the Asian USD bond issues, rendering dim sum bonds a competitive asset class for investors. We observe that recent dim sum bonds are issued at coupon rates more indicative of their credit profiles, and a higher proportion of issues being rated by international rating agencies with restrictive high-yield covenants. We expect this converging trend driven by institutional investors' more active involvement in the dim sum bond market to continue.

REFERENCES

Fung, Hung-Gay. 2009. "Financial Steps in an IPO for a Small or Medium-Size Enterprise," *QFinance*, London, UK: Bloomsburry Information Ltd., 540–542.

Mehta, Dileep, and Hung-Gay Fung. 2004. *International Banking Management*, Oxford, UK: Blackwell.

Stowell, David P. 2010. *An Introduction to Investment Banks, Hedge Funds, and Private Equity: The New Paradigm*. Burlington, MA: Academic Press.

Stroock & Stroock & Lavan, LLP. 2002. *Regulation S*. Retrieved from www.stroock .com.

CHAPTER 6

Case Studies of Landmark Issues

This chapter provides the pertinent information on cases of the landmark dim sum bond issues and benchmark issues of long-dated dim sum bonds. These cases represent milestones for the journey that this nascent market has traveled thus far at the time of writing. Landmark issues have played a pivotal role in the internationalization of the renminbi (RMB) as well as in the projection of market development trends. These landmark issues illustrate the deliberate efforts of the Chinese government, and financial institutions and corporations that capitalized on the impediments in the domestic market arising from regulation, for example, regulated interest rates and cross-border capital control, and how issuers rode with the underlying trend of the appreciating RMB during the period 2007–2012. We describe the pertinent and distinctive attributes of each landmark issue, including the general bond information, issuer background, and use of proceeds. For each landmark case, we highlight the risks that are peculiar to each landmark dim sum bond issue, recognizing that dim sum bonds are vulnerable to all other risks that are common to fixed-income securities, that is, credit risk, interest rate risk, foreign exchange risk, liquidity risk, and legal risk. Moreover, we discuss the significance of each landmark issue. Finally, we describe a couple of landmark cases in which the innovative credit enhancement structures enable the issuers to circumvent the regulatory red-tape, gaining access to offshore funding.

6.1 LANDMARK ISSUES

Table 6.1 lists the landmark issues of dim sum bonds since the inception of the market in July 2007 to the end of 2012. It is noted that many of the landmark issues and issuers are associated with the Chinese government, reflecting the Chinese government's push in the early development of the dim sum bond market. In addition, we present three benchmark issues that were used to help establish the yield curve for this nascent market.

TABLE 6.1 Landmark Dim Sum Bond Issues (2007–2012)

Date of Issue	Issue	Issuer	Amount (RMB million)	Coupon (% p.a.)	Tenor	Ratings: Moody's/ S&P
Jul-07	First dim sum corporate bond	China Development Bank	5,000	3	2	NR*
Jun-09	First dim sum bond by a PRC-incorporated foreign bank	Bank of East Asia (China)	4,000	2.8	2	NR
Oct-09	First dim sum floating rate notes	HSBC Bank (China)	1,000	4.5751	2	NR
Oct-09	First dim sum government bond (three tranches) (Tranche C - First 5-year dim sum bond)	Ministry of Finance	6,000	2.25, 2.7, 3.3	2, 3, 5	Aa3/ NR**
Jul-10	First dim sum corporate bond by a nonfinancial, foreign entity	Hopewell Highway Infrastructure	1,380	2.98	2	NR
Jul-10	First dim sum certificate of deposit	CITIC Bank International	500	2.68	1	NR
Sep-10	First dim sum corporate bond by an MNC	McDonald's	200	3	3	A2/A
Oct-10	First dim sum corporate bond by a red-chip corporation	Sinotruk (Hong Kong)	2,700	2.95	2	NR
Oct-10	First dim sum bond issued by a supranational# (Also, First 10-year dim sum bond)	Asian Development Bank	1,200	2.85	10	Aaa/AAA
Feb-11	First dim sum corporate bond by a China-incorporated company listed in Hong Kong (H-share)	Beijing Capital Land	1,150	4.75	3	NR
Aug-11	First dim sum bond with credit enhancement by a bank	Hai Chao Trading Co. Ltd.	900	2	3	NR

Date of Issue	Issue	Issuer	Amount (RMB million)	Coupon (% p.a.)	Tenor	Ratings: Moody's/S&P
Oct-11	First dim sum *sukuk* bond (Islamic bond)	Danga Capital BHD	500	2.9	3	NR
Oct-11	First dim sum subordinated bond	ICBC Asia Ltd.	1,500	6	10	NR/A-&
Nov-11	First dim sum corporate bond by a mainland China non-financial corporation	Baosteel Group Corp Ltd.	3,600	3.125, 3.5, 4.375	2, 3, 5	A3/A
Jan-12	First 15-year dim sum bond	China Development Bank	1,500	4.2	15	NR
Feb-12	First dim sum bond by a Latin American company	América Móvil S.A.B. de C.V.	1,000	3.5	3	A2/A-
Jul-12	First dim sum corporate bond by a PRC-listed company (A-share)	Gemdale Corporation	1,200	9.15	3	Ba3/BB-
Aug-12	First 20-year dim sum bond	China Development Bank	1,000	4.3	20	NR
Nov-12	First dim sum bond publicly issued by a Latin American financial institution	Banco Santandar Chile	500	3.75	2	Aa3/A

* NR = Not rated.

** For 3 and 5 years.

& A– is Fitch rating instead of Standard & Poor's (S&P).

First dim sum bond listed on the Hong Kong Stock Exchange.

We highlight eight cases to illustrate and analyze dim sum bonds issued by different types of issuers. These cases will help readers, prospective issuers, and investors understand the risk and return trade-off of dim sum bonds. Data of these landmark issues are primarily drawn from the offering circulars/prospectuses, if available, at the time these dim sum bonds were offered to the market along with information from various media sources.

Landmark issues discussed in this chapter include fixed-rate dim sum bonds first issued by:

- A mainland Chinese Bank (China Development Bank).
- The Chinese central government (China's Ministry of Finance).
- A Chinese entity incorporated outside China but listed in Hong Kong, that is, a red-chip company (Sinotruk [Hong Kong] Limited).
- A Chinese entity listed in Hong Kong as H-share (Beijing Capital Land Ltd.).
- A mainland China–listed (A-share) entity (Gemdale Corporation).
- A China-incorporated foreign bank (Bank of East Asia [China] Limited).[1]
- A foreign multinational corporation (McDonald's Corporation, a U.S. multinational corporation).
- A supranational agency (Asian Development Bank).

Each landmark case or benchmark issue indeed sets up a leading example for others to follow in issuing dim sum bonds in a particular sector or industry. Dim sum bonds issued by different entities from various sectors and industries make up a vibrant market, providing choices and diversity to investors. Features of the landmark dim sum bond issues are summarized in Table 6.2.

6.1.1 Benchmark Issues with Longer Tenors

For a bond market to be fully developed, it is important to establish a term structure of interest rates that includes not only the short-term but also the long-term debt instruments. Since most of the dim sum debts are of short-term duration, it is thus instructive to highlight the development of the long-tenor dim sum bonds. We present issuers that have issued the long-dated dim sum bonds. Benchmark issues with long tenors, which include 10-year, 15-year, and 20-year bonds, are used to establish the yield curve for the offshore RMB-denominated bond market.

---

[1] HSBC Bank (China) Company Limited and the Bank of East Asia (China) Limited were the first two foreign banks incorporated in China allowed to issue dim sum bonds. They made the announcement to issue dim sum bonds only a few days apart.

TABLE 6.2 Landmark Issues Discussed in Chapter 6

Case No.	Issue Year	Issuer Name	Amount RMB (Mln)	Bookrunners	Coupon (%)	Maturity Date	Tenor (Years)	Moody's Rating	S&P Rating	Exchange Listed	Bearer Bond	Retail Bond
1	2007	China Development Bank	5,000	BOC/HSBCL	3	7/13/2009	2	n/a	n/a	No	Yes	Yes
2	2009	Bank of East Asia (China)	4,000	BKEA/BOC	2.8	7/23/2011	2	n/a	n/a	No	Yes	Yes
3	2009	Ministry of Finance, PRC (tranche A)	3,000	BKCOMM/BOC	2.25	10/27/2011	2	n/a	n/a	No	Yes	Yes
		Ministry of Finance, PRC (tranche B)	2,500	BKCOMM/BOC	2.7	10/27/2012	3	Aa3	n/a	No	Yes	No
		Ministry of Finance, PRC (tranche C)	500	BKCOMM/BOC	3.3	10/27/2014	5	Aa3	n/a	No	Yes	Yes
4	2010	McDonald's Corporation	200	SCB	3	9/16/2013	3	A2	A	No	Yes	No
5	2010	Asian Development Bank	1,200	BOC/DB	2.85	10/21/2020	10	Aaa	AAA	Hong Kong	Yes	No
6	2010	Sinotruk (Hong Kong) Limited	2,700	BOC/CICC/ICBKC	2.95	10/29/2012	2	n/a	n/a	No	Yes	No
7	2011	Beijing Capital Land	1,150	HSBCL	4.75	2/21/2014	3	n/a	n/a	No	Registered	No
8	2012	Gemdale Corporation	1,200	HSBCL	9.15	7/26/2015	3	Ba3	BB–	Singapore	n/s	No

TABLE 6.3   Long-Tenor Benchmark Issues

Tenor (Years)	Issuer	Maturity Date	Amount (RMB millions)	Coupon (%)	Ratings Moody's/ S&P
10	Asian Development Bank	10/21/2020	1,200	2.85	Aaa/AAA
15	China Development Bank	1/19/2027	1,500	4.2	Unrated/ AA–
20	China Development Bank	8/2/2032	1,000	4.3	Unrated/ Unrated

Benchmark issues can quickly establish a term structure of interest rates, providing yields spanning the entire spectrum of short-term and long-term maturity for various investors and issuers. Establishing a term structure of interest rates for the dim sum bond market is of paramount importance since it facilitates the pricing of out-dated bonds and encourages more active market arbitrage activities that ensure more efficient pricing of future dim sum bond issues. Moreover, a well-developed term structure of interest rates will enable market participants to engage in other derivative transactions with hedging facilities that further lead to the development of the market per se.[2] Table 6.3 lists the benchmark issues of the long-tenor dim sum bonds.

6.2 CASE 1: THE FIRST DIM SUM BOND AND THE FIRST CHINESE FINANCIAL INSTITUTION ISSUER—CHINA DEVELOPMENT BANK (AND THE FIRST 15-YEAR AND 20-YEAR BONDS)

The first-ever dim sum bond was issued in July 2007 by China Development Bank (CDB), a policy bank wholly owned by the Chinese government. CDB is the first Chinese financial institution issuer of dim sum bonds. Other CDB issues include the first 15-year and the first 20-year dim sum bonds.

6.2.1 General Bond Information

The CDB's first dim sum bonds were issued for an amount of RMB5 billion with a two-year tenor and 3 percent coupon, paid semiannually. The bonds

---

[2] See Bank of International Settlement (2006) and Ebias (2012).

were not rated by major credit rating agencies. The bond was a retail bond and the minimum denomination of the bond was RMB20,000, with a subscription price that was 100 percent of the principal amount of the bond. The handling fee paid to the placing banks[3] was 0.15 percent, which was the typical rate for retail dim sum bond issues in Hong Kong.[4] There was no sinking fund arrangement for the bond. The bond would not be listed on any stock exchange. The bond was issued in a bearer form as stated in the prospectus. All the bond and fiscal agency agreements were governed by the laws of Hong Kong SAR (Special Administrative Region). The joint lead managers and bookrunners of the bonds were the Bank of China (Hong Kong) Limited and HSBC, while there were 13 placing banks for this issue, as this was the first-ever retail dim sum bond directly sold to the public.

Given the CDB's close link with the central government and its policy role, its bond issues are considered close proxies for Chinese sovereign bonds. We believe the key role of the CDB issues is to promote the development of the dim sum bond market and help establish the benchmark yield curve in this market. From the CDB's perspective, the dim sum bond issues helped diversify its funding channels.

6.2.2 Issuer Background

The CDB was established in 1994 and is the only policy-oriented statutory financial institution in China designated as a ministry-level institution. Thus, unlike debt issued by other state-owned banks, CDB bonds are classified at the same level as sovereign debt by the government, enjoying the lowest rate of borrowing.[5] It supports China's policy to develop balanced growth goals between coastal, central, and western regions. Specifically, the CDB is mandated to (1) support the development of China's infrastructure, basic industry, key emerging sectors, and national priority projects; (2) promote coordinated regional development and urbanization by financing small business, education, health care, agriculture/rural investment, low-income housing, and environmental initiatives; and (3) facilitate China's cross-border investment and global business cooperation. The bank is wholly owned by

---

[3] Placing banks are commercial banks with many branches helping to distribute the bonds to retail investors in Hong Kong. For more details, refer to Chapter 5, section 5.5.

[4] The handling fee is not the fee paid to investment banks that advise the issuer, but to the placing banks for handling the subscription and distribution of retail bonds.

[5] According to Forsythe and Sanderson (2011), the sovereign status saved about 30 basis points in terms of CDB's borrowing cost.

China's central government, subject to the supervision and direction of the China Banking Regulatory Commission (CBRC) and People's Bank of China (PBOC), which is China's central bank. In 2012, the CDB was the largest Chinese bond issuer in Hong Kong, raising RMB6 billion, which included the first 15-year and 20-year bonds.[6]

6.2.3 Use of Proceeds

Proceeds from the sale of the bonds would be used to:

- Fund RMB-denominated loans in China.
- Finance infrastructure and industrial projects, such as the Three Gorges Dam and Shanghai Pudong International Airport.
- Fund working capital needs and general corporate uses.

6.2.4 Risks

The CDB's first dim sum bond was a retail bond, issuing to the public and allowing retail investors to subscribe via the placing banks. Given the small entry ticket, the perceived low credit risk in view of state ownership and the potentially decent return on the bond due to sustained RMB appreciation, it had rallied many retail investors in Hong Kong to line up outside the branches of the placing banks to subscribe for the bonds. Investors needed to pay the subscription price of the bond plus a handling fee to the placing bank. Investors could resell the bond after purchase in the over-the-counter market, given the placing banks would quote prices on the CDB bond as they agreed. The trading price of the bond would fluctuate depending on the prevailing market situations but the trading liquidity of the bond was expected to be limited. Thus, investors would face the risk that they might not be able to sell the bond without a huge price concession.

If the CDB dim sum bond defaults, that is, the CDB has failed to pay any interest or principal on the bond for 30 days after the payment date, CDB will be dissolved, merged or consolidated by the PRC authorities in transferring the material part of the bank's assets elsewhere. Bondholders may demand the principal of the bond to be due immediately. Moreover, CDB would issue individual bearer certificates for the bondholders. Bond investors are protected by standard bond covenants such as negative pledge; that is, CDB would not grant or permit the outstanding dim sum bonds to have claims on any mortgage, charge, lien on any of the present or future assets of CDB, provided the dim sum bonds remained outstanding. CDB

---

[6] See China Development Bank (2013).

bonds are considered proxies of Chinese sovereign bonds, as such investors generally presume the credit risk of CDB bonds is equivalent to that of the Chinese sovereign bonds, without putting too much emphasis on the CDB's stand-alone credit profile. Investors seem to be quite comfortable with the CDB's reputation and corporate governance.

The bond was not guaranteed by the Chinese government or PBOC. There was no limitation on other indebtedness by the bond and no credit rating available on the bond per se, but there are credit ratings on the issuing bank. The bondholders of the CDB bond could not enforce claims against the PBOC in case of default. However, it seems clear that given the CDB's policy role in the Chinese economy and its 100 percent Chinese government ownership status, it is highly unlikely that the CDB would default on its debt obligations while the Chinese government would not do anything in making good the obligations. CDB is rated on par with Chinese sovereign ratings on a senior unsecured basis: an "Aa3" rating by Moody's Investors Service, "AA–" rating by Standard & Poor's Ratings Group, and "A+" rating by Fitch Ratings Inc., although there were no issue-specific credit ratings for its dim sum bonds.

Investors from all over the world should have been aware that changes in China's policies as well as in its leadership used to roil the capital markets. Since the CDB is a policy bank that executes the government's economic policies, any changes in the government policy with regard to its policy-bank status or its leadership could change the bond price. In addition to this policy risk, investors—especially foreign investors—were also confronted with foreign exchange and interest rate risks in the dim sum bond investment as the bonds were denominated in RMB. If the RMB declined in value upon maturity of the bond, the investment value of the bond would diminish. If the Chinese government increased the domestic interest rates, the market value of the bond, which carried a fixed coupon rate, would decline in value, causing capital loss to investors if the bonds were to be sold at that time.

6.2.5 Significance of This Landmark Issue

The first-ever dim sum bond issued by the CDB is of historic value, the inauguration of a new market in the grand scheme of internationalizing RMB. The Chinese government uses the CDB as a conduit to issuing a series of dim sum bonds in Hong Kong to stimulate the growth of the offshore RMB bond market. Without providing a constant supply of dim sum bond issues and motivation for other Chinese firms to issue dim sum bonds, this offshore RMB bond market is not sustainable for future development and growth. In addition, the issuance of the two long-dated dim sum bonds establishes the long end of the yield curve for this nascent market, enabling proper pricing of

VIGNETTE 6.1 COMPLETE MARKET

In the finance literature, a complete market is one that has the same number of securities that can span the number of independent states. In other words, a complete market (or complete system of markets) is one in which the complete set of possible outcomes on future states of the world can be constructed with existing financial assets without friction or market impediments such as transaction costs. The complete market theory can be traced to the work of Kenneth Arrow and Gérard Debreu (Flood 1991). Firms in a complete financial market can maximize all shareholders' utility by use of the net present value rule for projects while different modes of financing do not affect investment decisions of the firms.

each financial instrument by "completing the market." Please see Vignette 6.1 for an explanation of a complete market.

Table 6.4 shows that the wide array of dim sum bonds issued by the CDB demonstrated the policy intention of the Chinese government. It is indeed a success story for the growth of the dim sum bond market. It is noteworthy that the CDB took the responsibility to issue long-term bonds since the market up to that point was primarily a short-term market. In the long run, to help a nascent debt capital market, a yield curve needs to be established.

6.2.6 Benchmark Issues of Longer Tenors (15-Year and 20-Year Dim Sum Bonds)

Since the debut of dim sum bonds in 2007, the CDB has issued a total of 44 dim sum bonds to raise additional funds (Table 6.4). As a policy bank of China, the CDB has also subsequently issued a couple of dim sum bonds serving as benchmarks for the dim sum bond market. It is imperative for a nascent market to have a complete yield curve for pricing subsequent issues. One such benchmark issue is the first ever 15-year dim sum bond, raising RMB1.5 billion ($237.60 million) in January 2012.

In addition, CDB has also established another benchmark dim sum bond issue for the longest maturity in the dim sum bond market. In August 2012, the CDB priced a RMB2.5 billion ($390 million) offshore RMB bond, comprising the longest-dated dim sum ever sold, an RMB1 billion 20-year bond that was priced to yield 4.3 percent. The 20-year bond attracted an

TABLE 6.4   China Development Bank Issues by Tenor 2007–2012

Tenor (Years)	No. of Issues	Amount RMB (Mln)	Average Amount RMB (Mln)	Average Coupon (%)	Average Coupon (Exclude Zeros and FRN)(%)
1	15	6,746.00	449.73	1.61	1.61
2	9	10,840.00	1,204.44	2.68	2.39
2.5	1	300.00	300.00	2.90	2.90
3	8	9,275.00	1,159.38	2.62	2.37
8.25	1	311.55	311.55	3.65	3.65
9	1	600.00	600.00	3.30	3.30
10	6	1,330.00	221.67	3.57	3.57
15	2	2,500.00	1,250.00	4.20	4.20
20	1	1,000.00	1,000.00	4.30	4.30
Total	44	32,902.55	747.79	2.57	2.47

RMB2.2 billion order book, including 42 percent from insurers, 34 percent from banks, 12 percent from fund managers, 10 percent from central bank and 2 percent from private banks. For regional distribution, Hong Kong and Taiwanese investors were each allocated 42 percent, EMEA (Europe, Middle East, and Africa) 10 percent, and Singapore 6 percent.[7] The Bank of China (Hong Kong) (BOCHK) was the sole global coordinator and book-runner for the bonds.

6.3 CASE 2: THE FIRST DIM SUM BOND ISSUED BY A CHINA-INCORPORATED FOREIGN BANK—THE BANK OF EAST ASIA (CHINA) LIMITED

The Bank of East Asia (China) Limited (BEA [China]), a wholly owned subsidiary of Hong Kong's Bank of East Asia Limited (BEA), was incorporated in mainland China. It is one of the first two China-incorporated foreign banks in China that issued dim sum bonds.

6.3.1 General Bond Information

BEA (China) issued its first dim sum bonds in the amount of RMB4 billion on July 23, 2009, with a two-year tenor, a short tenor similar to the average

---

[7] See Wee (2012).

tenor of all dim sum bonds issued to date. The minimum denomination of the bond was RMB10,000. The coupon rate on the bond was 2.8 percent, paid semiannually. As compared to the 3.33 percent of the three-year deposit rate in China at the end of 2008,[8] the 2.8 percent interest rate on the bond implied a lower financing cost for BEA to raise money from dim sum bonds in Hong Kong.[9] In addition, as a Hong Kong–based bank, BEA lacks a comprehensive branch network and a large RMB deposit base in China. This puts BEA at a disadvantaged position in the lending business competing with other Chinese banks. The dim sum issue helps partly address its relatively small RMB and CNH deposit bases.

The bond was in the form of bearer bonds, implying no tax withholding by the issuer. The handling fee paid by retail investors to the placing banks was 0.15 percent for the bond issue, which was the typical rate. The bond was available for both retail and institutional investors.

The joint lead managers and bookrunners for the bond issue were BOCHK and BEA. The lead arrangers were HSBC, China International Capital Corporation Limited (CICC), and Standard Chartered Bank (SCB) with 18 placing banks, including BOCHK; Bank of Communications Limited, Hong Kong branch (BCOMMHK); BEA; and China Construction Bank (Asia). The total fees paid to bookrunners/managers were 0.2 percent of the total amount of the issue.

As BEA's headquarters is located in Hong Kong, it is relatively easy to estimate the cost of issuing bonds in Hong Kong dollar or in U.S. dollar as both are linked to the RMB by a pegged exchange rate. As such, the first goal of BEA's first issue of dim sum bonds was to tap the RMB deposits pool in Hong Kong for a lower interest rate, attempting to arbitrage between the mainland and Hong Kong interest rates. Because the bank lending rate was higher in the mainland, the cost of funding would be higher for BEA if RMB funding was financed in Hong Kong for use in the mainland, which had received prior approval from the Chinese authorities to transmit the RMB funds to the mainland to service the RMB loans, to provide working capital, and for general corporate purposes. Finally, BEA could avoid the exchange rate risk through the balance sheet hedge for RMB earnings generated in mainland China.

---

[8] Source: Bank of China. Retrieved from www.boc.cn/en/bocinfo/bi4/

[9] Typically, the onshore loan rate is 2 to 3 percent above the deposit rate in the mainland. Also, a few months later, in October 2009, the Chinese government issued a 2.7 percent coupon bonds of three-year maturity. Thus, the 2.8 percent coupon rate for the BEA (China) dim sum bonds could have been considered an attractive deal for the issuer.

6.3.2 Issuer Background

BEA (China) is one of the first two locally incorporated foreign banks in China that received approval for issuing dim sum bonds in Hong Kong in 2009. As early as 1920, BEA set up a branch in Shanghai and had 18 branches and 48 sub-branches in urban cities throughout China at the time of the bond issuance. Today, BEA (China)'s headquarters is housed in Shanghai and has 110 outlets including 25 branches and 88 sub-branches in 33 cities in China, providing a wide range of RMB and foreign services to customers in China.[10]

6.3.3 Use of Proceeds

As stated in the prospectus, the proceeds from the sale of dim sum bonds were used to support the RMB-denominated loans of the bank in China and elsewhere and for general working capital and corporate purposes. The use of dim sum bond proceeds to support its lending business in China is strategically important for BEA as it expands its business into China. As mentioned above, as a Hong Kong–based bank, BEA lacks a large RMB deposit base in China. This puts BEA at a disadvantaged position in the lending business competing with other Chinese banks. The dim sum bond issue can help BEA gain access to CNH liquidity in Hong Kong and CNY liquidity in China once the fund is remitted to the mainland. BEA could then lend CNY (since CNH funds remitted onshore become CNY funds) onshore to local Chinese entities, as well as to Hong Kong companies that have expansion plans in China, leveraging its existing banking relationship with them in Hong Kong.

6.3.4 Risks

The bond was not rated by major credit agencies, but Standard & Poor's assigned "A" and "A-2" respectively to the long-term and short-term counterparty rating to the firm itself. The bond was unsecured and unsubordinated and not guaranteed by BEA, the parent company, or by a third party. In addition to default risk, thin trading liquidity was considered one of the major risks since the bonds were unrated, as such the investor base could be smaller. Despite the five joint lead managers and bookrunners (BOCHK, CICC, BEA, HSBC, and SCB) had agreed to make a market and provide price quotes for investors, trading liquidity may not be sufficient to absorb large adverse volatility for investors, implying that investors might be subject to higher price risk if they sell the bond prior to maturity.

---

[10] Figures were obtained from www.prweb.com/releases/netdimensions-talentsuite/bank-east-asia/prweb10377186.ht, as of March 27, 2013.

6.3.5 Significance of This Landmark Issue

BEA (China) is one of the two foreign banks incorporated in China that received early approval to issue dim sum bonds; HSBC (China) is the other bank. BEA and HSBC are foreign banks that have had a long history of doing business in China. Having both banks on board early in the development stage would promote the dim sum bond market to global investors. The BEA (China) dim sum bond issue carries a historic landmark significance and exemplifies the potential of a lower-cost financing channel that can be obtained for entities outside mainland China (i.e., in Hong Kong) by taking advantage of the interest rate differentials. Moreover, the bond was in bearer form, implying anonymity and no withholding tax for investors. Bonds in bearer form are an important feature for bonds in the Eurobond market (see Vignette 6.2), which conceals the identity of investors. As China aspires to leverage the dim sum bond market to help internationalizing the RMB, emulating the bearer-form feature of Eurobonds seems to be a reasonable strategy in market development. This significance, however, needs time for validation.

VIGNETTE 6.2 THE EUROBOND MARKET

The Eurobond market is composed of investors, banks, borrowers, and traders that buy, sell, and transfer Eurobonds. Eurobonds are bonds issued by entities, denominated in currencies other than those of the countries in which the bonds are sold. Typically, they are denominated in a currency other than the issuer's, but they are intended for the broader international markets. For example, a USD-denominated bond issued by a German company in London would be a Eurobond. In the secondary market, Eurobonds are traded over the counter. Major markets for Eurobonds exist in London, Frankfurt, Zurich, and Amsterdam. Eurobonds made their debut in 1963, but did not gain international significance until the early 1980s. Since then, they have become a large and active component of international finance. Similar to foreign bonds, but with important differences, Eurobonds became popular with issuers and investors because they could offer certain tax shelters and anonymity to their buyers. They could also offer borrowers favorable interest rates, lowering the cost of borrowing after taking into consideration the exchange rate volatility, among other benefits (Ferri, Sugrue, and Yau 1991).

6.4 CASE 3: THE FIRST DIM SUM BOND ISSUED BY THE CHINESE CENTRAL GOVERNMENT

This bond issue was China's first RMB-denominated sovereign bond offering outside of the People's Republic of China (PRC) and the largest offshore RMB bond as of the time of the bond offering (November 2011). The Ministry of Finance (MOF) of the PRC acting on behalf of its central government issued the first sovereign dim sum bonds ever.

6.4.1 General Bond Background

The first MOF dim sum bonds were issued in three tranches on October 27, 2009, for a total amount of RMB6 billion:

- Tranche A was issued in the amount of RMB2.5 billion with a coupon rate of 2.25 percent with a two-year tenor.
- Tranche B (RMB3 billion) carried a coupon rate of 2.70 percent with a three-year tenor. Both Tranches A and B were targeted at retail investors.
- Tranche C was issued in an amount of RMB500 million with a coupon rate of 3.3 percent and a 5-year tenor. Tranche C was targeted at institutional investors.

The issue was well received by investors and three times oversubscribed. The bond extended the dim sum bond yield curve from three to five years. The differing interest rates for the various tranches by the Chinese government established benchmark interest rates for the dim sum bond market for different clienteles (retail and institutional investors) for future reference.

The two-year deposit rate in China at the end of 2008 was 2.79 percent, whereas in October 2010 it was 3.25 percent.[11] These two rates indicated that the deposit rates for the period between 2008 and 2010 would be somewhat between 2.79 percent and 3.25 percent because the Chinese government used a smoothing process in managing interest rates. As the central government issued the dim sum bonds in 2009 with 2.25 percent coupon, which was lower than both rates, suggesting that the issuing cost of this landmark bond to the central government was lower in the offshore bond market than in the domestic counterpart. Thus, we believe all the bonds in tranches A, B, and C carried a lower interest rate in the Hong Kong dim

---

[11] Rates were obtained for October 20, 2010, from the BOC. Retrieved from www .boc.cn/en/bocinfo/bi4/

sum bond market than that on the mainland, suggesting that the Chinese government had successfully demonstrated how to arbitrage a lower cost of financing by issuing dim sum bonds in Hong Kong.

The handling fee for the bond was 0.15 percent, which was based on the number of bonds purchased for which an investor paid a placing bank when submitting the application for purchasing the bond. The minimum denomination of the bond was RMB10,000 with a subscription price that was 100 percent of the par value of the bond. The bond was not listed on any exchanges. The BOCHK and BCOMMHK were joint lead managers and bookrunners.

6.4.2. Use of Proceeds

The central Chinese government could use the net proceeds of the dim sum bonds, after deduction of underwriting commissions and other offering expenses, for general governmental purposes. Thus, the money raised from the sale of dim sum bonds provided much flexibility for the Chinese government as there were few specific restrictions placed on the bonds.

6.4.3 Risks

This issue was the first sovereign dim sum bond. Sovereign risk is the major risk of the bonds. At the time of the bond offering, China had managed to avoid a hard landing for its economy amid of the global financial crisis. As such, the sovereign risk of the bond issue was very low at the time of the bond offering, echoed by the international credit rating agencies. Moody's, Standard & Poor's, and Fitch rated China as A1, A+, and A+, respectively, at the time of issuance. Also, the average growth rate of China since its economic reforms from late 1978 until 2007 had been 9 percent on average, an impressive rate. In addition, the government had accumulated a sufficient amount of foreign reserves (less gold), which was estimated to be US$2.3 trillion at the end of 2009.[12]

At the time of issuance, besides sovereign risk, the bond was vulnerable to inflation risk, interest rate risk, and foreign exchange risk for global investors. Inflation risk was most imminent as the growth rate of the Chinese economy seemed to slow down but inflation was rising. If the inflation rate increased, interest rates would rise, causing the bond price to drop. Moreover, rising inflation would drive down the exchange rate of RMB against the U.S. dollar, lowering the return on dim sum bond investments. The yield of sovereign bonds, especially those issued by countries with high credit ratings, are low as

---

[12] See www.chinability.com/Reserves.htm

a result of low credit spread over the risk-free rate, a premium to compensate investors for taking credit risk. Therefore, bonds issued by highly rated sovereigns such as China are particularly sensitive to interest rate movements.[13]

6.4.4 Significance of This Landmark Issue

This landmark issue was of historic significance because it represented the first offshore sovereign bond issued by the Chinese central government. From the market perspective, the fact that the first dim sum bond was a sovereign bond boosted investors' confidence in this new asset class and had provided the needed impetus for growth in this market.

However, there is a greater mission for this landmark issue. These dim sum sovereign bonds, denominated in the Chinese currency but issued in Hong Kong, were intended to achieve two major policy goals. First, the three tranches of the Chinese government bonds cover a two-year, three-year and five-year maturity, setting up benchmarks for the term structure of interest rates in the dim sum bond market in Hong Kong. In addition, given the sovereign status of these dim sum bonds by the Chinese government, future issues by other entities, banks or corporations, could be priced according to these benchmark issues. Second, in addition to the need to fund its own domestic projects, the Chinese government wanted to jump-start the fledgling dim sum bond market in Hong Kong, which would be used as a hub for the offshore RMB bond market. In the grand scheme of things, if the Chinese government wants to internationalize its own currency, it is important to have an active bond market denominated in RMB. Success of this dim sum bond market in Hong Kong will be an indicator to measure the progress of the RMB internationalization policy. So the issuance of the sovereign bonds in Hong Kong has important policy implications, and creation of the offshore RMB market is arguably an ingenuous approach to tackling the globalization of its currency.

6.5 CASE 4: THE FIRST DIM SUM BOND ISSUED BY A FOREIGN MULTINATIONAL CORPORATION—MCDONALD'S CORPORATION

McDonald's Corporation is the first foreign nonfinancial company that issued dim sum bonds in Hong Kong, representing the landmark issue of

---

[13] Lee, Xie, and Yau (2010) report that sovereign risk has a "shortening" effect on bond duration. The impact gets stronger for Asian USD sovereign bonds with lower ratings and in recessionary conditions.

dim sum bonds issued by a foreign multinational corporation (MNC). Subsequent to McDonald's dim sum bond, other U.S. companies, such as Caterpillar and Ford, have followed suit issuing dim sum bonds.

6.5.1 General Bond Information

McDonald's sold RMB200 million (US$32 million) of 3 percent dim sum notes with a three-year tenor on September 16, 2010, in Hong Kong. The bond's 3 percent coupon rate was well received in the market at that time because it was relatively higher than the RMB deposit rate (less than 1 percent per annum) offered to investors at the time in Hong Kong. In comparison, the interest rate in China was about 5.56 percent, which was much higher than the 3 percent coupon rate.[14] The dim sum bond issue offered by McDonald's was intended to tap into the large RMB deposits pool accumulated over the past few years in Hong Kong banks.[15]

Moody's rated McDonald's dim sum bond "A2," while S&P rated it "A," indicating that the bond was of high credit quality. The lead arranger for McDonald's dim sum bond was the SCB.

6.5.2 Issuer Background

McDonald's is a corporation organized under the laws of the State of Delaware, United States, on March 1, 1965, as the successor to an Illinois corporation formed in 1956. It primarily operates restaurants, providing food services in more than 110 countries globally. All restaurants are operated either by McDonald's or franchisees, including conventional franchisees under franchise arrangements, and foreign affiliates and developmental licensees under license agreements.

McDonald's business is managed as distinct geographic segments as reported in Table 6.5, including significant reportable segments such as the United States; Europe; Asia-Pacific, Middle East, and Africa (APMEA); and "Other Countries & Corporate" that includes operations in Canada and Latin America, as well as corporate activities. It can be seen from Table 6.5 that the growth in the number of system-wide restaurants, revenues, operating income, and assets between the end of 2010 (the year that McDonald's issued its first dim sum bond) and 2012, primarily came from the APMEA region, while other regions either experienced very little growth or negative growth in percentage terms. China is one of the three major markets in the

---

[14] See www.tradingeconomics.com/china/interest-rate
[15] The total RMB deposits in Hong Kong stood at about RMB217.1 billion at the end of October 2010 (Fung and Yau 2011).

TABLE 6.5 Geographical Breakdown of the Number of System-wide Restaurants, Revenues, Operating Income, and Assets

	2012		2010	
	No. of System-wide Restaurants/ RMB (in millions)	% of total	No. of System-wide Restaurants/ RMB (in millions)	% of total
United States	14,157	41.06	14,027	42.85
Europe	7,368	21.37	6,969	21.29
Asia-Pacific, Middle East, and Africa (APMEA)	9,454	27.42	8,424	25.73
Other countries and corporate	3,501	10.15	3,317	10.13
Total	34,480	100	32,737	100
Revenues				
United States	8,813.7	31.97	8,111.6	33.69
Europe	10,827.4	39.28	9,569.2	39.75
APMEA	6,391.1	23.18	5,065.5	21.04
Other countries and corporate	1,534.8	5.57	1,328.3	5.52
Total	27,567	100	24,074.6	100
Operating income				
United States	3,750.4	44	3,446.5	46
Europe	3,195.8	37	2,796.8	37
APMEA	1,566.1	18	1,199.9	16
Other countries and corporate	92.3	1	29.9	1
Total	8,604.6	100	7,473.1	100
Assets				
United States	11,431.6	32	10,467.7	33
Europe	14,223.3	40	11,360.7	36
APMEA	6,419.3	18	5,374	17
Other countries and corporate	3,312.3	10	4,772.8	14
Total	35386.5	100	31975.2	100

APMEA region and one of the six in the world for McDonald's in terms of total revenues. The growth in revenues in APMEA in 2011 and 2012 were attributed to the expansion in China. In terms of the number of restaurants, China is the third-largest market of McDonald's only after the United States and Japan. As at the end of 2012, there were 1,705 restaurants in China, up from 876 at the end of 2007.

6.5.3 Use of Proceeds

Proceeds from the dim sum issue would be used for the general purposes of refinancing of debts, capital expenditure (including acquisition and development of restaurants), payment of dividends, and stock repurchase program. Since McDonald's had obtained prior approval from the Chinese government to remit funds raised from the dim sum bonds to China, funds raised from dim sum bonds could be used as a balance sheet hedge[16] for McDonald's exchange risk exposure caused by the earnings from the mainland's operations. In other words, McDonald's RMB funds could pay for expenses of its China's operations. As discussed in its latest annual report, it is the company's financial policy to have its foreign operations to be self-funded; that is, McDonald's targets that cash flow from operations and financing activities, plus cash on hand of its foreign operations will sufficiently cover its operating expenses, capital expenditure and other funding requirements of its foreign operations.[17] During FY2010–2012, the non-U.S. market had contributed an average of 56 percent of its operating profit, and a significant portion of its operating cash flows was reinvested in foreign counties.

The company opened a record 250 outlets in 2012, after making a commitment to increase investment by 50 percent in 2011, without disclosing the financial details of the investment.[18] The company had 1,000 restaurants in 2010 in China and planned to double it to 2,000 in three years in 2013.[19] Thus, it will continue to build a foundation for long-term growth in China by opening over 300 new restaurants in China by the end of 2013.[20] The large investment outlays apparently require additional financing and proceeds from dim sum bonds could just meet the financing needs for this

---

[16] Balance sheet hedge refers to hedging against the exchange risk by financing the foreign operations in the same currency as the foreign revenues.

[17] McDonald's Corporation, *Annual Report 2012*.

[18] See *China Daily*, February 29, 2012.

[19] See Reuters, www.reuters.com/article/2010/12/15/us-mcdonalds-china-idUSTRE6 BE0VJ20101215

[20] McDonald's Corporation, *Annual Report 2012*, p. 14.

planned expansion. As the first dim sum bond issued by McDonald's would mature in September 2013, the company had planned to launch the second dim sum bond issue to refinance the retiring bonds in Hong Kong. However, no further news has been released as of the time of writing.

6.5.4 Risks

McDonald's, a foreign corporation that has operations in the mainland, has major exposure in exchange rates since its revenues are in RMB but its home currency is in U.S. dollars. Thus, investments in McDonald's dim sum bonds are subject to exchange risk, among other risks such as default risk, legal and political risks. Appreciation of RMB is no longer a one-way bet after the strong performance of Chinese currency over the past several years. Given high domestic inflation rates in China, it is possible that the RMB will depreciate to reflect the inflation premium. As McDonald's is a U.S. company, issuing U.S.-dollar denominated bonds will be preferable for avoiding the exchange rate fluctuations. In particular, if the RMB depreciates, the exchange rate risk will be an important factor for McDonald's to consider. However, given a 3 percent coupon rate on the dim sum bonds, which is relatively inexpensive for a financing option and the proceeds can be used to finance its operations in China, this action seems financially sound as compared to the U.S. financing option.

Because the dim sum bonds are unsecured, if McDonald's defaults on the bond, or in the event of a bankruptcy, liquidation, or reorganization, then, to the extent that McDonald's has granted security over its assets, the assets that secure those obligations will be used to satisfy the obligations before McDonald's could sell or otherwise dispose of those assets in order to make payment on the dim sum bonds.

6.5.5. Significance of This Landmark Issue

McDonald's is one of the most well-known MNCs from the United States with a very strong global franchise. The significance of this issue is to open a funding channel for MNCs to raise RMB funds for business expansion in China without risking a currency mismatch. The McDonald's case demonstrates to other MNCs the advantage of raising RMB funds in the dim sum bond market to finance their operations in China, providing a natural or balance sheet hedge against the exchange risk. Although the RMB has appreciated against the U.S. dollar for a number of years, it could reverse its trend at any time. Providing a means to hedging the currency risk with the dim sum bond financing, this landmark case encourages MNCs to invest and/or expand their business in China. This landmark case signals to global issuers that dim sum bond proceeds in RMB can be remitted to China and used internally in China. As foreign firms in China require financing for their business expansion, cash flow has become a critical factor for expansion. If dim sum bonds can be issued to raise cash, it helps alleviate the financing constraints faced by MNCs doing business in China. Unlike small and medium-sized corporations which are less well-known to global investors, McDonald's participation in the dim sum bond market represents a vote of confidence by a major MNC. With McDonald's long-term business development plans to expand in the mainland Chinese market, this dim sum bond issue boosted the confidence of global investors in dim sum bonds, which might not even have collateral and credit protection for bondholders. Investors could only rely on the creditworthiness of the issuer in the assessment of the riskiness of the bonds.

6.6 CASE 5: THE FIRST DIM SUM BONDS ISSUED BY A SUPRANATIONAL AGENCY—ASIAN DEVELOPMENT BANK (AND THE FIRST 10-YEAR DIM SUM BOND)

The Asian Development Bank (ADB) participated in the dim sum bond market in Hong Kong in October 2010 as the first supranational issuer as well as the issuer of the first 10-year tenor bond.

6.6.1 General Bond Information

The triple-A-rated ADB issued the first 10-year dim sum bond in the amount of RMB1.2 billion (US$181 million). This issue is of historic significance because it signifies confidence in this nascent market by a triple-A-rated supranational agency. More important, it helps establish the long-term yield curve for the dim sum bond market. Thus, the dim sum bond yield curve is able to extend from primarily a short-term horizon to a 10-year horizon for dim sum debt instruments.

ADB was able to sell the dim sum bond with an annual coupon of 2.85 percent, which was 57 basis points below the Chinese government bond yield at that time.[21] Reputable foreign and Chinese investors were unable to arbitrage the interest rate differential between the onshore and offshore Chinese markets earlier because of China's strict capital controls for funds flow across the borders. With this newly developed offshore dim

---

[21] See "ADB Issues Landmark Renminbi Bond," *Financial Times*, October 19, 2010. Retrieved from www.ft.com/intl/cms/s/0/5ca536cc-db7a-11df-ae99-00144feabdc0 .html#axzz2OlvvtsYu

VIGNETTE 6.3 PANDA BONDS

Panda bonds are RMB bonds issued by foreign entities in mainland China. The first Panda bonds were issued by the Asian Development Bank and International Finance Corporation of the World Bank Group in 2005 in mainland China after obtaining approval from the State Council of China for an amount of RMB2.13 billion. The second issue of Panda bonds for an amount of RMB1 billion (US$147 million) was issued in December 2009 to improve China's capital market and help make it global. The proceeds from the bond, which carried an annual coupon rate of 4.2 percent and a maturity of 10 years, were used to fund private sector clean energy and energy efficiency projects.

sum bond market, a well-known supranational agency such as the ADB can indeed take advantage of the market impediments as it previously did in the Panda bond market. The 2.85 percent coupon of ADB's dim sum bond was clearly below those of the Panda bonds issued earlier in China by ADB, demonstrating the comparatively cost advantage for ADB in issuing dim sum bonds in Hong Kong (see Vignette 6.3).

The ADB's dim sum bond, which will mature in 2020 and carries a triple-A credit rating, was the longest-dated and the highest-rated RMB-denominated bond sold to international investors at the time of issuance. They extended the horizon of the dim sum bond yield curve from 5 to 10 years. Subsequent to the ADB's issue, International Finance Corporation and other supranational agencies had also issued dim sum bonds in Hong Kong, demonstrating the influential impact of the ADB issue on other issuers.

The ADB's dim sum bond was unsecured and subordinated debt. In other words, investors might face risk in recovering the investment principal if the bond were in default because of huge claims by senior debtholders. However, the highest possible credit ratings assigned by Moody's (Aaa) and Standard & Poor's (AAA) suggest that the ADB bond was of high credit quality with a minimal probability of default.

The ADB's dim sum bond was also listed on the Hong Kong Stock Exchange, making it the first RMB-denominated security to be traded and settled on the bourse. This dim sum bond would act as a useful benchmark for other potential supranational borrowers, helping develop the offshore RMB bond market into an important long-term source of financing for infrastructure, environmental and developmental projects, such as the clean energy (wind power) and water treatment projects in China. The ADB has been proactive in facilitating the development of local currency bond markets as a liquid and deep domestic capital market can harness domestic savings and reduce dependence on external funding. Local currency bonds provide the ADB with the proper financing tool to minimize currency risks faced by borrowers in the region and at the same time help stimulate the growth of the local dim sum bond market, which is also a goal for the ADB to accomplish.

The ADB's dim sum bond received strong demand from the order book-building process and was distributed to a wide range of investors across the globe (i.e., investor demand for the ADB dim sum bond was twice the amount on sale), supporting the ABD's mandate in helping develop local currency debt markets.[22]

The bond was in bearer form, implying anonymity of investors. Deutsche Bank, AG (the Hong Kong branch) and BOCHK were joint lead managers for the deal.

6.6.2 Issuer Background

Founded in 1966, the ADB, similar to other regional development banks, is a not-for-profit organization striving to improve people's lives in Asia and the Pacific regions. By targeting its investments wisely, in partnership with its developing member countries and other stakeholders, the ADB alleviates poverty of local people and help create sustained and inclusive growth in the regions. The ADB is committed to helping developing member countries evolve into thriving, modern economies that are well integrated with each other and the world. The ADB has been cautious in using its funds histori-cally and maintains sound and sustainable economic goals.[23]

6.6.3 Use of Proceeds

The proceeds from the sale of the dim sum bonds would be treated as part of the ordinary capital sources and would be used for ordinary operations of the bank.

6.6.4. Risks

The dim sum bond issued by ADB entails similar types of risks as any dim sum bonds issued by other entities. The risks generally depend on a number of factors, including financial, economic, and political events of which ADB

---

[22] For an account of the development history of the Asian Development Bank, see Yau (1994).

[23] Ibid.

has no control. The ADB's dim sum bond program was rated "Aaa/P-1" by Moody's, "AAA" by Standard & Poor's, and "AAA" by Fitch Ratings. The bond would be listed on the Hong Kong Stock Exchange, improving the liquidity of the bond.

6.6.5 Significance of This Landmark Issue

This landmark issue has many "firsts": (1) the first dim sum bond issued by a supranational agency; (2) the first 10-year dim sum bond; (3) the first dim sum bond listed on the Hong Kong Stock Exchange; (4) the first dim sum bond receiving the highest ratings (Aaa and AAA by Moody's and Standard & Poor's, respectively); and (5) the first foreign entity to issue both onshore CNY bonds (i.e., Panda bonds) and offshore RMB bonds (dim sum bonds in Hong Kong).

With all these "first" honors, this landmark case is unquestionably significant for several reasons. First, it provides a benchmark for the long end of the yield curve of the dim sum bond market, a result supporting the CDB's efforts to set up the longer term spectrum of the market that has focused primarily on the short-term offerings. In addition, when more dim sum bonds are to be listed on exchanges for trading, the liquidity of the market will improve, further attracting more investors. It is clear that the listing of dim sum bonds on exchanges provides an impetus for the growth of exchange-traded funds (ETFs) of dim sum bonds for global investors. As more investors participate in this market, the depth of the market will improve. Finally, this landmark case would likely encourage other supranational agencies to issue dim sum bonds in the future, pushing the frontier of this emerging market.

6.7 CASE 6: THE FIRST DIM SUM BONDS ISSUED BY A CHINESE COMPANY, INCORPORATED OUTSIDE MAINLAND CHINA AND LISTED IN HONG KONG (RED-CHIP CORPORATION)—SINOTRUK (HONG KONG) LIMITED

Sinotruk (Hong Kong) Limited was the first issuer of dim sum bonds issued by a "red-chip" corporation, which is a mainland Chinese company incorporated outside mainland China and listed on the exchange in Hong Kong.

6.7.1 General Bond Information

Sinotruk (Hong Kong) Limited issued the RMB 2.7 billion dim sum bonds on October 29, 2010, with a two-year tenor, which is the typical tenor for dim sum debt instruments to date. The bond carried a 2.95 percent coupon rate, implying a loan rate higher than 3.25 percent since the two-year deposit rate was 3.25 percent on October 20, 2010 on the mainland.[24] Thus, the 2.95 percent coupon on the dim sum bond represented a lower cost of financing in Hong Kong for Sinotruk as compared to financing on the mainland.

The bond was in bearer form and thus no taxes were withheld on the bonds. The bond as an offshore offering outside the United States issued under Regulation S, was not allowed to be offered within the United States. The bond was not listed on any exchanges. The bond was not rated by credit agencies and was an unsecured and subordinated debt obligation for Sinotruk.

6.7.2 Issuer Background

Sinotruk (Hong Kong) Limited is owned 51 percent by Sinotruk (BVI) Limited, which in turn, is a wholly owned subsidiary of China National Heavy Duty Truck Group (Group) from mainland China. The Group is China's largest heavy truck manufacturer and a state-owned enterprise (SOE). Sinotruk (Hong Kong) Limited owns many subsidiaries that deal with exports and imports, design, and financing of truck business.

The Group, the ultimate owner of the issuer of the bond, an SOE, and a conglomerate related to the truck segment, has a high degree of vertical integration in its production chain, produces most of the engines for its truck production, and sells truck, industrial, and construction machinery engines to third parties. Most of the Group's sales are domestic sales but it has expanded its sales to other countries. The operations of the Group are organized into three operating segments: (1) services to a wide range of customers from all major industries that utilize heavy-duty trucks, including infrastructure, construction, container transportation, logistics, mining, steel, and chemical industries; (2) production of heavy-duty truck engines and other key heavy-duty truck parts and components; and (3) financing facilities for the purchase by its domestic end users and customers.

6.7.3 Use of Proceeds

The proceeds of the dim sum bond issue would be used for working capital requirements, general corporate purposes, and on-lending to Sinotruk's onshore subsidiaries in China. Sinotruk received regulatory approval to remit the funds raised from the bond to the mainland to refinance maturing loans.[25]

---

[24] Source: www.boc.cn/en/bocinfo/bi4/
[25] See "Sinotruk Leads the Red-Chip Way to Hong Kong" (2010).

6.7.4 Risks

The Sinotruk dim sum bond was unrated by any international rating agencies, like many of the dim sum issues at that time, although the default risk is considered low given its SOE background. Among other risks, the legal risk of the issuer that is a red-chip entity is more of a concern to investors as major operations and assets of red-chip entities are in mainland China. As compared to an issuer with major operations and assets in Hong Kong or countries where the bankruptcy law is more transparent and established, the legal risk of an issue by a red-chip issuer is higher because of the uncertainties in enforcing the offshore claim in mainland China and the offshore creditors' claim at the holding company level is subordinated to those of onshore creditors at the operating company level.

Moreover, the bond was not listed on any stock exchange and would be issued in bearer form. These attributes would somewhat limit the bond's investor base and adversely affect the trading liquidity of the bond.

6.7.5 Significance of This Landmark Issue

This case is a landmark issue because it is the first dim sum bond issued by a red-chip entity that is a Hong Kong–listed company incorporated outside mainland China but its parent or major business is located in mainland China. Sinotruk can choose to issue dim sum bonds in Hong Kong or foreign currency bonds, such as the U.S. dollar in the Asian debt capital market, since a red-chip corporation can issue offshore bonds in any currencies without prior approval from the Chinese regulators.[26]

The choice of the RMB-denominated bond issue was likely based on the considerations for lowering the funding cost, creating a natural hedge against the foreign exchange risk, the greater appeal to global investors who looked for a good investment alternative to the U.S. market after the 2007–2009 global financial crisis, obtaining short-tenor financing, and diversifying its funding channel. For example, Sinotruk could have saved 0.3 percent in issuing dim sum bonds at that time when the onshore interest rate was 3.25 percent (the average U.S. prime rate in 2010)[27] and the coupon rate was 2.95 percent. Moreover, investors invested in dim sum bonds

---

[26] Since July 2010, due to government policy liberalization, non-Chinese entities have been able to issue dim sum bonds at their own discretion. However, they still need approval from the Chinese authorities if they want to remit the RMB funds raised from the dim sum bond market to mainland China for use.

[27] Source: Federal Reserve Board. Retrieved from www.federalreserve.gov/releases/h15/data.htm

since the debut of dim sum bonds could have earned an annualized rate of 4 percent in currency appreciation in addition to the coupon yield on the bonds.[28] Since Sinotruk generates the majority of its sales domestically and its assets are mainly based in China, issuing dim sum bonds would provide a natural hedge to foreign exchange risk. Furthermore, Sinotruk's target for obtaining short-tenor financing (its dim sum bond has a two-year tenor) without the need to go through the credit rating process in contrast to issuing USD bonds made the dim sum bond market a more cost-effective and efficient funding channel for Sinotruk. The offshore RMB-denominated bond market helped diversify Sinotruk's funding channel. This is in line with the Chinese government's policy goal of encouraging SOEs to diversify their funding sources away from the domestic banking sector, so as to avoid over-concentrated credit risk in the domestic banking market.

A dim sum bond issued by a red-chip entity has significant implications on the risk perception of the issuer and management of risk from the investor perspective. Red-chip entities are different from their mainland Chinese counterparts, although the core business of the red-chip entity is derived primarily from the mainland operating entities. Red-chip entities are incorporated in locations outside mainland China, including Hong Kong, and thus are under different legal jurisdiction than those in mainland China. While bond covenants and bankruptcy procedures are more transparent and well understood in international investing community, subordination risk of dim sum bonds exists as the claim priority of creditors of a red-chip entity is behind those of secured and unsecured creditors of onshore operating subsidiaries of the red-chip entity. Put another way, the structural subordination risk of a red-chip issue is higher as operating assets and cash flow are onshore (in China) while creditors have a claim only on the offshore entity.

The bankruptcy proceedings in China have been quite opaque and the treatment of offshore investors has been quite unfavorable in some of the previous bankruptcy cases, such as Asia Aluminum and investment trust companies owned by municipal governments. When the jurisdiction of the dim sum bond issue falls outside mainland China, it is generally believed that the rule of law outside the mainland, such as in Hong Kong, provides better protection to investors. Thus, dim sum bonds issued by red-chip entities in particular have different implications on investors from default and

---

[28] The currency appreciation for the period October 2007–October 2010 was computed from the average exchange rates RMB7.5035/USD (October 2007) and RMB6.6685/USD (October 2010), respectively, obtained from www.oanda.com/currency/average

VIGNETTE 6.4 THE FIRST DIM SUM BOND WITH CREDIT ENHANCEMENT (BANK GUARANTEE)

Hai Chao Trading Co. Ltd., a wholly owned subsidiary of Hangzhou Zhongce Rubber Co. Ltd., a mainland Chinese company, issued a dim sum bond in 2011 for an amount of RMB900 million with an annual coupon of 2 percent and a three-year tenor. The bond was unrated and not listed on any exchange. The priority claim of the bond was senior and unsubordinated. However, the bond was guaranteed by the Export and Import Bank of China (Chexim). As such, this bond is the first dim sum bond with credit enhancement provided by a Chinese policy bank, improving the creditworthiness of the bond and helping reduce the funding cost. The low 2 percent coupon rate on an unrated bond issued by a relatively unknown issuer in the international debt capital market reflects the effect of such credit enhancement. Subsequently, there have been more issues with bank guarantees—one more issue guaranteed by Chexim and two issues guaranteed by foreign banks: the Export-Import Bank of India and Abu Dhabi Commercial Bank. (For these three cases, please refer to Chapter 2, section 2.2.7.2).

credit risks, which are very different from dim sum bonds issued by the Chinese banks or Chinese government in mainland China.

In addition to the preceding landmark cases, the first dim sum bond with credit enhancement—a bank guarantee—was issued by Hangzhou Zhongce Rubber Co. Ltd. in 2011 (see Vignette 6. 4). In the following, we present two cases with innovative credit enhancement structures that enable issuers to get access to offshore funding in the dim sum bond market.

6.8 CASE 7: THE FIRST MAINLAND CHINESE CORPORATION LISTED IN HONG KONG (H-SHARE) ISSUER OF DIM SUM BONDS—BEIJING CAPITAL LAND LTD.

The first mainland Chinese corporation listed on the Hong Kong Stock Exchange (H-share) issuer of dim sum bonds is Beijing Capital Land Ltd. (BECL). H-share issuers have limited access to offshore funding. As such, BECL has used an innovative offshore guarantee structure that circumvents the regulatory constraint on overseas funding in its first dim sum bond issue.

6.8.1 General Bond Information

The general bond information on this landmark issue is summarized in Vignette 6.5.

6.8.2 Issuer Background

Based in Beijing, BECL is a property developer in China, primarily engaging in the development of medium to high-end residential properties. Over the years, BECL has built a significant presence in Tianjin and Shenyang in the Bohai region, Chengdu, Xian, and Chongqing in central and southwestern China, Foshan in the Pearl River Delta region, and Wuxi and Huzhou in the Yangtze River Delta region.

VIGNETTE 6.5 SUMMARY TERMS OF BEIJING CAPITAL LAND LTD.'S FIRST DIM SUM BOND

Issuer:	BECL Investment Holding Ltd., incorporated in Hong Kong and wholly owned by the guarantor.
Guarantor:	Beijing Capital Land Ltd., incorporated in China and listed on the Hong Kong Stock Exchange.
Issue Size:	RMB1.15bn.
Coupon:	4.75 percent.
Ranking:	Senior and secured with charge on the interest reserve account.[a]
Covenants:	No standard high-yield covenant.
Rating:	Not rated.[b]
Issue date:	February 21, 2011.
Maturity:	February 21, 2014.

---

[a] On the issue date, Beijing Capital Land was required to deposit into the interest reserve account RMB54.625 million, or the amount equivalent to the two coupon payments. The obligations of the issuer under the bonds and the trust deed and of the guarantor under the guarantee are secured by a fixed charge over the interest reserve account given by the issuer in favor of the trustee pursuant to the charge over account.

[b] Beijing Capital Land was unrated when it issued this dim sum bond; the company's subsequent bonds are rated Ba2/BB+ by Moody's/S&P.

VIGNETTE 6.6 CHINA SECURITIES REGULATORY COMMISSION (CSRC)

The CSRC was granted by China's Securities Law the authority to implement a centralized regulation on its securities market. The CSRC oversees China's centralized securities supervisory system, with the power to regulate and supervise securities issuers and to impose penalties for illegal activities related to securities and futures.

The functions of CSRC include:

- Formulation of policies, laws, and regulations for the securities and futures contracts.
- Oversight of the issuing, trading, custody, and settlement of equity shares, bonds, and investment funds.
- Supervision on the listing, trading, and settlement of securities and futures contracts.

BECL was listed on the Hong Kong Stock Exchange in June 2003 as an H-share company, that is, a company incorporated in China but listed in Hong Kong. Its controlling shareholder is Beijing Capital Group Ltd. (Capital Group), which controlled 47.34 percent of BECL's issued share capital. Capital Group is a state-owned company under the direct supervision of the Beijing municipal government and has played a significant role in the long-term development of Beijing.

BECL's H-share status has, to some extent, limited its access to offshore funding channels as funding exercise of China-incorporated entities requires approvals and notifications of regulatory bodies such as the China Securities Regulatory Commission (CSRC) and State Administration of Foreign Exchange (SAFE).[29] Specifically, any guarantee on offshore obligations by a China-incorporated entity must be approved by the SAFE. The approval process could be lengthy and subject to the vagaries of the regulatory environment.

6.8.3 Offer Structure

The dim sum bond was issued by BECL's wholly owned special purpose vehicle (SPV), BECL Investment Holding Ltd., which is incorporated in

---

[29] The regulatory functions of CSRC and SAFE are presented in Vignette 6.6 (this chapter) and in Vignette 2.1 (Chapter 2), respectively.

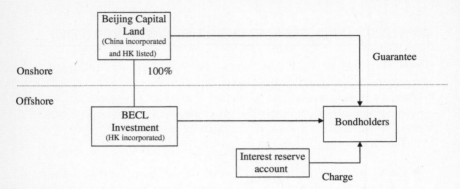

FIGURE 6.1   The offer structure of Beijing Capital Land's first dim sum bond

Hong Kong.[30] As such, a bond issued by an offshore SPV does not require approval from the Chinese regulatory bodies. However, since the SPV has no material operating assets and source of income, BECL, which owns the operating assets, has to provide guarantee to the principal repayment and interest payments of the issuer.

Since any guarantee of offshore obligations by a China-incorporated entity is subject to approval by the SAFE, BECL obtained the approval on December 2010 from the Beijing bureau of SAFE to guarantee the indebtedness of BECL Investment incurred outside China of up to US$200 million equivalent. The approval was granted by the Beijing bureau of SAFE pursuant to the "Notice on Issues relating to the Administration of Foreign Security by Domestic Institutions" promulgated by SAFE on July 30, 2010 (the SAFE Notice). With the SAFE approval, the guarantee was presumably enforceable under the PRC law. Additionally, the guarantee was approved on a rolling basis; that is, BECL can refinance this bond with the same guarantee structure without reapplying for the approval.

6.8.4 Major Risks of the Offer Structure

Given that the offshore guarantee structure is the first of its kind and the SAFE Notice is relatively new, the administration of the SAFE Notice is subject to policy discretion and hence the enforceability of the guarantee has not been tested. The uncertainties in the bond structure might probably explain why this offer structure had to be kicked off by a company with substantial backing, like state ownership.

---

[30] See Chapter 3, footnote 1, for the definition of a special purpose vehicle (SPV).

The approved guarantee will cover the principal repayment and interest payments up to US$200 million equivalent. However, if the RMB appreciates significantly during the tenor of the dim sum bond, the U.S. dollar equivalent of the principal repayment and interest payments could exceed US$200 million.

6.8.5 In the Wake of the Issue

In the wake of this issue, another H-share company, Guangzhou R&F Properties Co. Ltd., which is a privately owned property developer, issued a dual-tranche (dim sum and USD) offshore bond with a structure similar to that of BECL. However, partly because one of the key policy objectives of the Chinese government in the past years was to cool down the property market, the approval process for offshore guarantees for dim sum bonds as well as Asian USD bonds, especially those issued by property companies, had slowed down. As such, the debt capital market soon came up with a new bond offer structure, the "keepwell deed," to circumvent the approval requirements. Both BECL and Guangzhou R&F have subsequently tapped the dim sum bond market through the keepwell deed structure. We discuss the debut dim sum bond issue with this kind of innovative offer structure next.

6.9 CASE 8: THE FIRST PRC-LISTED (A-SHARE) ISSUER OF DIM SUM BONDS—GEMDALE CORPORATION

Gemdale Corporation is the first PRC-listed (A-share) issuer of dim sum bonds. Similar to the H-share issuers, A-share issuers have limited access to offshore funding. As such, Gemdale Corporation has used an innovative offer structure to circumvent the regulatory constraint on offshore funding, entailing the use of the "keepwell deed" in contrast to the offshore guarantee offer structure used by BECL.

6.9.1 General Bond Information

The general bond information on this landmark issue is summarized in Vignette 6.7.

6.9.2 Issuer Background

Established in 1988, Gemdale Corporation is a large-scale residential property developer in China. It is headquartered in Shenzhen, Guangdong province, and has built a significant presence in first-tier cities, such as Beijing,

VIGNETTE 6.7 SUMMARY TERMS OF GEMDALE CORPORATION'S FIRST DIM SUM BOND

Issuer:	Gemdale International Holding Ltd., incorporated in Hong Kong and wholly owned by Gemdale Corporation.
Credit enhancement:	Guarantee from Famous Commercial Ltd. (a wholly owned subsidiary of Gemdale Corp.) and several of its subsidiaries, keep-well deed, and deed of equity interest purchase undertaking.
Issue size:	RMB1.2 billion.
Coupon:	9.15 percent
Ranking:	Senior and secured with charge on the interest reserve account.[a]
Covenants:	Maintain total equity of not less than HKD100 million. No standard high-yield covenant.
Rating:	Ba3/BB–.
Issue date:	July 26, 2012.
Maturity:	July 26, 2015.

[a] 2x interest payments. First priority fixed charge over interest reserve account in favor of bondholders.

Shanghai, Shenzhen, and Guangzhou and second tier-cities, such as Tianjin, Ningbo, Nanjing, Hangzhou, Zhuhai, Changsha, Changzhou, and Dalian. Gemdale has been listed in the Shanghai Stock Exchange since April 2001. It is one of the largest A-share property developers by market capitalization. It was founded by Shenzhen Futian Investment & Development, which is wholly owned by the government of the Futian district in Shenzhen and under the supervision of the Shenzhen State-Owned Assets Supervision and Administration Commission.

As a Chinese company listed on a domestic PRC stock exchange, Gemdale's access to offshore funding is limited as compared with non-China-incorporated counterparts. Funding exercises of China-incorporated entities require approvals and notifications of the regulatory bodies, such as the CSRC and SAFE. The approval process could be lengthy and subject to the vagaries of the regulatory environment. Gemdale's debut dim sum bond issue of July 2012 has an offer structure with the "keepwell deed" and "deed of equity interest purchase undertaking," allowing the company to have access to the debt capital market without prior regulatory approval, unlike the case of BECL's debut dim sum bond issue for which BECL had obtained prior approval from the SAFE for providing an offshore guarantee. Regulatory approval for Gemdale's issue will be required only when events of default trigger the execution of the keepwell deed and the deed of equity interest purchase undertaking.

6.9.3 Offer Structure: Guarantees from Famous and Several of Its Subsidiaries

The bond is guaranteed by Famous Commercial Ltd. (Famous), a wholly owned subsidiary of Gemdale Corporation, and several of Famous's subsidiaries (subsidiary guarantors) that own 100 percent stakes of the onshore project companies in Foshan and Shenyang, China. Since Famous and subsidiary guarantors are incorporated in Hong Kong, they do not need approval from the Chinese regulatory bodies for providing guarantee for Gemdale's offshore bond issue.

6.9.3.1 Keepwell Deed Gemdale entered into a keepwell deed in connection with the dim sum bond issue. Upon the occurrence of an event of default, Gemdale will make sufficient funds available to Famous under the keepwell

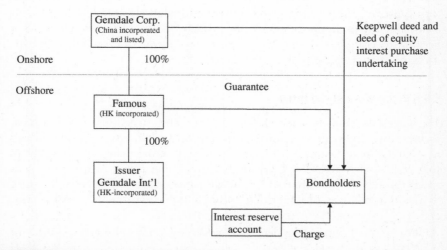

FIGURE 6.2 The offer structure of Gemdale Corporation's dim sum bond

deed. Although the keepwell deed is not a guarantee, Gemdale is legally obligated to provide sufficient funds to Famous to help avoid bankruptcy proceedings. If Gemdale has to remit funds offshore to fulfill its commitments under the keepwell deed, it will have to obtain prior consent or approval from authorities, including the National Development and Reform Commission (NDRC), Ministry of Commerce (MOFCOM), and SAFE.[31]

6.9.3.2 Deed of Equity Interest Purchase Undertaking   In addition to the keepwell deed, Gemdale had entered into a legally binding deed of equity interest purchase undertaking, under which Gemdale agreed to acquire from the offshore subsidiaries of Famous the equity interests in certain China-incorporated subsidiaries at a purchase price not lower than the amount sufficient to cover the principal and accrued interest obligations should an event of default occur. In other words, Gemdale was committed to inject sufficient money into Famous, the guarantor, to cover the principal and accrued interests in case of default. That said, Gemdale would need to obtain approval from the MOFCOM and SAFE and registration with the State Administration for Industry and Commerce (SAIC) as well as other necessary tax clearance prior to the completion of the equity acquisition.

6.9.4 Risks of the Offer Structure

The keepwell deed is not a guarantee. Gemdale is not obliged to assume payment obligations. However, the risk is somewhat mitigated by the deed of equity interest purchase undertaking, which is legally binding. However, enforcement of this undertaking deed is subject to various rounds of regulatory approval, authorization, and consent and is largely untested. If Gemdale is not able to obtain the necessary approvals from the authorities, it may not be able to complete the equity interest acquisition as required under the deed of equity interest purchase undertaking.

6.9.5 In the Wake of the Issue

The Gemdale issue has established a new offer structure for the China-incorporated companies to tap the offshore debt capital markets. In addition to Gemdale's subsequent USD and dim sum bond issues respectively in July 2012 and March 2013, Guangzhou R&F and BECL, which previously issued through the provision of offshore guarantees, have also successfully issued dim sum bonds with the keepwell and equity interest purchase undertaking

---

[31] Please refer to Chapter 2 for detailed discussion on credit enhancement, including keepwell deeds.

deeds. In addition, Gemdale presented its financial information in the bond offering circular in accordance with the PRC generally accepted accounting principles (PRC GAAP), instead of the International Financial Reporting Standards (IFRS) with which international investors are familiar. The success of the Gemdale issue has shown that international investors are willing to accept financial disclosure based on the PRC GAAP. This has paved the way for PRC-listed entities to tap the offshore RMB-denominated bond market without the necessity to go through the time-consuming procedure to prepare another set of financial information under IFRS for international investors.

6.10 CONCLUSION

In this chapter, we illustrate and analyze eight landmark dim sum bonds issued by different types of issuers. These historic cases illustrate the historical development of this emerging market and signal trends of market development. We demonstrate the flexibility of these bond issuers that capitalize on the domestic market impediments of regulated interest rates, and how the issuing firms rode with the underlying currency appreciation trend of the RMB during the period 2007–2012. In other words, all issuing firms exploited the lower funding cost in the offshore dim sum bond market as compared to the onshore funding cost and other impediments such as regulatory restrictions. We also present two landmark issues with special structural credit enhancements. This information helps prospective issuers and investors understand the risk and return of dim sum bonds.

These landmark cases highlight areas for future development and opportunities that requires closer examination. Chinese policymakers who want to further strengthen the market potential may want to consider the implications of these landmark cases we describe in this chapter. A good understanding of the implied exchange rate risk, the interest rate differential between the domestic market and offshore markets, and the subtle nature of credit risk as perceived by investors in the debt capital market has tremendous implications for the continued growth of the dim sum bond market.

REFERENCES

Bank of International Settlement. 2006. "Asian Bond Markets: Issues and Prospects." BIS working paper, No. 30. Retrieved from www.bis.org/arp/conf_0403.pdf
China Development Bank. 2013. *Annual Report 2012.*
Ebias, Jun. 2012. "Dim Sum Needs a Push to Lengthen Maturities." *Euroweek— Offshore RMB Market: A Maturing Global Market,* 26–27.

Ferri, Michael G., Timothy F. Sugrue, and Jot Yau. 1991. "Differential Market Reaction to Eurobond Financing." *Global Finance Journal*, Spring/Summer: 1–10.

Flood, Mark D. 1991. "An Introduction to Complete Markets." *Review*, Federal Reserve Bank of St. Louis, March/April.

Forsythe, Michael, and Henry Sanderson. 2011. "China Inc.'s Banker." *Bloomberg Markets*, June: 83–88.

Fung, Hung-Gay, and Jot Yau. 2011. "Chinese Offshore RMB Currency and Bond Markets: The Role of Hong Kong." *China and World Economy* 20(3): 1–16.

Lee, Hei Wai, Yan Alice Xie, and Jot Yau. "The Impact of Sovereign Risk on Bond Duration: Evidence from Asian Sovereign Bond Markets." *International Review of Economics and Finance* 20(3): 441–451.

"Sinotruk Leads the Red-Chip Way to Hong Kong." 2010. *IFR Asia* 672, October 30.

Wee, Denise. 2012. "Dim Sum Bonds for CDB and Sinotruk Reflect Investor Favouritism." *FinanceAsia*. Retrieved from www.financeasia.com/News/310113, dim-sum-bonds-for-cdb-and-sinotruk-reflect-investorfavouritism.aspx? eid=11&edate=20120731&utm_source=20120731&utm_medium= newsletter&utm_campaign=daily_newsletter

Yau, Jot. 1994. "Asian Development Bank," in *Great Events from History II: Business and Commerce*. Pasadena, CA: Salem Press. (Republished in *Chronology of Twentieth Century History: Business and Commerce*, F. N. Magill (ed.). London: Fitzroy Dearborn Publishers, 1996.)

CHAPTER 7

Conclusion

The Hong Kong dim sum bond market is a nascent offshore RMB debt capital market outside mainland China that has experienced a phenomenal growth. As the first offshore market for RMB-denominated capital assets, it has and will continue to play a pivotal role in the internationalization of the RMB. Although recently there have been some offshore RMB activities in London, Taiwan,[1] and Singapore, the Hong Kong dim sum bond market still leads the way as the primary offshore RMB bond market.

In this book, we presented the development, opportunities, and challenges of this nascent Asian debt capital market from several vantage points of view. We analyzed the market's supply from the issuer's perspective, demand from the investor's perspective, and development from the Chinese government's and investment bankers' perspective. We envisage the market will continue to grow with challenges along the way. In this final chapter, we conclude by discussing the opportunities and challenges that confront the various dim sum bond market participants. In our opinion, the prospects of the dim sum bond market remain "cautiously optimistic."

7.1 REVIEW AND PREVIEW OF THE DEVELOPMENT AND GROWTH OF THE DIM SUM BOND MARKET

In Chapter 1, we discussed and presented the various policies of the Chinese government that helped establish and promote the first offshore renminbi (RMB) bond market, that is, the dim sum bond market. We also described developments in various offshore RMB markets, such as the currency, currency swap, and deposit markets. In summary, we find that the phenomenal growth of the dim sum bond market has been fostered by several factors. First, relentless efforts made by the Chinese government in terms of continual

---

[1] See A. Wong (2013).

policy changes geared toward promoting the use of RMB outside mainland China and favoring Hong Kong as the primary offshore RMB market have been instrumental to the development and growth of the dim sum bond market. As the Chinese government vies to gain global reserve currency status for the RMB, the dim sum bond market is part of the grand scheme to help internationalize RMB, including establishing the offshore RMB (CNH) deposit and currency swap markets and RMB currency trading centers, among others. Second, the 2007–2008 global financial crisis and the European crisis gave significant impetus to the growth of the dim sum bond market as global investors were turned away from the U.S. and European markets looking for viable alternatives in Asia. China has remained one of the few major markets that still display some growth momentum amid the global economic slowdown; dim sum bonds appear to be an appropriate candidate for investment that came into being at the opportune time.

In 2012, the RMB appreciation against the U.S. dollar slowed down after a 30 percent rise in value since 2005 when the Chinese central bank ended the peg to the U.S. dollar. Now that the RMB appreciation is no longer taken for granted, institutional investors, including insurance companies, asset managers, and investment banks, need to work hard to look for potential value and growth opportunity in this six-year-old market, a much-needed step to reflect that the market is growing toward maturity. In contrast to the past, when dim sum bonds mostly appealed to retail investors for higher returns as a one-way bet on currency appreciation, the slowdown of the RMB appreciation requires dim sum bonds to offer something more and valuable to investors, who are now demanding quality, flexibility, and higher return in the bonds.

Given China's national policy on the internationalization of the RMB and liberalization of cross-border RMB transactions between the mainland and Hong Kong as well as the adoption of RMB as the trade settlement currency, the use of RMB-denomination in new financial products, dim sum bonds as collateral in the repo market, and the growing size in the offshore RMB (CNH) deposits in Hong Kong, it is reasonable to expect a sustainable upward trajectory in the growth of the dim sum bond market. We believe this market will gradually develop into a mature debt capital market in Asia.

Participants in this market, including investors, issuers, the Chinese government, and investment bankers, will keep playing different roles in the future development of the market. In previous chapters, we presented the perspectives of major participants, who help drive the development of the dim sum bond market. There are, however, pending issues as to how and under what situations that the dim sum bond market will sustain its trajectory of growth over time. For example, is the growth of the dim sum bond market secular and sustainable? What needs to take place to ensure dim sum bonds would develop into an acceptable asset class going forward? What should participants be concerned about this market, knowing that there are many challenges ahead of them? Would these challenges be a catalyst or an inhibitor to the development of the dim sum bond market? Would other financial centers such as Taiwan, Singapore, and London compete with Hong Kong? These are some of the issues concerning investors, issuers, investment bankers, regulators, and policymakers that we explore in this concluding chapter.

7.1.1 Market Prospects and Outlook

As mentioned earlier, the prospects of the dim sum bond market remain "cautiously optimistic." While there are favorable underlying factors that will help this market grow, its future depends very much on the Chinese government policy changes in response to changes in the global economy and other noneconomic factors.

First of all, the growth momentum in the offshore RMB (CNH) market will continue because of China's relentless efforts to internationalize the RMB under its policy of making the RMB a global reserve currency. RMB cross-border settlement will therefore continue to expand to more countries as China promotes the use of RMB for trade settlement, leading to a rise in the offshore RMB deposit base and ongoing demand for investment options. Thus, the dim sum bond market will continue to grow as long as the offshore RMB (CNH) pool is growing. In the case where sufficient RMB investment options becomes available, dim sum bonds will just have a smaller market share of the growing CNH pool.

Market developments may bring the supply and demand for dim sum bonds out of balance. For example, the recent approval by the National Development and Reform Commission (NDRC) for Guangdong Nuclear Power Group to borrow RMB3 billion directly from an offshore bank, Bank of China (Hong Kong) (BOCHK), suggests that the offshore RMB deposit pool in Hong Kong can be drained rather quickly by a change in policy. This may easily balance out the excess supply of offshore RMB deposits relative to available investment options that absorb the offshore RMB deposits.

Second, a change in the policy regarding the Renminbi Qualified Foreign Institutional Investor (RQFII) program may disrupt the balance in the offshore RMB markets. Under the RQFII program, the RMB funds raised in Hong Kong can be invested in the mainland securities market.[2] The RQFII program will certainly expand the investment channels for RMB funds raised in Hong Kong, and the approved quota for the program has been increasing

---

[2] For the difference between RQFII and QFII programs, see Chapter 1, section 1.3.4.2.

to keep up with the demand of the market.[3] The program was first opened to domestic fund managers familiar with the A-share market and securities companies' subsidiaries in Hong Kong. Although at present the program is available only to approved institutions in Hong Kong and one institution in the United Kingdom, the plan will expand to Singapore, Taiwan, and other locations. This is part of the strategy for internationalizing the RMB and will challenge Hong Kong's position as the primary offshore RMB center. Offshore RMB funds that could have been invested in dim sum bonds can be invested in the mainland China's stock market, diverting the offshore RMB funds away from the dim sum bond market. Nonetheless, we expect the dim sum bond market and CNH pool to continue to grow, but dim sum bonds will likely have a lower share of the growing CNH pool. We also expect that Hong Kong can leverage on its "first-mover advantage" to maintain its position as a leading offshore RMB center, taking a cue from the fact that Hong Kong's stock market remains the exchange listing of choice for Chinese corporations, despite the fact that they can list their shares in other financial centers such as London, New York, and Singapore. One way for Hong Kong to cement its position is to work more closely with foreign firms and governments to initiate new types of landmark dim sum bonds or to make wider use of dim sum bonds by the investment community including the use as collateral.

Third, recent developments of dim sum bond funds will further promote the dim sum bond market. Guggenheim, which has assets exceeding $119 billion (as of September 22, 2011), launched the Guggenheim Yuan Bond ETF, a fund that provides access to the dim sum bond market. This move signals that there is opportunity to benefit from the appreciation potential of the RMB. Another example is the PowerShares Chinese Yuan Dim Sum Bond Portfolio, which is an ETF based on the Citigroup Dim Sum (Offshore CNY) Bond Index.[4] The fund normally invests at least 90 percent of its total assets in dim sum bonds that comprise the index. Moreover, Blackrock, Inc., Van Eck Global, and Invesco Ltd. have launched mutual funds or exchange-traded derivatives targeting investors looking for exposure to dim sum bonds.

---

[3] At the time of this writing, the QFII quota has increased to US$150 billion, while the RQFII quota stands at RMB270 billion (US$44 billion) (Tan, 2013).

[4] The Citigroup Dim Sum Bond Index includes fixed-rate securities issued by governments, agencies, supranationals, and corporations. Bonds must have a minimum of one-year maturity, fixed-coupon bonds (no zero coupon), and no minimum rating, and bonds must have RMB1 billion outstanding. The index is based on market capitalization and updated monthly.

Finally, currency exposure to RMB gained through dim sum bonds may act as a complement to a stock, bond, and/or cash portfolio, broadening overall portfolio diversification (see Chapter 4, section 4.2.3). Foreign companies are also allowed to issue shares denominated in RMB, thus broadening the scope of offerings in financial products in the Chinese stock market. For instance, Pharo Management, the US$4 billion global macro hedge fund manager headquartered in London, became the first hedge fund manager to offer US$500 million worth of shares in its investment vehicles denominated in RMB. This share offering was targeted at both mainland and Hong Kong-based Chinese investors and non-Chinese investors.[5] In addition, in April 2011, Hui Xian Real Estate Investment Trust, a subsidiary of a Hong Kong's major property developer, Cheung Kong Holdings, was the first company listing an RMB-based financial product in Hong Kong and outside the mainland China. In October 2012, Hong Kong–listed Hopewell Highway Infrastructure, which was also the first Hong Kong–listed company to issue a corporate dim sum bond in June 2010, became the first company to adopt a dual-currency regime for its shares that trade in Hong Kong dollars and offshore RMB (CNH). Under the dual-currency regime, investors who own the company's Hong Kong dollar-denominated shares are able to convert them into offshore RMB-denominated shares and vice versa.[6]

A tightened onshore credit environment and a low offshore interest rate regime could support a steady growth of the dim sum bond market.[7] We believe it is the objective of the Chinese government policy to encourage mainland companies and banks to issue dim sum bonds as the Chinese government sees the development of the dim sum bond market an important step toward the internationalization of the RMB. Additionally, the development of the dim sum market will also help avoid the systemic risk resulting from the concentrated credit risk in the Chinese banking sector.

7.1.2 Debt Maturity Profile and the Pipeline of Supply of Dim Sum Bonds

One major determinant of the growth of the dim sum bond market is the future supply of dim sum bonds in the pipeline. Should we be able to forecast the supply of dim sum bonds, we can have a better prediction on the future of the dim sum bond market. However, we are by no means be able to accurately forecast the supply of new dim sum bonds as we have learned from experience that there are too many moving parts in the bond supply,

---

[5] See *Financial Times*, January 14, 2011, p. 21.
[6] See Jönsson (2012).
[7] See Davis (2012a).

especially in Asia. In the Asian debt capital markets, the vast majority of new bond issuances are for expansion, which is a discretionary capital investment in contrast to refinancing, which is mandatory. The supply of new debt issues in the Asian debt capital markets will therefore be less dependent on the "rigid supply" from issuers with refinancing requirements, but more on issuers with discretionary expansion plans. As such, the supply of new dim sum bonds is more a function of the macroeconomic environment (e.g., the interest rate), onshore liquidity, and regulatory environment, among other factors. Thus, issuers in Asian debt capital markets can afford to be more cost sensitive. A greater supply of new bonds will come to the market if the market backdrop is strong, the funding cost is low, and regulations are loosened.

Although forecasting the supply is difficult in the dim sum bond market, we look at the debt maturity profile for clues on the potential supply of dim sum bonds in the future. Figure 7.1 depicts the RMB amount and number of dim sum bonds maturing in the future as at the end of 2012, suggesting an estimated potential supply of new dim sum bond issuance if the maturing dim sum bonds are being refinanced. As shown in Table 7.1, RMB118.59 billion, RMB93.30 billion, and RMB58.05 billion worth of dim sum bonds will mature in 2013, 2014, and 2015, respectively. They represent 42.91 percent (342), 16.06 percent (128), and 10.41 percent (83) of the issues for 2013, 2014, and 2015, respectively. Thus, if issuers decide to refinance their maturing dim sum bonds, the next few of years would be quite busy for the dim sum bond market, particularly the short-term CDs, majority of which are from Chinese banks. The wave of new CD issuance resulting from rollovers is likely to create a pricing benchmark for future dim sum bond issues, fueling

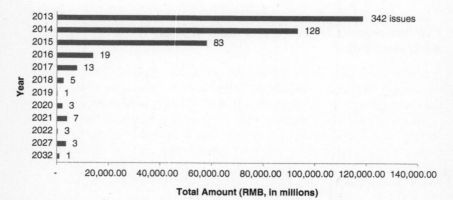

FIGURE 7.1   Maturity profile of dim sum bonds (as of the end of 2012)

TABLE 7.1   Maturing Dim Sum Bonds by Year (as of the end of 2012)

Year	No. of Issues	Market Share (%)	Total Amt RMB (Mln)	Market Share (%)	Average Coupon (%)	Average Tenor (Years)
2013	342	42.91	118,586.85	29.53	2.73	1.14
2014	128	16.06	93,301.00	23.24	3.46	2.55
2015	83	10.41	58,051.00	14.46	4.04	3.04
2016	19	2.38	14,006.50	3.49	3.16	5.00
2017	13	1.63	7,770.00	1.94	3.96	5.00
2018	5	0.63	2,520.00	0.63	3.84	6.72
2019	1	0.13	200.00	0.05	4.20	7.00
2020	3	0.38	2,111.55	0.53	3.27	9.08
2021	7	0.88	3,930.00	0.98	4.25	9.86
2022	3	0.38	350.00	0.09	4.26	10.00
2027	3	0.38	3,500.00	0.87	4.18	15.00
2032	1	0.13	1,000.00	0.25	4.30	20.00
Outstanding Subtotal	608	76.29	305,326.90	76.04	3.15	2.24
Matured	189	23.71	96,190.00	23.96	1.54	1.18
Total/ Wt.Avg.	797	100.00	401,516.90	100.00	2.77	1.99

more capital market activity in the offshore market. Given the anticipated sizable volume of CDs issuance, this could act as an alternative benchmark rate for dim sums bonds rather than offshore China government bonds.[8] While we expect an increase in the dim sum bond issuance driven by financial institutions' rollovers of maturing bonds, issuance by corporations, quasi-sovereign entities and supranational agencies may decline because of lower dim sum bond yields as compared to Asian USD bonds, broader emerging market risk aversion, and higher onshore deposit rates in China.

Offshore RMB bonds are likely to grow in popularity due to the increasing acceptance of offshore RMB usage, including the settlement of international trade obligations, and such usage has been facilitated by the corresponding development of financial infrastructure for offshore RMB in Hong Kong.

---

[8] See C. M. Wong (2013b).

In contrast to the thriving dim sum bond market, two other offshore RMB markets are doomed to disappear—in fact, one of them has already disappeared. The one that has come and gone is the synthetic RMB bond market.[9] Since investors can obtain offshore RMB (CNH) directly to take advantage of the RMB appreciation, the synthetic RMB bonds have lost their appeal as the only option for fixed income investors to play directly on RMB appreciation. Synthetic RMB bonds have since been phased out as dim sum bonds become the prevalent choice.

The second market that may be adversely affected and disappearing is the market for the nondelivery RMB forward (NDF) contracts traded in Hong Kong and Singapore, which have been a popular hedging instrument for the RMB.[10] The NDF market was built on the premise that the RMB is not convertible. As RMB becomes more widely used and easily accessible, and other substitutes such as the RMB futures contracts become available,[11] the NDF market is likely to disappear.

7.2 MARKET PARTICIPANTS

In previous chapters, we presented the attributes of the dim sum bond market by way of the discussion of the perspectives of the players on the dim sum bond market. Issuers provide the supply of dim sum bonds to the market, whereas investors provide the demand for these bonds. Issuers are expected to be driven by the incentive to take advantage of cheaper funding costs (e.g., the lower coupon for dim sum bonds compared to straight Asian USD bonds), while investors are expected to focus more on the credit quality of dim sum bonds in light of slowing down in the RMB appreciation. Issuers need to comply with what investors are asking for, and in particular, they are seeking credit ratings on bond issues and better creditor protection.[12] Investors' appetite for RMB-appreciation betting positions is also expected to slow down against the backdrop of a waning Chinese economy. Investment banks playing the intermediation role and matching the issuer and investor interests within the rules set by the Chinese government are in general enthusiastic in seeing the dim sum bond market flourish as it will provide a variety of RMB-denominated investment products to increase transaction flows in the market. The Chinese government has been doing everything necessary to help promote the dim sum bond market favoring Hong Kong

---

[9] See Chapter 2, section 2.1.2.
[10] See Fung, Leung, and Zhu (2004).
[11] See Ferguson (2012).
[12] See Fung, Tzau, and Yau (2013).

in every aspect of the policy implementation in light of the grand scheme of internationalizing the RMB.

7.2.1 Issuers

Credit quality has become an increasingly important consideration in issuing and pricing dim sum bonds. In particular, if the bonds received quality ratings from credit rating agencies, they will clearly add appeal to investors. However, the challenge is that investors in the dim sum bond market have not been very discriminating in bond pricing according to the bond's credit risk. Particularly for well-known Chinese issuers, such as BOC and CCB, their investor base is local investors who have not been concerned about credit ratings. In other words, investors tend to ask for the same yield without differentiating the credit quality of bonds. Some issuers, for example, Germany's Landesbank Baden-Württemberg, lament that they pay a higher yield for the bank's credit quality, which is undifferentiating from other lower quality issuers.[13] In the future, issuers of dim sum bonds are likely to add more protection to their bonds to attract investors as waning RMB appreciation expectations weigh on sales. Issuers have already started to include keepwell and EIPU deeds in place of guarantees as we discussed in Chapter 6. In addition to performing an important role to enhance bond protection, these deeds enable the issuer to get around regulations that hinder the timely issuance of dim sum bonds.

Although it has been widening in terms of credit spectrum, the dim sum bond market is still constrained in terms of tenors. There are a handful of long-dated bonds from China's Ministry of Finance (MOF), but long-dated bonds are still rare as compared to the latent demand from investors that are looking at the dim sum bond market as a currency play for a longer horizon (see Chapter 2, section 2.2.4). The supply of dim sum bonds with longer tenors is expected to rise as both policy banks and corporates continue to show interest in the market, helping to develop the yield curve beyond five years.[14]

Some issuers that have found difficulty in obtaining onshore financing, for example, major property developers in China mainly fund their land acquisitions with offshore funding, are particularly interested in tapping the market for larger and longer-tenor deals. For seasoned issuers who come to the dim sum bond market for refinancing, we expect to see larger deals as they have become better known to investors in this market, for example, foreign multinational (MNC) issuers that come back for the second time.

---

[13] See Chatterjee (2013).

[14] See C.M. Wong (2013a).

As the market begins to mature, we expect the average size of dim sum bond deals to get larger over time, approaching those of Asian USD bonds.

Currently, the majority of the issuers are Chinese banks and state-owned enterprises (SOEs), and Hong Kong and foreign corporations, including many MNCs (see Chapter 3, section 3.2). The profile of issuers has become more diverse than before. For example, the dim sum bond market has attracted Chinese regional and municipal SOEs that have found themselves squeezed out of the onshore market by firms with closer links to central government.[15] More foreign corporations and supranational agencies, as well as sovereign and subsovereign entities from different geographical regions, have started to join the rank of issuers. For example, the province of British Columbia in Canada was poised to be the first foreign subsovereign issuer of a dim sum bond for at least RMB500 million. Despite British Columbia's failed attempt, the dim sum bond market has raised international awareness, opening the door for more to follow.[16] Likewise, in terms of industry, issuers now come from a more diverse industry background (see Chapter 3, section 3.3). As the dim sum bond market matures over time, issuers can also first issue dim sum bonds and swap them to other currencies (such as the U.S. dollar). The higher the CNH cross-currency swap rate, the better opportunity issuers would look to raise money via the dim sum bond market. During the term of the swap, it will receive the CNH swap rate and pay U.S. dollar London Interbank Offered Rate (LIBOR) to the swap counterparty. The total cost of funding, of course, also depends on the coupon level that an issuer promises to give to the investor. Foreign issuers are concerned about swap liquidity since they swap back to other currencies, for they do not have onshore demand for the RMB.

Last, but not least, from the issuer perspective, will the dim sum bond market be a sustainable alternative market for raising capital? The answer to this question depends very much on market risks, and the risk of future changes in the direction of government policy, which we discuss in section 7.2.4.

Regarding risks, existing and potential issuers are concerned about the following specific risks. First, issuers in the dim sum bond market will face more refinancing pressure given the short tenor of dim sum bonds and a small investor base that may not have many long-term investors. Second, for foreign issuers that have a genuine need for onshore liquidity for their operations, the transparency and certainty of the approval process for remitting the money onshore has been their concern that holds them back.

---

[15] See Walker (2013).

[16] See Davis (2012b). At the time of this writing, the deal slated for the first quarter of 2013 was postponed due to unfavorable economics.

Issuers are concerned about changes in the cross-border remittance policy. In general, they are quite confident that they can send U.S. dollars onshore under the U.S. dollar offshore borrowing quota—the quota system in the form of intercompany loans. However, they are not sure whether they can remit the offshore RMB onshore under the "offshore borrowing quota," since the quota is small compared to that of the U.S. dollar. Some find that it is equally difficult to move the funds (U.S. dollar or RMB) onshore since typically any remittance into China is subject to a case-by-case basis approval. We believe that more clear-cut and simplified policies for the remittance of RMB funds into mainland China from the dim sum bond market in Hong Kong will help address this concern.

7.2.2 Investors

Since the inception of the dim sum bonds, some investors are eager to invest in these bonds without rigorously differentiating the credit quality of issuers and the bond structure as most of these bonds are short-term bonds and these investors focused on the RMB appreciation potential. They were willing to tolerate lower coupons at the beginning since they invested in dim sum bonds primarily as a one-way bet on currency appreciation. However, as the Chinese currency's appreciation slows down, credit profiles of issuers are more diverse, and the average duration of the dim sum bonds becomes longer, investors become more selective about the credit quality of the bonds. Investors have started to compare yields of different credits and demand a higher yield on those names with lower credit quality. For instance, HSBC data show that high yield and nonrated corporate dim sum bonds were yielding around 6 percent versus 3 percent for Chinese government bonds as at the end of October 2012.[17]

Institutional investors are attracted to the dim sum bond market as they can bet on a broader array of issuers with diversity in yields based on credit fundamentals. That is, investors will look for better credit ratings from agencies to ensure proper information on the bonds or higher yield for lower quality bonds. If there are sufficient interests from institutional investors in building up dim sum bond ETFs, the breadth of the market will grow, the investor base will expand, and the growth of dim sum bond market will sustain in the long run.

The important element for market sustainability is the long-term interest in the market. That is, issuers and investors must rationalize the dim sum bond pricing and valuation in a logical manner. Valuation of the bonds must be based on risk and return, rather than on herd and spontaneous

---

[17] See Ho (2012).

reaction on the bond behavior. A relatively large-sized market can provide stability in the trading volume and liquidity, which is critical to the proper valuation of the bonds. Poor liquidity is the biggest concern for dim sum bond investors; it is quite challenging to actually invest in the market if the liquidity is not there. The increase in market size has led to more brokers participating, and dealing sizes have also increased (from RMB15 million to RMB25 million).[18] Pundits however point out that it is important not to exaggerate the significance of the dim sum bond market since it is relative small as compared to since the domestic onshore corporate bond market is between RMB5 trillion and RMB6 trillion.[19]

Some of the traditional buyers of long bonds such as the pension funds and insurance companies are also not active in the dim sum bond market (see Chapter 4, section 4.1). This is because insurance companies do not write policies in offshore RMB, and pension savings are not yet denominated in offshore RMB, so there is no real demand for ultra-long-dated dim sum bonds from these types of investors.[20] At the time of writing, a potentially large and important group of long-term investors has just emerged— the central banks. For example, the Reserve Bank of Australia announced that it plans to invest 5 percent of its total foreign currency assets in Chinese sovereign bonds, making the currency its fifth-largest reserve currency after the U.S. dollar, euro, Japanese yen, and Canadian dollar.[21] This group of investors is exactly the target investors that the Chinese government aims to pursue in the policy of making the RMB a global reserve currency.

7.2.3 Investment Banks

Compared with other financial instruments, investment bankers do not receive hefty fees for the dim sum bond issuance because the issuing size of the dim sum bond is relatively small. A pertinent question is whether the dim sum bond market will soon become a lucrative market, which is largely dependent on the macroeconomic and market conditions affecting the supply and demand of dim sum bonds. Investment banks have recently created transactions that stimulate growth of the dim sum bond market by providing a swap market for the existing and future dim sum bonds.

The creation of a swap market is of interest and its importance can be illustrated with several cases. First, ANZ Banking Group issued an RMB1 billion dim sum bond, which yielded 2.9 percent, and swapped to LIBOR

---

[18] See Walker (2013).
[19] Ibid.
[20] See Wee (2013).
[21] See Li and Wang (2013).

plus 90 basis points in early August, 2012.[22] Second, Hyundai Capital of Korea was in the market with an 18-month senior unsecured dim sum bond of RMB500 million ($78 million) that offered a yield of 3.45 percent. It swapped the proceeds first to three-month LIBOR plus 105 bp in U.S. dollars and then to 3 percent in Korean won. Third, IFC, a member of the World Bank group, also closed a RMB500 million two-year SEC-exempt global bond and swapped the proceeds to U.S. dollars. The coupon was fixed at 1.875 percent and the notes reoffered at 99.854 to yield 1.95 percent, which was deemed to be very tight pricing for the bonds that could have been taken by the bank.

In addition, investment banks need to provide and develop more derivative products on the dim sum bonds including new ETFs and swap options on dim sum bonds and credit default swaps. After the swap market emerges, the creation of swaptions in the dim sum bonds market will provide a special feature that has yet to develop.

7.2.4 Chinese Government and Its Policy

Continued support by the Chinese government in terms of favorable policy stance would help the dim sum bond market continue to grow. Several policy and regulation areas relating to dim sum bonds warrant attention from the government.

First, making dim sum bonds as widely acceptable collateral in the Asian repo market[23] will help expand the investor base considerably. Such a move will endorse the willingness of banks, prime brokers, and other financial intermediaries in the region to accept dim sum bonds to support their short-term funding needs. In fact, in June 2012, the HKMA launched a tri-party cross-border collateral management platform in conjunction with JPMorgan and Euroclear, and in August, 2012, a Hong Kong dollar tri-party repo deal was done between BOCHK and Barclays Bank. The early use of dim sum bonds and other local securities as collateral for cross-border repurchase agreements indicates a good prospect that Asia's repo market will likely develop. At least two other repo deals would be done on the HKMA tri-party collateral management platform by the end of 2012: one involving the borrowing of CNH-denominated funding, and the other involving the pledging of dim sum bonds as collateral for funding in another currency.

Second, encouraging the use of RMB as collateral for margin trading across the world will increase investors' willingness to hold the RMB. *Financial Times* reported that the CME Group, the world's largest futures

---

[22] See Wee (2012).
[23] See Lee (2012).

exchange, would allow international investors to use the RMB (including RMB deposits in Hong Kong or other financial centers outside mainland China) as collateral for margin trading in all its futures products up to US$100 million effective January 2012.[24] This move by the CME group clearly recognizes the wider use of RMB, a significant step toward the success of internationalizing RMB. If other markets similarly use RMB bonds as collateral, it clearly suggests that the dim sum bond market will continue to flourish.

Third, encouraging other sovereign governments, especially governments of Asian countries that have significant trade relationships with China, to issue sovereign dim sum bonds will make this market more vibrant.[25] As mentioned above in section 7.2.1, there are foreign sovereign and sub-sovereign issuers which have shown interests and explored the opportunity in the dim sum bond market. Sovereign issuers would add a lot of market clout to this nascent market and they would open the door for more to follow. Moreover, if the Chinese banks can encourage issuers of dim sum bonds to swap into Asian sovereign bonds, the dim sum bond market will expand even more.

Fourth, further expanding the geographical coverage of RMB trade settlement will increase the worldwide use of RMB. Currently, about 12 percent of China's total trade is settled in RMB. Different incentive schemes will be helpful to this end, for example, the Chinese government may provide rebates or tax break for exporters or importers who would use RMB in trade settlement. Recently, a discussion on the bilateral local currency swap agreement between China and France was held. France leads the Eurozone in offshore RMB payments. France is ranked fourth in the world in terms of the value of offshore RMB payments—excluding Hong Kong and the mainland, trailing behind the United Kingdom, Singapore, and Taiwan, according to SWIFT.[26] Prior to this, China had signed a three-year bilateral local currency swap agreement with the United Kingdom's Bank of England in March 2013.

Fifth, developing multiple hubs without letting one particular center winning business at the expense of the other in its effort to internationalize the RMB will promote cooperation rather than competition between offshore RMB hubs. There is a general recognition that a new offshore RMB center or hub means more liquidity, more trading, and more internationalization, which is to the benefit of everyone trying to develop an offshore

---

[24] See Cookson (2011).

[25] Foreign governments have issued USD bonds to raise capital before. Therefore, it is conceivable that other Asian governments can issue bonds in renminbi.

[26] See Li and Wang (2013). SWIFT is the Society for Worldwide Interbank Financial Telecommunication, a member-owned cooperative.

RMB market. Several developments related to offshore RMB markets across financial centers (London, Taiwan, Singapore, and Paris) may pose potential threats to the Hong Kong dim sum bond market. These cities are potential competitors to Hong Kong's dim sum bond markets but at the same time, they are rivalries to each other, especially between London and Paris for the business in Europe, and Taiwan and Singapore in Asia.

London, a potential offshore RMB bond center after Hong Kong, can tap business in European countries. The London market is still in the very early stage of development, but if it grows quickly to capture the needs of RMB in Europe, it will certainly pose a threat to the Hong Kong's dim sum bond market as well as to Paris, a long time rivalry. London has started early and in fact jump-started with a dim sum bond issued and settled in London without the explicit blessing of the Chinese government. Paris has come lately in the race for being the offshore RMB bond hub in the Eurozone, challenging the position of London. However, Paris might have the qualifications. It is the home to the second-largest amount of RMB deposits in Europe (RMB10 billion compared to London's RMB35 billion). Moreover, nearly 22 percent of the trade between France and China is already denominated in RMB, making it the sixth-largest center for RMB payments after Taiwan, Singapore, the United Kingdom, China, and Hong Kong.[27] Several large international companies based in Paris have already demonstrated a keen interest in settling their international trade and making investments in RMB.[28] Furthermore, French companies have also issued RMB7 billion (US$1.1 billion) in dim sum bonds, an amount nearly equals Germany's and doubles the volume from the U.K. borrowers.[29] In addition, the French investment banks also have experienced in issuing offshore RMB bonds; for example, BNP Paribas was ranked fourth in the dim sum bond bookrunners league table (see Table 5.2).

In contrast, London benefits from being one of the largest financial centers in the world for all asset classes and currencies, with a world-class infrastructure. London also has the "early first-mover advantage," which might be more about publicity generation than any real power (such as the "real" experience in issuing offshore RMB bonds in London), although some believe that the momentum is with London.[30]

---

[27] See SWIFT (2013).

[28] See Yiu (2013).

[29] See Cushnie (2012).

[30] Some people think that London does not have the real experience in issuing offshore RMB bonds because the first and only offshore RMB bond issued in London was a product issued by the City of London Commission and not by a real issuer (Cushnie, 2012).

The rivalry between Taiwan and Singapore is not as intense as the one between London and Paris. Taiwan had been less aggressive than Singapore in terms of pursuing the opportunity to become the second offshore RMB center in Asia after Hong Kong, but it came ahead of Singapore in having a local RMB clearing bank approved by the Chinese government.[31] At the time of writing, Taiwan and Singapore have both started issuing their offshore RMB bonds. Their exchanges have also prepared to introduce RMB-denominated products.

7.3 ONGOING DEVELOPMENTS AFFECTING THE DIM SUM BOND MARKET

Several ongoing developments directly or indirectly affecting the dim sum bond market are noteworthy. First, the first group of Hong Kong banks has received the green light in January 2013 to issue RMB loans to onshore mainland companies as a significant step to globalize the RMB.[32] Fifteen Hong Kong–based banks including HSBC, SCB, and BEA signed an agreement to issue loans of up to RMB2 billion (US$321 million) to Chinese enterprises in the Qianhai district of Shenzhen (near Hong Kong) for 26 projects. These banks have already significant RMB business in China. Tenors and interest rates of the loans can be set independently of the benchmark rates set by the PBOC. This is the first time China has opened its domestic lending market to offshore competition. The program will likely foster the development of the offshore RMB market and further open up China's capital account to bolster demand for RMB loans and RMB liquidity between the mainland and Hong Kong. This will indirectly benefit the dim sum bond market.

Second, discussions on policies relating to the opening up of capital account and the liberalization of exchange rates—full convertibility of the RMB—are intimately related to the future success of the dim sum bond market. It is quite revealing to see what "full convertibility" means. Zhou Xiaochuan, China's central bank chief, in a December 2012 speech, made it clear that the country's capital account convertibility does not necessarily mean 100 percent convertibility, a free-floating currency with cross-border asset transfers without control, or zero financial supervision. Thus, even when the RMB is fully convertible and the capital account opened up, it does not rule out the necessity of maintaining certain existing filing procedures, cross-border financial transactions, financial supervision, and

---

[31] For a brief account of the development of the offshore RMB market in Taiwan and Singapore, see Fung and Yau (2013).

[32] See Liu (2013).

certain capital controls to prevent money laundering and tax avoidance. In addition, the Chinese government believes capital controls are also necessary under certain circumstances to fend off financial risks brought by "hot money" inflows.[33] Thus, for China, capital account liberalization is a natural progression from current account convertibility.[34] The Chinese government hopes that liberalization of the RMB will push more offshore investors to put their money to work in the mainland, which will eventually lead to a convergence of onshore and offshore fixed-income markets. However, capital flows may have undesirable impacts on China's economy, just like in other emerging markets. In other emerging markets, capital inflows, particularly short-term loans and portfolio flows, can easily go into reverse and create a major liquidity crisis as it happened during the Asian financial crisis of 1997–1998.[35] Sequencing of reforms is crucial and the right sequence to introduce substantial exchange rate flexibility before opening up the capital account to financial flows in a major way is the lesson learned from emerging market financial crisis in the last 20 years.[36]

Another ongoing development concerns the integration of onshore and offshore RMB bond markets. If the two markets were integrated, it might provide different opportunities and risks to issuers and investors. Some suggests that the onshore and offshore markets are likely to converge, partly driven by policy initiatives and partly by increased balance between the inward and outward flows to and from the mainland.[37] However, it is not clear *when* the two markets will be integrated. We believe as long as there is still control on the capital account, the onshore and offshore markets will not converge as quickly as anticipated.

Apart from the convergence of the onshore and offshore RMB markets, the convergence between the dim sum bond and Asian USD bond market is going on. The catalyst for this move toward convergence is that Chinese companies tap both markets for capital. For MNCs having operations in mainland China, they can raise funds in RMB or USD. This funding arbitrage will make the dim sum bond market converge with the USD bond market as we pointed out in section 7.2.1.

Finally, as we pointed out in Chapter 1, a change in the government's policy regarding the RQFII program may pose a threat to the dim sum bond market. If the RQFII program was extended to other countries, it would take

---

[33] See Wang (2012).

[34] See Muk and Waite (2013).

[35] See Beim and Calomiris (2001).

[36] Ibid.

[37] See Walker (2013).

some business from Hong Kong's dim sum bond market.[38] Despite it is a concern for Hong Kong to worry about losing its edge as the world's choice RMB offshore center, we expect Hong Kong can leverage on its "first mover advantage" to maintain the position as a leading offshore RMB center.

7.4 FINAL REMARKS

The dim sum bond market is the first offshore RMB bond market. It was established as a tactical move to complement the strategy for the internationalization of the RMB. As the internationalization of the RMB is complete or close to complete, a question regarding the viability of the dim sum bond market has been raised. If the Eurodollar or Asian dollar market for the United States is any indication, it seems clear that the dim sum bond market will stay even after the RMB becomes fully convertible. The Eurodollar bond market has been strong and sustainable today even after the United States removed the barriers of capital flows restricted by the Interest Equalization Tax Law established in 1963. Given the current policies and commitments as revealed by the top Chinese officials to support the Hong Kong's dim sum bond market, we do not expect this market to disappear soon.

This book outlines the existing and future forces that support the development of dim sum bonds, which is part of the RMB internationalization process. In light of the ardent support by the Chinese government, increasing trade settlement using RMB, the dim sum bond market is likely to grow. While the spread of the RMB trading centers in London, Taiwan, Singapore, and Paris facilitates worldwide circulation and use of the RMB in trade and investment settlement, the supply of and the demand for offshore RMB currency and bonds will increase. Thus, we are optimistic that the growth of the dim sum bond market will continue.

We believe the Chinese government will continue to explore ways to promote the RMB as a desirable alternative to the U.S. dollar in global trade and finance and China as the top destination for international listings. As part of the grand scheme under the national policy for internationalizing the RMB, Hong Kong has been pivotal in the internationalization process by relying on Hong Kong's established capital market infrastructure. As China plays a greater role in the global economy, the RMB will likely become a global reserve currency in the future. As such, it should not be a surprise to see that dim sum bonds will eventually become an alternative asset class in global asset allocation.

---

[38] At the time of this writing, the RQFII program has already been extended to other cities. See Chapter 1, footnotes 25 and 26.

REFERENCES

Beim, D. O., and C. W. Calomiris. 2001. *Emerging Financial Markets*. New York: McGraw-Hill/Irwin.

Chatterjee, S. 2013. "Credit Ratings Elbowed Aside in Hunger for Yield." Reuters, May 9.

Cookson, Robert. 2011. "CME to Allow Renminbi as Collateral." *Financial Times*, December 6: 22.

Cushnie, Lorraine. 2012. "Paris Should Aim for More than Being London's Achilles Heel—Opinion." *Asiamoney PLUS*, December 10.

Davis, Anita, 2012a. "Covenant Breach Is Welcome Development for Dim Sum—Opinion." *Asiamoney,* August.

Davis, Anita. 2012b. "British Columbia Opens Door for Sovereign CNH Issues." *Asiamoney*, December 10.

Ferguson, N. 2012. "Hong Kong Sets Start Date for Renminbi Futures Market." *AsiaFinance*, August 23.

Fung, Hung-Gay, Derrick Tzau, and Jot Yau. 2013. "A Global Chinese Renminbi Bond Market: The Dim Sum Bond Market," in *Frontiers of Economics and Globalization*, H.-G. Fung and Y. Tse, eds., Volume 13, Elsevier, forthcoming.

Fung, Hung-Gay, and Jot Yau, 2013. "The Dim Sum Bond Market and Its Role in the Internationalization of the Renminbi." *European Financial Review*, February–March: 64–67.

Fung, H. G., W. K. Leung, and J. Zhu. 2004. "Nondelivery Forward Market for Chinese RMB: A First Look." *China Economic Review* 15, 348–352.

Ho, Min. 2012. "Investors Flock Back to Feast on Dim Sum Bonds." *AsiaInvestor*, December 11.

Jönsson, Anette. 2012. "Hopewell Highway Sells New Shares in Offshore Renminbi." *FinanceAsia*, October 25.

Lee, Georgina. 2012. "Asia Investor Dim Sum Bonds Tipped to Boost Nascent Repo Market." *AsianInvestor*, September 13.

Li, X., and X. Wang. 2013. "France Leads Eurozone in Offshore RMB Payments." *China Daily*, April 27. Retrieved from www.chinadaily.com.cn.

Liu, Lillian. 2013. "China Opens Onshore Market to Foreign Lenders." *FinanceAsia*, January 29.

Muk, E., and S. Waite. 2013. "Execs Welcome Prospect of Full RMB Convertibility." *AsianInvestor*, May 8.

SWIFT. 2013. "France Leads Euro Countries in Chinese Payments with a 249% Increase." Press Release, April 25.

Tan, Clement. 2013. "China Plays the Long Game in Latest Investment Quota Expansion." Reuters, July 17.

Walker, R. 2013. "Integration of the Renminbi Bond Market Is Inevitable." *FinanceAsia*, March 8.

Wang, X. 2012. "Full RMB Convertibility Ruled Out." *China Daily*, December 18. Retrieved from http://chinadaily.com.cn.

Wee, Denise. 2012. "Dim Sum Bonds Offer Borrowers Arbitrage Opportunity." *FinanceAsia*, August.

Wee, Denise. 2013. "Greentown Taps Dim Sum Arbitrage Opportunity." *FinanceAsia,* May 8.

Wong, Andrea. 2013. "HSBC Shuns Formosa Debut as Taiwan Funds Cut Yield: China Credit." Bloomberg, February 27.

Wong, Chien Mi. 2013a. "Longer-Dated Dim Sum Supply to Increase in 2013." *AsiaMoney*, January 3.

Wong, Chien Mi. 2013b. "Dim Sum Yields to Reference CDs on Heavy Supply in 2013." *AsiaMoney*, January 4.

Yiu, E. 2013. "Paris Bids for Top Spot in Europe's Yuan Business." *South China Morning Post*, April 29.

About the Authors

Hung-Gay Fung, PhD, is Curators' Professor of Finance, Dr. Y. S. Tsiang Endowed Chair Professor of Chinese Studies, and department chair in the Finance and Legal Studies Department, College of Business Administration, University of Missouri–St. Louis. His areas of research and teaching include international finance, financial risk management, and banking. He has published over 150 scholarly papers in various journals. He has also published seven books, numerous book chapters, and many teaching cases.

He is currently the editor of *Chinese Economy, International Journal of Business and Economics,* and *International Review of Accounting, Banking and Finance.* He has served on several other editorial boards and has served as president in many Chinese organizations in St. Louis, including the Mid-West Chinese American Science and Technology Association, the Chinese Culture Day at the Botanical Garden in St. Louis, Organization of Chinese Americans, and St. Louis Chinese Association.

■ ■ ■

Glenn Ko, CFA, is an executive director of the UBS Asian Credit Research team, covering corporate credits. He focuses on Chinese properties and industrials. He has extensive experience in Asia's straight and convertible bond markets, with previous work experience in proprietary trading desks, sell-side research, and rating advisory at financial institutions, such as Daiwa, JPMorgan, and HSBC. Prior to these, he worked at Moody's as a credit rating analyst.

■ ■ ■

Jot Yau, PhD, CFA, is Dr. Khalil Dibee Endowed Chair in Finance at the Albers School of Business and Economics, Seattle University. Since joining Seattle University in 2001, he has served as the Robert D. O'Brien Chair of Business, chair of the department of finance and MSF program director. He has published numerous articles and chapters in finance journals and professional books. He is the coeditor and coauthor of two books. He has served on several editorial boards, and was the associate editor and special editor (Risk Management) of the *Journal of Alternative Investments*. He cofounded Strategic Options Investment Advisors Ltd., a Hong Kong–based investment advisory firm. He served on the board of directors of Group Health Credit Union and of the Northwest Hedge Fund Society, where he was also the treasurer.

Index